ZEN CATHOLICISM

Also by DOM AELRED GRAHAM

Books:

THE LOVE OF GOD
An Essay in Analysis

THE FINAL VICTORY
A War-Time Meditation

THE CHRIST OF CATHOLICISM
A Meditative Study

CATHOLICISM AND THE WORLD TODAY

CHRISTIAN THOUGHT AND ACTION
The Role of Catholicism in Our Time

Contributory Studies:

THE CHURCH ON EARTH
(*The Teaching of the Catholic Church*)

THE PERSON AND TEACHING OF OUR LORD JESUS CHRIST
(*A Catholic Commentary on Holy Scripture*)

ZEN CATHOLICISM

A SUGGESTION

DOM AELRED GRAHAM

Prior of the Benedictine Community
Portsmouth, Rhode Island

"If useless things do not hang in your mind
Any season is a good season to you"
—*Lines from a Zen Poem*

A Harvest Book

HARCOURT, BRACE & WORLD, INC.   NEW YORK

NIHIL OBSTAT: D. GREGORIUS STEVENS, S.T.D.
                  CENSOR CONGREG. ANGLIAE O.S.B.

IMPRIMI POTEST: RR. D.D. CHRISTOPHORUS BUTLER
                  ABBAS PRAESES

NIHIL OBSTAT: AUSTIN B. VAUGHAN, S.T.D.
                  CENSOR LIBRORUM

IMPRIMATUR: ✠ FRANCIS CARDINAL SPELLMAN
                  ARCHBISHOP OF NEW YORK

16 January 1963

The nihil obstat and imprimatur are official declarations that a book or pamphlet is free of doctrinal or moral error. No implication is contained therein that those who have granted the nihil obstat and imprimatur agree with the contents, opinions or statements expressed.

TO THOSE

WHO WITH THE INSIGHT OF THE EAST

SET IN THE GREAT TRADITION OF THE WEST

MAY EVEN IN THIS PAINFUL WORLD

BE HAPPY

What had to be fully known, that I have fully known;
What had to be developed, that I have developed;
What was to be forsaken, that I have forsaken.
Therefore, O Brahmin, I am the Buddha.

—From *Buddhist Scriptures*,
TRANSLATED BY EDWARD CONZE

The Light, the true Light
That illumines all mankind,
Was on its way into the world—

Was *in* the world, which came to be through Him,
And the world did not know Him—
Came to His own,
And His own did not take Him to themselves.

—From *St. John's Gospel*,
TRANSLATED BY E. V. RIEU

INTRODUCTION

This book has no message. In its original draft, it bore the title
Zen Catholicism?—but I have allowed myself to be persuaded
that the tentative note, the interrogative mood, emerge with
sufficient clarity from the subtitle. A question, not a proposal
or a thesis, is here conveyed. Were that question as important
as I think it is, its public discussion may turn out to be of some
general consequence, even though the themes unfolded are too
far-reaching to be brought neatly to a conclusion. The word
Zen means "meditation"; which sounds simple enough. No one,
presumably, would object to a more meditative Catholicism.
Zen, however, is Buddhist, and Buddhism is commonly regarded as a religion on its own account. The religious aspect,
a later development, of the Buddha's teaching will not concern us. The questions to be discussed are whether what is
essential to Buddhism, with its Zen emphasis, does not have
its counterpart in Catholicism; whether Catholics might not
be helped, by the Zen insight, to realize more fully their own
spiritual inheritance; and whether Zennists need be as exotic
as they are.

It is sometimes said that Zen is now taken more seriously
in Europe and America than in its native Japan. But this
could have as little relevance as to say, for example, that
Kierkegaard receives greater attention in the Paris salons than

from his Danish compatriots; or that Thomism is better understood by hundreds of American college students than by the average citizen of Rome. Whatever may be its associations in the popular mind, Zen has venerable antecedents; it represents something permanent to the human spirit; it cannot be dismissed as merely the latest intellectual and aesthetic fad, *à la mode* among bohemians and beatniks. That Zen has become the theme of best-selling novels may be indicative of its appeal to many who are seeking, unconsciously perhaps, an ultimate viewpoint. Not having found this in their own Western tradition, they try, some of them, to discover "reality," in terms of a life-enhancing experience, among the local equivalents of Kerouac's "poetic Zen Lunatic Dharma Bum friends of San Francisco." The worldly-wise will smile, but others may think it worth considering that such an experiment can end, if only as the conclusion of a story, with—"And I said 'God, I love you' and looked up at the sky and really meant it. 'I have fallen in love with you, God. Take care of us all, one way or the other.' "

Similarly, J. D. Salinger, fascinated by Zen, consciously reaches to the deep things of the spirit, the central thesis of *The Cloud of Unknowing,* when he portrays his character Franny Glass in total revulsion against the omnipresent ego, against the scramble to be successful at all costs, against the urge to cut a figure in the world. She turns in disgust from the only concept of a wise man ever presented to her at college—that of a wealthy stockbroker attaining the status of an elder statesman, being called to Washington to act as adviser to the President.

The quest is for "wisdom," for the ultimately *real;* and to attain the goal not hereafter but now. There are five things, according to Buddhist tradition, which no power in the universe can bring about.

What five things are those? That what is subject to old age should not grow old, that what is subject to sickness should not be sick, that what is subject to death should not die, that what is subject to decay should not decay, that what is liable to pass away should not pass away.[1]

To be reconciled, not blindly but with a mind enlightened, to the inevitable—that, if I have rightly understood, is the heart of Zen Buddhism. But this also, in its depths at least, is the message of Catholicism. Such, at any rate, is the "suggestion" offered in these pages. Nothing in the way of religious syncretism is called for; the aim is to evaluate, sympathetically, Zen from a Catholic point of view; and in the process, though incidentally, to present Catholicism at its mature level. The approach is not that of an orientalist, for which I have no competence, but of one formed in the oldest monastic tradition of the West, familiar with a truly "existential" Christian philosophy, and really interested in the contemporary world.

The reader is not being invited to embark on a daring theological adventure, to explore new spiritual frontiers, but to look into his own nature, and that of the Church. Hence this essay, though superficially avant-garde, is in a deep sense conservative. It aims at throwing light on what is before everyone's eyes, though often overlooked. No new program is proposed, no prophetic vision unveiled. The only change that might be in order, should anyone think it applies, is a change of heart; which, it could be argued, is the sole effective basis for reform. There is no bishop-baiting; as is indulged in, unmaliciously, in certain quarters nowadays. The Catholic hierarchy, discharging its rightful function, is taken for granted. One becomes more grateful, as understanding grows, to those who, in the face of immense difficulties, maintain the Church's constitutional structure and so preserve intact the heritage of the West. Awareness that this heritage is linked also with the East is evident where one might expect it to be. In his essay *East and West,* the late Ananda Coomaraswamy describes certain words of Pope Pius XII as "an almost literal summary of the true philosophy of Work as it has been propounded by

---

[1] Quoted from Ananda Coomaraswamy, *Buddha and the Gospel of Buddhism* (Bombay: Asia Publishing House, 1956), p. 84.

Plato and in the *Bhagavad Gita.*" More recently Pope John
XXIII emphasized the point by a significant act. On November
18, 1962, "the Pope received 28 Japanese Buddhist monks in
a special audience in his library. He told the monks that both
Roman Catholicism and Buddhism work for peace, seek the
betterment of man and honor God."[2]

To me, at least, it seems that an underlying harmony is discoverable, as one ponders the Buddha's "holy truths," the Zen
concern for seeing into one's own nature, and the insights of
St. Thomas Aquinas. The resulting emphasis is on Catholicism; not as a religious cult, nor as an ecclesiastical system organized for man's eternal salvation, though neither of these
aspects is forgotten, but as a way of life, an answer to one's
problems here and now. The outcome may be of some general
interest—no work quite of this kind, so far as I know, having
been attempted before. Nearly twenty-five years ago, I published
my first book, *The Love of God,* still in some demand in its
paperback edition. The present essay, in its author's eyes, handling related topics more mellowly, is a sequel, at least as
regards its main chapters. The three "Supplementary Discussions," though slightly specialized, amplify subjects touched on
in the preceding text which are currently much talked about.
The concluding Postscript is mainly addressed to the cogno-
scenti. A recently published critique of religion and philosophy
has been loudly acclaimed, in academic circles, as a noteworthy
achievement. Were its basic contentions valid, they would not
only nullify most of what is substantial to this book, but un-
dermine the entire structure of Catholic theology. They seem
deserving of attention.

By way of acknowledgment, it should be recorded that the
first chapter was read as a paper at the 1962 national meeting of
the Catholic Commission on Intellectual and Cultural Affairs
at Fordham University. An informed and encouraging discussion followed, notable contributions being made by the Rev-

2 The New York *Times,* November 19, 1962, p. 1.

erend Thomas Berry, C.P., and Professor William Theodore de Bary of Columbia University. What was there said has affected constructively points of emphasis in the subsequent chapters. I am grateful also to Dom Alban Baer of the Portsmouth Priory Community, who read carefully through the manuscript, offering a number of valuable suggestions. No one except the author, of course, is responsible for any errors of fact or judgment or arising from sheer inadvertence.

AELRED GRAHAM

The Priory
Portsmouth
Rhode Island

ANALYTICAL CONTENTS

CHAPTER THREE
HAVING ONE'S OWN WAY p. 43

Duality between conscious ego and true self is caused by a
grasping desire or craving, p. 43. The need is not for world-
renouncing asceticism but for nonattachment, pp. 43–4. The
ambivalence of having one's own way, p. 44. The theology
of the Fall, p. 44. Guilt and egocentricity, pp. 44–5. Difficulty
of looking at things as they are, p. 45. Danger of living in
an imaginary world in which the conscious ego is supreme,
pp. 45–6. All lies in sympathetic insight, p. 46. Egoism of
the mind, p. 47. "Try not to seek after the true," pp. 47–8.
In the way of Truth, "nothing is easy, nothing hard," p. 48.
Looking and listening, p. 48. Enhancing the ego by grasping
and clinging, p. 49. Living on the spot where we are, p. 50.
Corporate and professional loyalties, p. 51. These illustrated
by the clerical profession, pp. 51–2. The priestly state, p. 52.
Positions of power and prestige, p. 53. Anti-clericalism, p. 54.
Speaking and writing about religion, pp. 54–5. The Church
in process of self-realization, p. 55. Clerical preoccupations
not to be equated with religion itself, p. 56. The Church's
"ego," p. 57. The sacraments, pp. 57–8. The Eucharist, p.
58. Spiritual direction, pp. 59–60. Doing what one pleases,
pp. 60–1.

CHAPTER EIGHT

ANY SEASON A GOOD SEASON p. 136

attention without tension, p. 144. *Zazen*—"to sit and meditate," p. 145. Zen meditation, p. 145. Remarks by St. John of the Cross, p. 145. *The Cloud of Unknowing* on contemplation, p. 146. Contemplative state not an exclusive pre-occupation with God, since God excludes nothing, p. 146. *Sat-Cit-Ananda:* Being-Knowledge-Bliss, p. 147. The Catholic's satori, p. 147. Christian *agape* and Buddhist *karuna,* pp. 147–48. "The enlightened have no likes or dislikes," p. 148. Remarks on death, pp. 148–49. Living in the present is *the* secret of happiness, p. 149. Lines from Ben Jonson, p. 149. The reality of time, pp. 149–50. But Catholicism's *raison d'être* is beyond time, p. 151. We can live in a continuous present, p. 151. Catholic spirituality and the Hindu-Buddhist-Zen tradition, p. 151. "Nothing exists of time except *now,*" p. 152. We have to become "children of time present," p. 152. Eternity not everlastingness, p. 152. Sanctity is willing what happens to us by God's order, p. 153. No salvation outside the soul, pp. 153–54. Facing Reality with complete awareness makes every season a good season, p. 154. Spirit of Zen congenial to Catholicism, p. 154. Satori of Mother Juliana of Norwich, p. 155. Whatever is of permanent value in Zen is not Japanese but Buddhist, p. 155. The Buddhist insight is something universal, p. 155. Buddhism in Japan on the decline, pp. 156–57. The Zen insight may cleanse the Christian mind a little, p. 157. Zen uniting Martha and Mary, action and contemplation, pp. 157–58. Catholics becoming more "mindful" of what they already know, p. 159. All that is required of us is not to harden our hearts, p. 159. To live as one's true self—egolessly, p. 160.

THREE SUPPLEMENTARY DISCUSSIONS

POSTSCRIPT

INDEX OF NAMES

ZEN CATHOLICISM

CHAPTER ONE

OUTSIDE IN TO INSIDE OUT

What is here being initiated is not an academic enquiry; the point of interest is an "existential" one. Christianity originally proclaimed itself as a way of life; Catholicism, in particular, has developed, schematically at least, as an all-embracing philosophy. How real is that "way," how vital is that "philosophy," to the average man and woman, even among the Church's adherents, today? How adequate to humanity's needs, physical, mental, moral, and spiritual, is the Catholic message as it now presents itself?

The simplest and most obvious answer to these questions is that nobody knows. There is plenty of evidence to show that, besides persuading vast numbers of the faithful to attend Sunday, and even weekday, Mass, Catholicism at one level is succeeding impressively. Those who derive satisfaction, or advantage, from church-sponsored variants of rotarian "togetherness" are provided for. Such requirements are easily met. But what of the others? Or, rather, what of all of us—including, indeed especially they, the gregarious ones—when we are alone, quietly, if it ever can be quietly, by ourselves? Kierkegaard, though a decided oddity, observed truly that to be linked emotionally with "the crowd" is to be involved in unreality. "The larger the crowd, the more probable that that which it praises is folly, and the more improbable that it is truth, and the most improbable of all that it is any eternal truth."[1] But whether we are alone or with the crowd, a relevant question remains—how satisfying an insight into the problems that burden most of us do we derive from our understanding of Catholicism?

At the normal level of consciousness we are at a loss to account for our depressions. Yet how overwhelming, for many, the anxiety can be: the sense of foreboding and frustration, the feelings of insecurity that dog the lives of thousands, which bring them in their extremity to the psychiatric clinic or mental home, or, beyond a given point of desperation, to suicide. Many, perhaps most, of these unhappy victims are well enough endowed with this world's goods. To outward appearances, one would say, they should not have a care in the world; yet they are full of care.

And, then, the external tangible sufferings: bad health, disease, poverty, domestic upheavals, marital breakdowns, social disgrace, the calamitous "mistakes," intensified by a harrowing guilt and self-accusation; the impossible situations from which, it seems, there is no way out; the unattainability of what, so we tell ourselves, we cannot do without. The robust-minded may affect to smile at the pervading anxiety, the *angst,* which characterizes our age; but the weight of human sadness cannot be smiled away. The paramount need is that the situation be understood; and then, having ourselves learned through suffering, become mellowed by an age-long wisdom, we may, perhaps, compassionately smile a little.

Except in rare cases these problems cannot be solved, in the present climate of opinion, by the promise of future alleviation and reward. The prospect of heaven hereafter, even if it be believed, is not enough. Nor does Catholicism seriously maintain that it is. Present sorrows call for present assuagement. How this may be effected—to make the seemingly unbearable not only tolerable but fundamentally accepted—is what we have to explore. Catholicism, so those who know it

[1] S. Kierkegaard, *Purity of Heart;* quoted from Ralph B. Winn, *A Dictionary of Existentialism* (New York: Philosophical Library, 1960), p. 20.

from the inside would say, has unique resources for calming the troubled human spirit. It could be, however, that, owing to a variety of circumstance for which no one in particular is to blame, these resources are not being brought sufficiently to light.

At the risk of appearing to digress, I must stress the point that no one, even by implication, is being criticized. Criticism of Catholics by Catholics can be an extremely wholesome exercise; but it is uncalled for here. The integrity of the present essay would be impaired by any pretensions on the part of its author to superior insight; the only heart he has presumed to search has been his own. An implied condition of the reflections that follow is that they should be conducted, not as exemplifying an eccentric piece of personal "research," but as illustrating the central tradition of Catholic theology long since accessible to all. The hierarchic structure of the Church, for example, though hardly calling for discussion,[2] is taken for granted as providing the necessary framework. No doubt much that is to be said will apply to ecclesiastics, but they must make the application for themselves. Where it touches them, it is not as a challenge to responsible officials but as food for thought to those who are fellow Christians with the rest of us.

This having been stated, it may be suggested that the cultural atmosphere of our time, by which Catholics like everybody else are affected, is not favorable to the acceptance of the Church's doctrinal teaching as this is normally offered to the faithful. Again, let me hasten to add that we are not now considering the inadequacies, if such they be, of the Catholic educational tradition. As occasion arises, we doubtless need to be spurred on in our efforts, culturally and scientifically speaking, to keep up with the Joneses. But here we are concerned with

[2] At the late editor's invitation, I have, in fact, discussed it at length in an essay entitled "The Church on Earth" in *The Teaching of the Catholic Church*, edited by Canon George D. Smith, D.D., Ph.D. (London: Burns, Oates & Washbourne; second—two volumes in one—edition, 1952), pp. 691-732.

something, as I see it, both different and more important. Even
if it be conceded that the manner of the Church's proclama-
tions might sometimes be made more attractive, substantially
they cannot be altered. They are part of what is given, aspects
of "the faith that was once for all delivered to the saints" (Jude
3). Yet it may still fairly be asked whether anything further
can be done, not necessarily by the Church's hierarchy, but by
experts at lower levels, to arouse the minds of ordinary believers to a more fruitful response.

The difficulty should not be underestimated. Those who are
undisposed to reflect may well be content with the objective
facts: Almighty God, transcendent in His heaven, has revealed
Himself in the course of history, most significantly of all in
the person and lifework of His coequal Son, our Lord and
Saviour Jesus Christ. By Him the Catholic Church was instituted, having Simon Peter as its first pope; down the centuries
the Church has endured to our own day, as described by the
orthodox historians. This outline, so summarily stated, is not
here in dispute. Needing to be noted, however, is what happens to the individual when he subscribes to the Christian
creed. It is in the actual acceptance of the articles of belief
that both the personal satisfaction and the possibility of problems arise. Once the act of faith has been made, Catholicism
is no longer something "out there" to which we adhere; it has
become part of the furniture of our minds. As it affects the
individual believer, religion, even a universal religion, operates
effectively only within the distinctive personality of each.
Faith, love, spiritual growth, final salvation itself, exist nowhere save as individualized in this particular man or woman.
Catholicism, needless to say, has not thus been transformed
into an entirely subjective affair; its objectivity remains un-
touched; but it is *partly* subjective—since, faith being a form
of knowledge, here clearly is applicable the principle recalled
by St. Thomas Aquinas precisely in this context: "the thing
known is in the mind of the knower according to the measure
[*modus*] of that mind" (*Summa Theologica*, II-II, 1, 2).

What is the relation between the believer's mind and the "external" facts of the Christian revelation as proposed by the teaching Church? Obviously this relation will differ in accordance with the mental capacity and equipment of each: a Catholic who knows, for example, something of the history of ideas will understand his religion differently from one whose instruction derives mainly from the catechism. But our immediate concern is with a more manageable topic. Accepting the deliverances of the Church's teaching authority, and giving due weight to what the theologians have to tell us, what can we do to "realize" the doctrine effectively in our everyday lives? The question, therefore, is the highly "existential" one of the individual's response to what the Church has to say. Faith comes from outside ourselves, by hearing (Galatians 3:2; Hebrews 5:11); each one's awakening to the divine light, however, prompted though this be by grace, can only come from within his own spirit. The Christian Creed may be sung congregationally, but its commitment, by one man, one vote, is personal, not collective—*"Credo": "I* believe."

Today countless factors conspire to make the individual rather than the group the focal point of interest. Democracy itself, theoretically at any rate, is a vindication, in the name of the people, of the rights of the one, if not against the many, at least against despotism. It is not so much the uniqueness of each, as that each must be regarded as a center of initiative, which characterizes our Western way of life. This situation has both its attractions and its drawbacks, but there are few signs that it arouses any widespread desire for change. Existentialism, with its emphasis on independent choice, psychoanalysis, with its stress on the individual as the plaything of circumstance, may be regarded respectively as active and passive aspects of the same phenomenon. In the face of these secularizing forces, religious approaches which ignore the individual's prized, yet dreaded, aloneness, but strive to regiment him, in the name, let us say, of "brotherly love," into some community of believers, betray unawareness of the basic problem. If mod-

ern man is to be persuaded to take seriously his relationship
to God, his aspirations must be met with complete realism and
careful particularity.

Confronted by this state of affairs, there are few signs that
the Christian "churches" experience an exhilarating sense of
their own adequacy. On the contrary, public heart-searching
and breast-beating are the order of the day. Catholics themselves, or the more sensitive among them, are casting about for
ways and means to enhance the appeal of their message in the
eyes of those most needing help. Friendly glances are even being turned to other denominations, with the implied enquiry:
What do they have that we don't have? The question is still
being actively debated: Which was the greater mistake—the
Reformation or the Counter-Reformation? Nor need the search
for reunion all round stop here. Not only the politicians but
also, it would seem, Church functionaries and theologians must
take account equally of the susceptibilities of Catholics, Prot-
estants, and Jews. A radical divergence of view on the existing
nature of man and basically opposing standpoints with regard
to the person and message of the Founder of the Christian religion are obstacles that, apparently, can easily be overcome,
given sufficient good will and the urgency of forming a united
front against the common enemy: skepticism, general immorality, communism, or whatever it may be.

It would be an indication of regrettable levity to be skittish
about these *rapprochements*. All the more so as it is one of the
purposes of this essay to examine the bases, and stress the need,
for greater human unity. Perhaps it is a nagging sense, amounting almost to a conviction, that what our present situation calls
for is an analysis in depth which leaves one with only a qualified interest in a "dialogue" between the sects. Interdenomi-
national camaraderie under quasi-official auspices no doubt
brings its benefits, not least to that social entity known as the
"organization man"; but what is of more immediate concern
is man and woman simply as they are—or, to say the same thing
in another way, as they stand before God.

To one who has lived over half a century within the Church's fold, blessed with the happiest opportunities for studying Christianity's sources and seeing it lived, Catholicism's abiding fascination lies in its hidden spiritual riches. Compared to these, jurisdictional questions, which must inevitably arise in, for example, ecumenical discussions, stand on the periphery. No decisive step toward the reunion of the Christian denominations can be taken until it is generally recognized that the Roman Church, as it exists today—whatever its members' readily admitted defects—testifies uniquely to the ancestral faith of Christendom. With promoting this recognition, however, we are here, at the most, only incidentally concerned. More to the purpose is it to enquire how the Church's inner resources can be made available to those who urgently need them. They are accessible to all; they are not "mysterious"; every school child, in a sense, knows about them. And yet there is plenty of evidence to suggest that they hardly influence the lives of the majority, even among the faithful. What seems to be required is that Catholicism, to put it extravagantly, should be able to turn itself inside out.

The point here being made is other than the truism that the world would be a pleasanter place to live in if Catholics acted less inconsistently with their beliefs. This goes without saying. What is being submitted is that a prerequisite of any improvement is not, in the first place, better intentions and increased good will, but a greater insight into the doctrines subscribed to. Verbal professions need to become more meaningful in the light of a deepened awareness. Are there any means by which this process can be assisted?

Traditional Christianity, with its respect for the validity of human reason, has in the past elucidated its own position with the aid of rational philosophy. Such an undertaking is perhaps more congenial to the Catholic mind than scholarly discussions on the Bible, or enquiries into the foundations of Church authority; since these give rise to controversial issues which, though well worth examining, are usually irrelevant to the basic needs of the human spirit. Catholicism, unhampered by any sense of sectarian insecurity, has utilized, and allowed itself, within limits, to be influenced by, the intellectual and cultural fashions of the day. The enormous part played by Platonism and Stoicism in the work of the Greek Fathers is universally admitted. In the Latin Church, St. Augustine's vast productivity would have been unthinkable without his debt, openly acknowledged, to the neo-Platonists. As for the Middle Ages, all the world knows that St. Thomas Aquinas "baptized" Aristotle, that is to say, utilized him for his own admirable purposes: with the result that the Church's theological and philosophical textbooks are to this day, for better or worse, impregnated with the thought and terminology of Aristotle.

Thus we are led to the question, or, to be more accurate, the tentative line of suggestion, which will occupy us from now on. Can a philosophy of life which originated in India centuries before Christ—still accepted as valid, in one or other of its many variants, by several hundred millions of our contemporaries—be of service to Catholics, or those interested in Catholicism, in elucidating certain aspects of the Church's own message? The possibility cannot be ruled out. To the point is St. Ambrose's well-known dictum, endorsed by St. Thomas Aquinas, being a gloss on 1 Corinthians 12:3, "All that is true, *by whomsoever it has been said,* is from the Holy Ghost."[3]

Sociologists may be left to account for the widespread interest now being displayed, both in America and Europe, in Hinduism, with the related cult of "Yoga," and in Buddhism, especially in its Chinese, and more specifically Japanese, development known as Zen. It is with this last that we shall concern ourselves: both because it is considered by many qualified judges to reach uniquely to the heart of the matter, and because, as will appear, it seems likely to provide the most fruitful point of contact with Catholic spirituality.

[3] Quoted from Ananda K. Coomaraswamy, *Am I My Brother's Keeper?* (New York: The John Day Company, 1943), p. 42.

In order that we may proceed in an intelligible manner, the historical antecedents of Zen must be touched on, however briefly; even though we can agree with an observation made by Julius Evolva in his essay "Zen and the West": "It is sufficiently well-known that Zen, in its spirit, may be regarded as a return to the Buddhism of the origins."[4] The word "Buddha" means simply the "Enlightened One"; so understood, there have been many "Buddhas." As Dr. Edward Conze[5] points out: "In the official theory, the Buddha, 'the Enlightened,' is a kind of archetype which manifests itself in the world in different personalities, whose individual particularities are of no account whatsoever." From this point of view, Jesus of Nazareth would undoubtedly be accorded the title "Buddha," since He is revealed, according to St. John, as both uniquely "Enlightened" and the "Enlightener." In this context, we may note in passing that St. John Damascene, in his eighth-century narrative, *Barlaam and Ioasaph,* had no difficulty in accepting as genuinely Christian what appears actually to have been a version of the life of the Buddha. That there is indeed some affinity between the Buddhist and Christian ethos can be allowed, without pressing the similarities to the point of religious syncretism. Here Christians may note, not perhaps without a prick of conscience, a remark by the late Ananda Coomaraswamy: "Our position in relation to Christians and other faiths can be stated by saying that 'even if you are not on our side, we are on yours; and that is something all your zeal cannot take away from us.' "[6]

The "historical Buddha"—Gautama, or Shakyamuni (*The sage from the tribe of the Shakyas*)—lived probably between 560 and 480 B.C., in the northeast of India. The traditions con-

[4] *Anthology of Zen,* edited by William A. Briggs (New York: Grove Press, 1961), p. 207.
[5] See Edward Conze, *Buddhism: Its Essence and Development* (New York: Harper & Brothers, Torchbook edition, 1959), pp. 34-35.
[6] Ananda K. Coomaraswamy, *Indian Culture and English Influence* (a lithoprinted address published by Orientalia, New York, 1946), p. 33.

cerning the Buddha and his alleged "sayings" (*sutras*) are, of course, sacred to Buddhists; but it must be remembered that the historic existence of Gautama as an individual is of little importance to Buddhist faith. The Buddha is a type embodied in this individual—and it is the type, as an ideal to be repeated or reproduced, which interests the religious life. Thus Buddhists consider the Buddha as a spiritual principle, and as such they call him *Tathagata* (which means "He who has thus come," *i.e.,* as other Buddhas have come), or speak of his *Dharma-body*.[7]

The relation between Buddhism and the Hindu background from which it sprang continues to be a matter of debate among scholars. "The more superficially one studies Buddhism," writes Coomaraswamy,[8] "the more it seems to differ from the Brahmanism in which it originated; the more profound our study, the more difficult it becomes to distinguish Buddhism from Brahmanism. . . . The outstanding distinction lies in the fact that Buddhist doctrine is propounded by an apparently historic founder, understood to have lived and taught in the sixth century B.C. Beyond this there are only broad distinctions of emphasis."

What may safely be said is that Buddhism arose as a reaction to the speculations and ritualism which were the chief preoccupation of India's ancient priestly caste. Buddhism, as had Hinduism before it, later developed into a "religion," with its characteristic dogmas, moral code, ritual, and even scholasticism. Considered in itself, however, such underlying philosophy

---

[7] Hindu and Buddhist terminology is, often deliberately, ambiguous. "*Dharma, dharmas:* (1) The one ultimate Reality; (2) an ultimately real event; (3) as reflected in life: righteousness, virtue; (4) as interpreted in the Buddha's teaching: doctrine, Scripture, Truth; (5) object of the sixth sense-organ, *i.e.,* of mind; (6) property; (7) mental state; (8) thing; (9) quality." Quoted from glossary of technical terms in *Buddhist Scriptures,* selected and translated by Edward Conze (Harmondsworth, England: Penguin Books, 1959), p. 245.

[8] Ananda K. Coomaraswamy, *Hinduism and Buddhism* (New York: Philosophical Library, 1943), p. 45.

as may seem to be present in Buddhism is merely incidental, as
will be shown by its development in Zen. The Buddha broke
with Hinduism by his refusal to interest himself in metaphysical questions. He was concerned, not with laying down propositions about the nature of the universe, but, rather, with the
practical problem of making human existence bearable and
eventually—for those who would allow themselves to be "enlightened," and so attain "Buddhahood"—blissful. The Buddha's last injunction to his disciples ran: *All conditioned things
are impermanent. Work out your salvation with diligence.* The
chief means to salvation are not outward deeds, though a conduct of life is implied, but contemplation and meditation effected through a controlling of the mental processes.

It should be remarked that, while there exists an enormous
bulk of authoritative writings, the Buddhists possess nothing
that corresponds to the New Testament. For the first five hundred years the Buddha's teachings were orally transmitted.
There is thus no equivalent to the "initial tradition" of Christianity, only a "continuing tradition"—which, however, scholars agree in regarding as reliable, at least with respect to the
central matter which must now claim our attention. In substance, this matter, which is the heart of Buddhism, has to do
with the painfulness inherent in the human situation and the
means to its relief. It is sometimes described as "the sorrow of
existence," which, on close inspection, is seen to arise from a
general state of restlessness, agitation, craving, and heedlessness
of reality. It is by way of comment, so to speak, on this state of
affairs that, "Next to the Buddha, the Dharma"[9]—the *Dharma,*
in this context, meaning "doctrine."

The essence of the doctrine, accepted by all schools, lies in
the Four Holy (or Noble) Truths, which the Buddha first
preached at Benares immediately after his enlightenment:

    *1. What then is the Holy Truth of Ill? Birth is ill, decay
is ill, sickness is ill, death is ill. To be conjoined with*

[9] See footnote, p. 12.

*what one dislikes means suffering. To be disjoined from
what one likes means suffering. Not to get what one
wants, also that means suffering. In short, all grasping
at any of the five Skandhas[10] involves suffering.*

*2. What then is the Holy Truth of the Origination of
Ill? It is that craving which leads to rebirth, accompanied
by delight and greed, seeking its delight now here, now
there, i.e. craving for sensuous experience, craving to perpetuate oneself, craving for extinction.*

*3. What then is the Holy Truth of the Stopping of Ill?
It is the complete stopping of that craving, the withdrawal from it, the renouncing of it, throwing it back,
liberation from it, non-attachment to it.*

*4. What then is the Holy Truth of the steps that lead to
the stopping of Ill? It is this holy [noble] eightfold Path,
which consists of right views, right intentions, right
speech, right conduct, right livelihood, right effort, right
mindfulness, right concentration.[11]*

It would be presumptuous to remark upon the depth of
insight revealed in these statements. They have no parallel,
that I know of, in the religious literature of the West. Not surprisingly, systematic meditation on the four Holy Truths, as
on the basic facts of life, is Buddhism's central task. From the
Christian, as indeed from the Buddhist, point of view they call
for comment and elucidation. The underlying thought is different from that which preoccupied the authors of the Catholic
creeds. There is no reference to God; but neither do the four
Holy Truths contain any hint—and this should be noted—of
"atheism."[12] It seems that there is only one topic on which we

10 The five *Skandhas* are what Buddhism conceives to be the constituents
of the personality: (i) form = body; (ii) feelings; (iii) perceptions; (iv)
volitional impulses; (v) consciousness.
11 Quoted from *Buddhist Scriptures,* pp. 186-87.
12 "The just word on the Buddhist position with regard to God has been
spoken by René Guénon, who, more than any other European, is qualified
for the office of interpreter of the traditional doctrines:—

 " 'In reality, Buddhism is no more "atheistical" than it is "theistic" or

need momentarily pause at this stage, having regard to our present undertaking—which is to concentrate attention on those features of Buddhism, and its particular development in Zen, that serve to illuminate, and are compatible with, traditional Catholic spirituality. There is a reference to "rebirth," with its overtones of the Hindu doctrine of "transmigration." Though even this may be passed over, with Coomaraswamy's illuminating comment: "The Lord is the only transmigrator."[13]

Organized Buddhism, as a consequence of persecution by the Hephtalitic Huns, and later by the Mohammedans, was extinguished first in Gandara, and then in the whole of Northern India. But the essence of the doctrine has lived on to this day in the land of its birth; under the name of Vedanta, it is still the official doctrine of Hinduism at its highest level.

Buddhism does not speak with one voice; it has many sects and a variety of schools; though all subscribe to the doctrine of the Four Holy Truths. Among the various developments, there is one—though this, again, has split up into a number of subdivisions—that particularly interests us. This is a more liberal version of Buddhist tradition known as the *Mahayana* —meaning, approximately, the *"great career"* or *"great vehicle,"* by way of distinguishing it from the more conservative *Hinayana:* the *"lesser"* or *"inferior vehicle."* As Dr. Conze points out: "The Mahayana seemed *great* for many reasons —chiefly because of the all-embracing nature of the sympathy, and emptiness which it taught, and because of the greatness of the goal it advocated, which was no other than Buddhahood itself."[14]

It was probably not until about the beginning of the ninth

"pantheistic"; all that need be said, is that it does not place itself at the point of view where these various terms have any meaning.' " Marco Pallis, *Peaks and Lamas* (London: Cassell & Co., 1939), p. 177.
[13] See *Hinduism and Buddhism*, p. 16, where copious references are given.
[14] *Buddhism: Its Essence and Development*, p. 121.

century, with the decline of official and monastic Buddhism in India, that the Mahayanists began to outnumber the Hinayanists. The form of Buddhist faith that was carried to Tibet, China, and Japan was the Mahayana. The Hinayana took root only in Ceylon, Burma, Cambodia, and Siam, where it still prevails. The coming of the Mahayana to China brought about its fusion with the native Taoism, so that *ch'an*[15] is as much Taoist as Buddhist. The Chinese word *ch'an* means "meditation," of which the Japanese form is *Zen*. The tradition of Zen Buddhism in Japan, marked by a rich variety of cultural fruits, reaches back to the twelfth century. About these developments something must now be said.

The name associated with the origin of Taoism is Lao-tzu, an older contemporary of Kung Fu-tzu, or Confucius, who died in 479 B.C. Lao-tzu is said to have been the author of the celebrated *Tao Tê Ching,* of which a literal translation is *The Book of the Way and Its Virtue,* but which is often rendered more freely as *The Way of Life.* It is a short collection of aphorisms, setting forth the principles of the Tao and its effectual power.[16] The Chinese Tao, like the Greek Logos, is one

[15] The Chinese *ch'an* renders the Indian *dhyāna* (meditation) ; whence, later, the Japanese *zazen* (to sit and meditate) .

[16] See "The Philosophy of the Tao," being the first chapter of Alan W. Watts's *The Way of Zen* (New York: Pantheon Books, 1957) . Few students of Zen, at least among those who are not professional orientalists, can fail to be indebted to Mr. Watts; and it is a pleasure to record one's gratitude here. In his later work, however, Mr. Watts appears to stress unduly those characteristics of Zen which he conceives, perhaps rightly, to conflict with Christianity. This he sadly oversimplifies—*e.g.,* ". . . our Hebrew-Christian spiritual tradition identifies the Absolute-God with the moral and logical order of convention" (*op. cit.,* p. 11)—and, indeed, shows himself surprisingly unfamiliar with, or perhaps merely uninterested in, the subtler aspects of its theology. He emphasizes differences rather than similarities, and there are passages in his writings which are strongly marked by the antinomian, quietistic bias, which some have found in Zen. As the present essay appeals to the same sources in support of, rather than opposition to, the traditional religion of the West, I take the opportunity, with considerable regret, to cite a relevant comment on one of Mr. Watts's most recent

of those richly ambiguous words, with multiple meanings, none of them exact, for which there is no precise equivalent. Here is how it is spoken of in the *Tao Tê Ching:*

> The Tao that can be expressed is not the eternal Tao;
> The name that can be defined is not the unchanging
> name . . . .
> There is a thing inherent and natural,
> Which existed before heaven and earth.
> Motionless and fathomless,
> It stands alone and never changes;
> It pervades everywhere and never becomes exhausted.
> It may be regarded as the Mother of the Universe.
> I do not know its name.
> If I am forced to give it a name,
> I call it Tao, and I name it as supreme. . . .[17]

Attempting to place it within a Christian context, the suggestion has been made that if John 9:3 be translated, as by E. V. Rieu[18]—"What was desired was that through this man *the way in which God works* should be made manifest"—the italicized words would convey something of what is implied in the Tao. In general, it should be noted that impatience with such indefiniteness, to demand clear verbal equivalents for ideas that are no less clear, is to make difficult an appreciation of Zen.

---

works, *This Is It:* "Mr Watts has been regarded for many years as a professional expert on Zen. This must be a most difficult position to occupy, and its anomalies may account for the discomfort this reviewer feels in the presence of Mr Watt's essays. One of them, 'Beat Zen, Square Zen and Zen', is indeed famous in the United States. Any pundit is obliged to keep his personal end up; but any Zen vogues of any shape can easily be cut down to size by simply remembering that real Zen is Buddhist. About Buddhism there is none of the equivocation with which Mr Watts makes so much play." "The Appeal of Zen," author anonymous, the London *Times Literary Supplement,* December 29, 1961.

[17] From chapters 1 and 25, *Tao Tê Ching*, translated by Ch'u Ta-Kao (New York: The Macmillan Company, fifth edition, 1959), pp. 11, 37.

[18] *The Four Gospels* (Harmondsworth, England: Penguin Books, 1953), p. 218.

Oriental scholars point out that the structure of the Chinese language may provide one clue to the growing popularity of Ch'an (Zen) in the West. From deeply ingrained habit we tend to think in terms of the noun and its predicates, and are led to postulate as existing "out there" entities corresponding to abstract nouns. This intellectual approach has brought many benefits; but it has led to the widespread assumption that the structure of external reality is adequately represented by our mental processes, and even by the words in which those processes are expressed.

"It is our unquestioning adherence to a handful of abstract ideas," writes an authority already referred to,[19] "especially in the political and social spheres, that may be thought to be largely responsible for our present spiritual plight." The same writer continues,

The present-day cults of Beat Zen and Intellectual Zen are both to a large extent an attempt to breach the prison built by our language structure. The mere fact that the patterns of thought lying behind Chan are Chinese goes a long way to explain why it can serve as a protest against Western complacency. It also explains why Indian Buddhism, expressed in a language of similar structure to ours, in which highly abstract entities are hypostatized only to be negated, has not for us the appeal of Chinese Buddhism. One can legitimately interpret the whole of the Indian Prajna (Wisdom) literature as prolonged battle between Buddhism and the abstract noun.

The word Zen, as we have already remarked, means "meditation"; but Zen itself is indefinable. Echoing Confucius's cry —"I wish never to speak"—the Zen masters are fond of quoting the Buddhist dictum: *"Those who say do not know; those who know do not say."* Nevertheless, an astonishing amount has in fact been said. What is of interest from the Christian standpoint is that Zen is not a theology; it has nothing to tell us about a supernatural revelation, nothing therefore that needs to be "corrected." Zen is not a philosophy; it does not have to

[19] *Times Literary Supplement,* December 29, 1961.

be debated with or convicted of errors. Its exponents will tell
you that, in a profoundly literal sense, there is nothing in it.
Perhaps the best description is that conveyed by a single word
—"unself-consciousness."

Zen is an attitude of directness and simplicity, born of an
awareness of one's own nature. It is matter of fact and down
to earth. Zen's interest is not in words but in things. "When I
raise the hand thus, there is Zen," says Daisetz T. Suzuki. "But
when I assert that I have raised the hand, Zen is no more
there." There is little that is devotional or religious, in the
conventional sense, about Zen—only in the ultimate sense, in
as much as religion is an unimpeded relation to Reality. The
enlightenment (*satori*) which is the goal of Zen is not something that can be achieved by working at it; it comes to those
who dispose themselves to receive it. Or, rather, it is there already, if only our self-conscious little egos, cleansed from distracting thoughts and unclouded by emotion, would allow us
just to look at things as they are. "Awaken the mind without
fixing it anywhere." When we can do this, we have found the
"secret" of Zen.

Enough may have been said to make it clear that Zen is
something universal. Professor R. H. Blyth—who remarks that
"Zen, though far from indefinite, is by definition indefinable,
because it is the active principle of life itself"[20]—has shown at
length how the spirit of Zen can be illustrated by the great
works of English literature. To Christians it is pointed out by
orientalists that when Jesus of Nazareth invited his disciples
to "consider the lilies how they grow," this was an act of *direct
pointing,* the very hallmark of Zen.

Here is a famous Zen story. It is called: *Is that so?*

The Zen master Hakuin was praised by his neighbors as one living
a pure life.

A beautiful Japanese girl whose parents owned a food store lived

[20] R. H. Blyth, *Zen in English Literature and Oriental Classics* (Tokyo:
The Hokuseido Press, 1942), p. 2.

near him. Suddenly, without any warning, her parents discovered she was with child.

This made her parents angry. She would not confess who the man was, but after much harassment at last named Hakuin.

In great anger the parents went to the master. "Is that so?" was all he would say.

After the child was born it was brought to Hakuin. By this time he had lost his reputation, which did not trouble him, but he took very good care of the child. He obtained milk from his neighbors and everything else the little one needed. A year later the girl-mother could stand it no longer. She told her parents the truth—that the real father of the child was a young man who worked in the fishmarket.

The mother and father of the girl at once went to Hakuin to ask his forgiveness, to apologize at length, and to get the child back again.

Hakuin was willing. In yielding the child, all he would say was: "Is that so?"[21]

This is a typical illustration of the attitude of enlightened nonattachment at which Zen Buddhism aims; the story might have been told by a St. François de Sales.

The conclusion from what has so far been said appears to be that, in applying certain insights from Zen to Catholicism, we shall be in no danger of confusion. No foreign element is being injected into the situation. All we should be doing is to articulate the urgency of what is apt to be taken for granted. That a tentative effort of this kind would not be out of place could be indicated by a recent observation of Pope John XXIII. He alludes to the possibility, and points to the consequences, of the Church's doctrine on vital questions of the day meeting with no inward response from even the most responsible Catholics. "Should these teachings remain only a pronouncement without effect," the Pope warned, "strength would be given to the arguments of those who hold that the Church

[21] Quoted from *Zen Flesh, Zen Bones: A Collection of Zen & Pre-Zen Writings*, compiled by Paul Reps (New York: Doubleday & Company, Anchor Books, 1961), pp. 7-8.

is incapable of facilitating the solution of the most difficult problems of temporal life."[22] To the words of the outwardly proclaimed message must come the light of the Spirit within. Provided it be judiciously administered, perhaps none of us will take any harm from at least "a tongue-tip taste of Zen."

[22] Quoted from *Time*, February 9, 1962, p. 42.

CHAPTER TWO

WHY SHOULD IT HAPPEN
TO ME?

At first sight it is a child's question: Why should it happen to me? Yet children's questions often touch the heart of the matter. This one, as we grow older, we learn not to ask, aloud, too insistently. All lies in the luck of the game, we try to tell ourselves: that's just the way the ball bounces, or the cooky crumbles. There is much to be said for this hearty, good-humored fatalism. But, clearly, it cannot be the whole story. We are still left with the perplexing suspicion that things might equally well have been otherwise. Of those conspicuously less fortunate than ourselves, we commonly say: There, but for God's grace, go I. Yet there also, no less truly, in place of this or that notably "successful" person, given a little more of the same kind of grace, might I have gone.

The underlying problem is perhaps best posed in terms of the pleasant things that happen to us. Let us say that I am greatly interested in Wednesday of next week being fine and sunny, so interested that I pray for it. Wednesday comes and proves to be, from my standpoint, a perfect day. Naturally, I am grateful; my prayer has been answered. God has been good to me, is the spontaneous thought. But how true is it? It might have been better for my neighbor's vegetable garden, or for the town water supply, had it poured with rain. Did God forgo these larger benefits so as to execute the particular design of satisfying me? One would hesitate to think so. God's providential plan is not centered on my ego; but neither am I a mere pawn in a divine game of chess. The difficulty is to keep both these facts simultaneously in mind.

We shall not be able to come to grips with the problem until we have looked, more closely than we are accustomed to do, into our own nature. What is the "me" to whom things "happen"? Notice that it is only when we consider ourselves as an object of thought, as "me" rather than "I," that this question arises. When the "I" is fully engaged, wholly taken up in action or thought or both, this total absorption includes an undifferentiated self-awareness, but no self-preoccupation; that is to say, there is a high degree of consciousness without "self-consciousness." The "I" is functioning so wholeheartedly as not to be distracted by the "me." This distinction, within ourselves, between I and me is more than merely verbal; it corresponds to a psychological reality of great significance. The I and me are not, of course, separate entities; they represent respectively the self as subject and the self as object. They present a distinction without a difference, and can perhaps best be described as having a nondual relationship to one another.

According to Catholic tradition, man is a unity made up of soul and body; he is part spirit, part matter, but substantially a whole. The Church not having defined the nature of either spirit or matter, this generalized description of man, while answering to common-sense observation, permits of detailed filling in. Thus, from the psychological standpoint, we can look at ourselves in terms of our bodies, feelings, perceptions, volitional impulses, and consciousness—which are the chief aspects of the human personality as seen by Buddhism.

Feelings, perceptions, volitional impulses, and even our bodies manifest themselves at the level of our conscious egos. The level, that is to say, at which we are keenly aware of ourselves as distinct personalities, as separated from the world around

us. This awareness is obviously of great importance. Without
it we could not function purposefully, either in a manner leading to the gratification of our wishes as individuals, or as playing our part in the various groups—domestic, social, political,
religious—to which we belong. The ego, aware of itself, is what
places us in a subject-object relationship to ourselves, to other
people, and even to God.

Indispensable as is this self-conscious ego to our well-being,
it is also the condition and focal point of our deepest distress.
By it we function, but by it also we suffer. We suffer the sense
of alienation inherent in the subject-object relationship: alienation from self, alienation from the natural world and other
people, alienation from God. The feeling of not knowing where
one is, of not belonging, being ill-adjusted, forces us to play a
part, more or less successful according to circumstances. We
prepare a face to meet the faces that we meet. On the basis of
such insight as we have, we come to a working compromise
with life, adapting ourselves as best we may to the social round,
to the "one damned thing after another" which largely makes
up the world of space and time.

> Time for you and time for me,
> And time yet for a hundred indecisions,
> And for a hundred visions and revisions,
> Before the taking of a toast and tea.[1]

Daily life, for most people, consists of a series of personal encounters, pleasant, unpleasant, or neutral. The original meaning of the word "person" (*persona*)—as distinct from the
technical sense which it has acquired in Catholic theology—is
that of a mask used by actors. A person is someone who as-
sumes, in however slight degree, a disguise. As soon as the word
is extended to "personage," we have no difficulty in seeing the
point. A personage is an individual with a role; he must, like
an actor, project himself in accordance with the appropriate

[1] T. S. Eliot, "The Love Song of J. Alfred Prufrock," *Collected Poems,
1909-1935* (New York: Harcourt, Brace & World, 1936), p. 12.

"image." An aspiring politician is obliged to appear as simultaneously cheerful, confident, and statesmanlike; a movie star as arresting and sexually attractive; an ecclesiastic as at once grave and benign, with perhaps a hint of a bright clerical smile. These conventions are well understood and acceptable enough. They only become tiresome when the individuals concerned, forgetting that from the basic human standpoint they are merely playing a part, identify themselves with their role. This invariably leads to trouble both for them and for those associated with them.

Here in fact we are on the brink, according to an age-long wisdom, of humanity's chief source of trouble. Deep distress inevitably occurs whenever we identify what may be called our true self (the "I") with the assertive, separative ego (the often all-too-demanding "me") : when, in other words, we allow our lives to be immersed in a private sea of feelings, perceptions, desires, and aversions, whether physical or mental. This can involve us in a kind of counterfeit self-awareness, so vivid that we may mistake its contents for our very being: all we are is what we *feel* we are.

The tendency to this condition, from which our humanity must perpetually struggle to free itself, has always been regarded as a primary fact of life by the Hindu-Buddhist tradition which lies behind Zen. A comparable outlook, though not commonly expounded with a parallel depth of insight, is to be found in the Catholic doctrine of original sin. Contemporary psychoanalysis, while preferring not to talk about sin, is similarly preoccupied with its chief constituents: ignorance and wayward desire. In this context, Dr. D. T. Suzuki cites a pertinent observation by the novelist Nancy Wilson Ross:

In accounting for the present interest in Zen in the West one must look to the shaft struck into the Western mind by psychoanalysis; the grave warnings of psychologists in general about the unhappy effects of ignoring the deeper levels of human consciousness, the unfortunate results to be seen on every side of repressing the more subtle and invisible aspects of the human being in total favor of an externalized existence.[2]

Psychoanalysis, however, fruitful as its contribution may be, leaves the depths of the spirit unplumbed. Psychologists can help us to understand the anguish which necessarily results from an existence bounded by self-preoccupation. Such a condition, we are persuaded, is not consciously willed; there is thus little question of personal guilt, though the victim is apt to experience a strong sense of guilt. Moreover, we are all victims, to a greater or less degree; self-preoccupation is inescapable; the problems it gives rise to can only be resolved by our understanding the *self*. For, when we come to think of it, we are all bounded by our ego-awareness. Nothing happens to us except in terms of it. Even that which has its origin outside ourselves —other people's love, for example—brings satisfaction only as a subjective experience. It is not what they give, but what we receive, that counts.

Yet is this entirely true? Are we totally deceived when, at times, we believe we are looking at people and things objectively, without any subjective self-reference? An answer to this question may emerge as we proceed. What confronts us at the moment is the existence, as has already been remarked, of the self under two distinct aspects: the conscious ego, the demanding "me," calling for our own and others' attention; and that which, even in everyday speech, we refer to as the "true" or "better" self—at its truest and best when subdued to what it works in—the "I." The self so considered constitutes our being; by it we live; it is the source within us, not of egoism, but of all that is creative, whatever makes for happiness; and yet we can scarcely say anything about it other than that it *is*.

The true inner self is what Indian religious thought, which lies behind Zen Buddhism, calls the *Atman*. Here we must pause; for we are at the heart of our subject. To come to terms

[2] *The Essentials of Zen Buddhism Selected from the Writings of Daisetz T. Suzuki*, edited, and with an introduction, by Bernard Phillips (New York: E. P. Dutton & Co., 1962), p. 372.

with the inner self, or as Zen describes it, "seeing into our own nature," is very much more easily said than done. " 'The Self is not to be attained by one without fortitude, nor through slackness nor without distinctive marks of discipline'. To see the Self one must become 'calm, controlled, quiet, patiently enduring and contented.' "³ We should note that this highly desirable condition, according to the masters of the spiritual life, is indistinguishable from what is required to live consciously in the presence of God. "Man must first be restored to himself, that, making in himself as it were a stepping-stone, he may rise thence and be born up to God."⁴ There is thus the closest connection between being truly aware of ourselves and being aware, in some degree at least, of God.

This raises the interesting question: How far could one, as a Catholic, agree with a position which many expositors hold to be implicit in Buddhism, namely, that to become aware of the inner self (Atman) is to become aware of the Ultimate Self (Brahman) which is God? Succinctly the doctrine is expressed in the sacred Sanskrit formula *tat tvam asi* (That thou art) ; "The Atman, or immanent eternal Self, is one with Brahman, the Absolute Principle of all existence; and the last end of every human being is to discover the fact for himself, to find out Who he really is."⁵

We should be foolish to quarrel over words and descriptive terms. Provided we remember that our individual self is finite and creaturely, we may call it Atman, and call God Brahman. Indeed, God may even be regarded as the Ultimate Self—a thoroughly Augustinian notion, as well as being a fair paraphrase of Exodus 3:14 ("I am Who am"), or of St. Thomas's

³ Quotations from the Upanishads, as cited in *A Source Book in Indian Philosophy*, edited by Sarvepalli Radhakrishnan and Charles A. Moore (Princeton, N. J.: Princeton University Press, 1957) , p. 38.
⁴ St. Augustine, *Retract.*, I, viii, 3; quoted from Erich Przywara, *An Augustine Synthesis* (New York: Harper & Brothers, Torchbook edition, 1958) , p. 17.
⁵ Aldous Huxley, *The Perennial Philosophy* (New York: Harper & Brothers, 1944) , p. 2.

Ipsum esse subsistens. But it would impose too great a strain on the orthodox formulas to attempt to equate them with such a typical statement as the following: "The real which is at the heart of the universe is reflected in the infinite depths of the self. *Brahman* (the ultimate as discovered objectively) is *Atman* (the ultimate as discovered introspectively). *Tat tvam asi* (That art thou). Truth is within us."[6] Nor is there the least necessity to do so.

If Catholics may conceivably be helped by certain insights from Zen, expositors of Zen, for their part, will lose nothing by a consideration of why Christianity insists on the truth that the creature is really distinct from the Creator. Yet it may prove that the differences on this point, fundamental as they appear, could in their practical implications be more apparent than real. Nothing is clearer in the Christian revelation than that man's "self" has the closest affinity to God. We are made in God's "image" (Genesis 1:27); man's spirit is "the lamp of the Lord" (Proverbs 20:27); we are to be "perfect" with God's perfection (Matthew 5:48); being joined to the Lord, we are "one spirit" (1 Corinthians 6:17); by God's gift we are actually "partakers of the divine nature" (2 Peter 1:4). These texts do not indicate man's identity with God, though they point to the possibility of the closest communion with Him. They are the positive aspect of one of Christianity's basic teachings—that the only misfortune is to be separated from God.

The tradition behind Zen is not dissimilar. Authorities on Hinduism and Buddhism come out strongly against the "monism" which is often ascribed to them by Western critics. The doctrine of the Vedas (*i.e.,* the Hindu sacred writings), declares Coomaraswamy, is "neither pantheistic nor polytheistic, nor a worship of the powers of Nature except in the sense that *Natura naturans est Deus*[7] and all her powers but the names of God's

[6] *A Source Book in Indian Philosophy,* p. 38.
[7] St. Thomas Aquinas refers to God as *"Natura naturans"* in the *Summa Theologica,* I-II, 85, 6: "Deus a quibusdam dicitur *natura naturans"*—"God is said by some to be *the Nature Who makes nature."* It is clear from the context that St. Thomas finds the term quite acceptable.

acts."[8] In the same sense we find one of the leading exponents of Zen insisting, "Buddhism is often regarded as being pantheistic. This must be corrected. Buddhism is absolutely not pantheistic. Buddhism stands in itself and is not to be subsumed under any such category. Pantheism is apt to ignore differences, while Buddhism does not. Differences are differences and as such they remain. But there is something in the particular differences which makes them most intimately related to each other, as if they all come from one source."[9] This is hardly distinguishable from St. Thomas's position, that God exists in all things, not as part of their essence, but as the immediate cause of their being.[10]

Nevertheless there are possibilities of equivocation. Certain Zennists, unwittingly perhaps, contrary to the spirit of Zen (which is not a philosophy, but a pure experience), transform it into an ontology and, doing what the Buddha consistently refused to do, proceed to make categorical statements about the nature of reality. One such statement, though phrased as a negation, is that "there is no ego, no enduring entity which is the constant subject of our changing experience." It may be doubted whether so sharp an affront to common sense is made any more acceptable by the explanatory sentence which follows. "For the ego exists in an abstract sense alone, being an abstraction from memory, somewhat like the illusory circle of fire made by the whirling torch."[11] The implication here is that the only "self" is the Ultimate Self, that is to say, God. On this premise, the grounds for the individual's moral responsibility are, of course, removed, as the author does not fail to see. "But one must face the fact that, in its essence, the Buddhist experi-

---

[8] *Hinduism and Buddhism*, p. 3.

[9] *The Essentials of Zen Buddhism*, p. 64.

[10] See *Summa Theologica*, I, 8, 3, which concludes, "Therefore, God is in all things by His power, inasmuch as all things are subject to His power; He is by His presence in all things, as all things are bare and open to His eyes; He is in all things by His essence, inasmuch as He is present to all as the cause of their being."

[11] *The Way of Zen*, p. 47.

ence is a liberation from conventions of every kind, including the moral conventions."[12]

The operative word in the sentence just quoted is "conventions"; it is not the author's intention to dispense altogether with morality. It is true also, as we shall consider later, that the moral content of many social conventions may be much less than is often supposed. But it is well to take note of the Zen tendency to sit lightly to ethical obligation, and even to seek to rationalize this irresponsibility by an appeal to an implied philosophy of Buddhism. Furthermore Mr. Watts claims too much for his position, that there is no ego, when he says that it is "fundamental to every school of Buddhism." Dr. Edward Conze has pointed out that "belief in individuality" appears so intrinsically plausible that it might be expected "to have some kind of objective foundation somewhere." "Here was the weak spot in the Buddhist armour, and the problem that has harassed the Buddhist theoreticians throughout their history." He describes how the "heresy" of a belief in a self invaded the ranks. "The followers of one of the eighteen traditional sects— the Sammitiyas—were known as *Pudgala-vadins, 'Upholders of the belief in a person.'* " Dr. Conze adds, "The orthodox, in the end, were forced to admit the notion of a permanent ego, not openly, but in various disguises, hidden in particularly obscure and abstruse concepts"; and he shrewdly remarks, "As soon as the advice to disregard the individual self had hardened into the proposition that *'there is no self,'* such concessions to common sense became quite inevitable."[13]

All this is highly relevant to our present theme. Catholicism is at one with Zen in extolling the self-*less* life; but selflessness is an attitude of the human spirit resulting from its surrender to God, the Ultimate Self, not a denial of the existence of the creaturely ego. Zen enthusiasts in the West may profitably search their hearts on this point. Why do they find the "there-

[12] *Ibid.*, p. 107.
[13] *Buddhism: Its Essence and Development*, pp. 169-70.

is-no-ego" doctrine so attractive? As indicating the creature's relative insignificance before God, it could have meaning; as it has for the Catholic mystics—St. Catherine of Siena, for example: "Thou, O God, art an abyss of everything and I am an abyss of nothing." But divorced from a religious context, to what does it lead? To some kind of aesthetic intuitionism, perhaps. Not, however, so far as I can see, to "regeneration" or any deeply significant way of life. On the contrary, the evidence points to an old familiar degeneration, the path that leads to individualistic anarchy and spiritual rootlessness.

It should be noted also that the nonexistence of a created self or ego is not indicated by any one of the Buddha's Four Holy Truths, whatever the Hinduist assumptions that may be read into them. Gautama Buddha, as Aldous Huxley points out,[14] was one of those strictly practical teachers who had "no use for speculation and whose primary concern is to put out in men's hearts the hideous fires of greed, resentment and infatuation." This is a fruitful thought. Applied to Christianity, it transforms the somewhat abstruse metaphysic of the Creator-creature relationship into the highly rewarding practical truth, which dominates alike the Old and New Testaments: the truth, namely, that it is to God alone that man both appropriately may, and imperatively needs to, surrender his created self. "The thought of Thee stirs him so deeply," writes St. Augustine in the well-known opening to his *Confessions*, "that he cannot be content unless he praises Thee; because Thou didst make us for Thyself and our hearts find no peace until they rest in Thee."

We should observe that it is God Himself, not a "thought" about Him, that brings satisfaction. The thought may be helpful, but it may also be erroneous—in which case it is the reverse of helpful. Of necessity it must be inadequate. (See Isaiah 55:9.) It is not in the realm of thoughts about God, but in God

[14] *The Perennial Philosophy*, p. 1.

Himself that we live and move and have our being (Acts 17:28). He is present to us by His creative power, itself one with the divine substance, more intimately than it is possible to imagine. "Closer is He than breathing, and nearer than hands and feet." Our existence, though distinct, is rooted and grounded in God's existence. As an effect is, as it were, transcended and embraced by what causes it, so there is a sense in which we may say, echoing the thought of Augustine and Aquinas, that we exist more really in God than in our own being. What is needed, if we are to be at peace, is that we should be consciously aware of this fact. Such an awareness, as distinct from a theoretical knowledge based on inference, would constitute "enlightenment." Without amounting to a direct vision of God, it would bring us into harmony with the Principle behind the universe and so enable us, at last, to understand ourselves.

We have next to recall that, though it is fatally easy for us to became identified with our feelings and emotions—and the less creditable they are the easier it is—we cannot, from the nature of the case, "identify" with God. God has to take the initiative, our contribution being to correspond by not preferring darkness to the Light which is ready to "enlighten every man" (John 1:9). Furthermore, though the divine initiative is supremely free, it is characteristic; that is to say, it is wholly natural to God to "realize" Himself in creatures. The principle that self-diffusion is the mark of goodness is verified without qualification in God. What gives creatures their being is actually God's love extending itself to them: *"amor Dei est infundens et creans bonitatem in rebus."*[15]

From the rational standpoint of the human mind, God's activity toward us, His "realizing" His own *image,* takes place at two levels—that of nature and that of grace: though the whole process is in fact a "gracious" one, being independent of any merit on our part. God as the Author of nature *(Deus ut natura*

[15] *Summa Theologica,* I, 20, 2.

naturans) brings us into and sustains our existence. God as the Author of grace (*Deus ut sanctificator sanctificans*) integrates our personalities; in other words, provided our egos do not get in the way, He makes us whole, which is the same thing as "holy."

Grace perfects, and therefore presupposes, nature. The implications of this well-known theological axiom are worth considering. One most relevant to our present discussion is that unless we respond to the divine initiative at the natural level, we block its effectiveness in the order of grace. From which it follows that one cannot simultaneously be holy or whole and "unnatural." This conclusion, about which Zennists have no difficulty, might well occupy the attention of Catholics more than it commonly does. "O God who art ever the same," writes Augustine in his *Soliloquies* (II, 1, i) , "let me know myself, let me know Thee." Until we can see into our own nature, we cannot establish a satisfactory relationship with God. Though, by the same token, through relating ourselves appropriately to God we gain self-knowledge.

Looking into one's own nature, as here understood, is not an introspective effort at examining one's mental processes; still less does it require us to submit to the ministrations of a psychoanalyst. An inner task is certainly involved before we can experience what has been called the "opening of the third eye"; but this, again, is no psychological miracle. It is the gift, so simple yet so rarely possessed, of looking directly at reality, so that we see it as it is, in its "suchness." It is the capacity to bring all our powers of perception to bear on what is before us—including, be it noted, our own actions and experiences—without any subjective admixture of personal feelings, prejudices, alien thoughts, wishes, attractions, aversions, memories, hopes, fears, and, in general, that complex amalgam of emotions which habitually prevents us from observing what we are looking at, clear and unclouded. The result of such an "enlightenment" is to remove the sense of alienation from the natural world, from other people, from our selves, and consequently from God,

which lies at the root of our distress. Once a harmony has been
established, on the basis of that nature "which makes the whole
world kin," there is a sense in which the Christian also can
make his own the *tat tvam asi* (That art thou) , and, in enlightened compassion, find relief from an at times seemingly unbearable weight of suffering.

Among the factors that turn the existence of suffering into a
"problem," even for religious people (perhaps especially for
them) , is a tendency to apply to God their own notions of good
and evil, right and wrong. The expectation that the Almighty
will conform to a moral pattern laid down for Him in advance
by His creatures still endures, despite the whole weight of Biblical evidence to the contrary. The assumption that if one's
conscience is clear God must be on one's side explains the self-
righteousness that usually characterizes this or that "crusade"—
"we" being in the right, "they" hopelessly in the wrong—in
which the participants are confident that they are fighting the
battles of the Lord. Eastern religious thought, as well as mature
Christianity, takes a different view.

One of the deeper aspects of the Chinese wisdom underlying
Zen is the doctrine of *Yang-Yin*. These are the two great cosmic
forces, *Yang* (positive, masculine, dry, hot) and *Yin* (negative,
feminine, damp, cold) . As Dr. Hubert Benoit points out, "The
primordial dualism Yang-Yin includes all the oppositions that
we are able to imagine: summer-winter, day-night, movement-
immobility, beauty-ugliness, truth-error, construction-destruc-
tion, life-death, etc. . . ."[16] Here might also have been included,
good-evil, right-wrong, and any pair of opposites we choose to
think of. What this suggests is that no element in the created
world is absolutely positive or absolutely negative. But the opposites are held to be reconciled in a superior conciliatory principle—the Tao.[17] This all-embracing system of Yang and Yin
as reconciled in the Tao is often represented by an equilateral

[16] Hubert Benoit, *The Supreme Doctrine: Psychological Studies in Zen
Thought* (New York: The Viking Press, 1959) , p. 7.
[17] See p. 17.

triangle, with the Tao at the apex, and Yang and Yin respectively at the angles at the base.

Certain qualifications being made, this geometrical symbolism can be transposed into a Christian context, with God at the apex angle, good and evil at the two opposite base angles. A Christian truth which, often to our great detriment, we are for some reason reluctant to face is that God is implicated in created evil. "Shall there be evil in the city which the Lord hath not done?" (Amos 3:6). "I form the light and create darkness. I make peace and create evil. I, the Lord, that do all these things" (Isaiah 45:7). These texts from the inspired Scriptures are to be explained in the light of a consistent theology, but they are not to be explained away.

The clearest brief discussion of God's relationship to creaturely evil is to be found in the first part of the *Summa Theologica,* question 49, "On the Cause of Evil." Where the absence of an appropriate good—and this, fundamentally, is what constitutes evil—is due to an ineffective agent, then God cannot be its cause, since He is never ineffective. "But the evil which consists in the corruption of some things goes back to God as to its cause," says St. Thomas (article 2). "And this appears both with regard to natural things and voluntary things." God has created a universe in which His positive action (*Yang*), the generation of things, implies a corresponding negative (*Yin*), corruption or destruction. In order that man may live, part of the animal and vegetative world must die. Even moral evil, sin, falls within the divine plan. Though sin, being a defect in a creature's will, does not require God's causality, sin could not happen unless God permitted it. God, having created a race of frail human beings, takes account of the fact that large numbers of them will prove their frailty in action (article 3, reply 5). God's universe contains the built-in realities of physical and moral evil.

It is worth noting that Aquinas, in dismissing as absurd the notion that evil is caused by some intrinsically evil first agent, supposedly standing in opposition to God, faces the realities of

the situation with the same calmness as characterizes the Buddhist tradition.

Those, however, who upheld two first principles, one good and
the other evil, fell into this error from the same cause, whence also
arose other strange notions of the ancients; namely, because they
failed to consider the universal cause of all beings, and considered
only the particular causes of particular effects. For on that account, if
they found a thing hurtful to something by the power of its own nature, they thought that the very nature of that thing was evil; as, for
instance, if one should say that the nature of fire was evil because it
burnt the house of a poor man. The judgment, however, of the goodness of anything does not depend on its order to any particular thing,
but rather upon what it is in itself, and on its order to the whole universe, wherein every part has its own perfectly ordered place (article 3).

A commonly felt reluctance to face the fact that evil enters
into God's scheme of things is due to a mental confusion. God
is supremely good, we rightly say; therefore He can have no
part in evil. But the conclusion does not follow; as may be
gathered from St. Thomas's reasoning above. There is a distinction to be drawn between the ontological goodness, which
is one of God's attributes, and moral goodness, which is based
on conformity to an external norm. God is infinitely good because He lacks nothing of being, but His actions are not regulated by any norm other than His own inscrutable wisdom.
God's holiness, which means "wholeness," includes all that is
positive in moral goodness as we understand it; but what He sees
as beneficial to the universe as a whole may involve evil to individuals. If we are to discover our true self, which is our being
as harmonized with God, then we must learn to look upon
areas of evil, not with approval, but calmly and dispassionately.
What God tolerates we have no business to find intolerable.
Or, to state the same point in more positive terms, we should
seek to become increasingly identified with the attitude of
"your Father in heaven, Who makes His sun rise on the evil

and equally on the good, His rain fall on the just and equally on the unjust" (Matthew 5:45).

The dualism of positive and negative, *Yang* and *Yin,* exists within our own personalities. We are both good and bad, we see and approve the better but do the worse. As Dr. Benoit points out, "The belief in this bipartite composition expresses itself in all sorts of common sayings. 'I am master of "myself," ' 'I cannot prevent myself from . . . ,' 'I am pleased with myself,' 'I am annoyed with myself,' etc. . . ."[18]

Here is the familiar war within ourselves. Though it is worth enquiring how far our ignorance and lack of light are responsible for transforming the tension of necessarily opposing opposites into a "war." We take sides with the "good" self and do battle with the "bad"; we strain every nerve to be "in the right," so suffering anxiety and inner conflict. Or else we give way to our "bad" side, and become subject to a dispiriting sense of guilt, the reproach of the "good" self to the "bad" self. The only way out of this dilemma is to seek refuge in the superior conciliatory Principle where "good" and "bad" are reconciled. If, instead of clinging to our limited notions of the good, we allow God's goodness to realize itself in the created "self," we shall find that we are sharing also in God's mercifulness toward what is bad in us. This was St. Paul's way of release from a strain that had become beyond his capacity to bear. "Unhappy man that I am, who shall deliver me from the body of this death? The grace of God, by Jesus Christ our Lord" (Romans 7: 24-25. *Vulgate*).

Short of the state in which the human spirit is "oned" with God, by what St. Thomas calls *co-naturalness,* the sense of strain just alluded to never completely abates. In other words, until we are at one with God we cannot be at one with ourselves. As a result of this internal disharmony, the individual feels a sense of alienation from the people and things around him. When he cannot control or find pleasure in them, they

---

[18] *The Supreme Doctrine,* p. 153.

become, at least unconsciously, a threat, in that they diminish his ego. Feeling himself, or what amounts to the same thing, his interests threatened, he reacts by hostility, expressing itself in aggression or withdrawal. In either case the gulf between the conscious ego and reality widens, with a consequent intensification of distress.

These considerations help to explain why, even apart from humanity's burden of physical privation, suffering is endemic to the human situation. Our joys provide only an occasional respite. In this there is no blank pessimism, as if a more or less continuous state of happiness were impossible. What needs to be understood, however, is that happiness depends on the preliminary acceptance of a number of unpalatable facts. Chief among those facts is the practical knowledge, as distinct from airy theory, of what makes for happiness. This knowledge is especially hard to come by for us of the West, conditioned as we are to making large demands on our environment, and to entertaining the illusion that to raise the standard of living is equivalent to nourishing the human spirit.

Against this background, it must be acknowledged that the Buddha's teaching on the omnipresence of suffering and the means to its relief appears more relevant to our needs than not a few popular presentations of Christianity. We need to be reminded, as the Hebrew prophets insisted, that it is much easier to worship God than to do His will. Less self-giving is demanded to answer the summons to go regularly to church than to fulfill the requirement, of Christ and the Buddha alike, that we have loving-kindness and be compassionate. This is not to decry either popular Christianity or churchgoing, but to urge that we see both in due perspective. Until we do, Coomaraswamy's adaptation of Matthew Arnold's lines, as indicating the widely held Eastern estimate of Western civilization, may still apply:

> The East bowed low before the West
> In patient, deep disdain.

Despite a depressingly large number of appearances to the contrary, Catholic spirituality—at least as expounded in its most satisfying form by Aquinas—moves at the same profound level as the metaphysical tradition behind Zen Buddhism. God's all-embracing providence, as one might expect, is considered in terms of the splendid Biblical imagery of Wisdom. "Bold in her sweep from world's end to world's end, and everywhere her gracious ordering manifests itself" (Wisdom 8:1).[19] But God's providential control of things is not only world-embracing, it reaches to the minutest particular. Each individual, all that he is and has, including his thoughts and free choices, is totally subject to the God whose intent it is to enlighten us increasingly by His presence, if only we consent to let our eyes be opened. St. Thomas has no place in his philosophy for the autonomous personality, supposedly on his own, cut off from God and therefore from an insight into his own nature.

How the divinely ordained plan in fact works out is made known to us by daily experience. The circumstances of our lives, the calls of duty, the innumerable encounters, pleasant and unpleasant, with persons and situations, success and failure, honor and dishonor—these are the signs of what God wills to happen to us. We find, however, that we cannot be reconciled to life's inevitable difficulties, still less can we achieve the calm of an inner harmony, by a process of "adjustment" to each new turn of events. For this we have only a limited capacity; we grow weary or feel that we are not versatile enough. Nevertheless human nature is extremely flexible, its powers of resilience are often astonishing; we learn, too, to "roll with the punch," if not happily, at least with a display of good humor. In due course we discover that the ability to remain one's true self, amid harassment and multiple preoccupations, depends on our fidelity to an inner task. That task is to become awake,

[19] See *Summa Theologica*, I-II, 110, 2, where, quoting this text, St. Thomas argues that, alike in the order of nature and of grace, we are equipped with all that we need to respond easily and promptly to God's initiative.

to "realize" that God's providence operates most significantly, so far as we are concerned, not outside ourselves but within our own spirit.

Discussing the question "Whether everything is subject to God's providence," St. Thomas concludes, needless to say, with an unqualified affirmative. In the course of his argument he deals with an objection based on a text of Scripture: "God made man from the beginning, and left him in the hand of his own counsel" (Ecclesiasticus 15:14). It would appear, then, that God looks on, so to speak, as a spectator while man, as an independent agent, does what he chooses. Aquinas replies as follows:

When it is said that God left man to himself, this does not mean that man is exempt from divine providence; but merely that he has not a prefixed operating force determined to only the one effect; as in the case with natural things, which are only acted upon as though directed by another towards an end; and do not act of themselves, as if they directed themselves towards an end, as rational creatures do, through their having free will which enables them to take counsel and make a choice. Hence it is significantly said, *"in the hand of his own counsel"*. But since the very act of free will goes back to God as to its cause, it necessarily follows that everything that happens by the exercise of free will must be subject to divine providence. For human providence is included under God's providence, as a particular under a universal cause.[20]

Though God acts effectively, "by an interior inclination of the will,"[21] on our free choices, no violence is done to the will, as if it were under the alien control of some external force. God alone "glides into our minds" (*"sola Trinitas menti illabitur"*),[22] leaving their nature and activities wholly intact. God can do this because He is the "realization" of our true selves; or, as St. Thomas puts it, "God alone being the universal good, He only fills the capacity of the will and moves it suf-

[20] *Summa Theologica*, I, 22, 2, 4.
[21] *Ibid.*, I, 105, 4.
[22] *Ibid.*, III, 8, 8, 1.

ficiently as its object. Similarly the power of willing is caused by God alone. For to will is nothing but to be inclined towards the object of the will, which is universal good. But to incline towards the universal good belongs to the First Mover, to whom the ultimate end is proportionate; just as in human affairs, to him who presides over the community it belongs to direct his subjects to the general welfare."[23]

These detached, unemotional phrases, to those who will take the trouble to ponder them, convey more clearly than the rhapsodies of poets and mystics how close God is to man. God surrounds, envelopes, permeates us by the immediacy of His Being (*immediatione suppositi*), and this not only with respect to our nature, but as touching our every choice and all we do. What must further be noticed, St. Thomas himself drawing attention to it, is that the human will acts by benefit of an illumination from the mind. And here, again, God by His immediate activity is the enlightener of our minds. "God moves the created intellect, inasmuch as He gives it the intellectual power, whether natural or superadded; and impresses on the created intellect the intelligible species, and maintains and preserves both power and species in existence."[24]

Aquinas is at one with the expositors of Zen in emphasizing insight. The importance of this, that understanding must precede action or even good intentions, is not seldom overlooked.

[23] *Ibid.*, I, 105, 4.

[24] *Ibid.*, I, 105, 3. NOTE: The theory of knowledge underlying these statements is commended to students of intellectualist Zen. To a Western mind they sometimes appear rather naïve: in their enthusiasm for "enlightenment"—the *satori* experience—they pass over without discussion the serious epistemological problems involved. Plato and Aristotle have not been outmoded by "the San Francisco renaissance," or even by the admirable labors of D. T. Suzuki. More specifically, it may be found that the Aristotelian-Thomistic theory of the "active intellect" (*intellectus agens*) —involving an act of "illumination" antecedent to any reasoning process—will repay study. This is linked by Aristotle with the "potential intellect" (*intellectus possibilis*), itself having a capacity to become by knowledge everything (*est quoddamodo omnia*), so providing an intelligible frame of reference for a direct apprehension of reality boundless in its scope.

If love is more important than mere knowledge, for love to be effective it must still be "according to knowledge" (Romans 10:2). Genuine love is compounded of appreciation and sympathy, issuing eventually in action, but first in a kind of contemplative egolessness. In default of this we tend to deal with others not as they are, but as embodiments of our ideas of what they are, which is quite a different matter. Once more we recall the basic Hindu—and may we not say also, for practical purposes, Christian?—doctrine: *tat tvam asi:* "That art thou." Graced by God, we share His nature (2 Peter 1:4); in Christ, we are members one of another (Ephesians 4:25). Thus, in the final analysis, it is "unnatural" for us to experience separation, either from God or from other human beings.

Nonseparation is oneness. For the realization of this oneness Jesus Christ especially prayed—"that they all may be one, as Thou Father art in me, and I in Thee" (John 17:21). He seemed to imply that His life's work would have an element of failure until this unity became an accomplished fact—"that the world may come to believe that it is Thou Who hast sent me." Keeping this in mind, we have little difficulty in disposing of the question which gives its title to the present chapter. Things, good or bad, agreeable or disagreeable, happen to us because God wills it that way. United to God, we discover our true self, know our own nature, and thus are able to "identify" ourselves, certain conditions being fulfilled, with the very Author of events, whatever they are. When this state of harmony with, of nonalienation from, God and His creation is achieved, suffering may remain but there will be no sense of frustration. We shall "realize"—that is, experience with complete acceptance—that that is how it was meant to be.

> The perfect way knows no difficulties
> Except that it refuses to make preferences; . . .
> If you wish to see it before your own eyes
> Have no fixed thoughts either for or against it.[25]

[25] *Buddhist Scriptures*, p. 171.

CHAPTER THREE

HAVING ONE'S OWN WAY

The duality we experience, real or only apparent, between the conscious ego and our true self, is always ready to declare itself. According to Buddhist doctrine, and the Catholic Christian may readily concur, what chiefly accounts for the division within is a grasping desire or craving, either for what we do not yet have, or, having, fear to lose. This is, in fact, *the Holy Truth of the Origination of Ill*—a "craving . . . accompanied by delight and greed, seeking its delight now here, now there, that is, craving for sensuous experience, craving to perpetuate oneself, craving for extinction."

Here it is important to note that this diagnosis of the main source of human distress does not indicate a world-renouncing asceticism as the cure. There is no endorsement of a Mani-chaean or Jansenistic view of life, no prompting to harsh austerity. It is not what is craved, the delight, the sensuous enjoyment, that causes trouble, but the *craving* itself. The point, and the difficulty, is similar to, if not quite identical with, what St. Paul is saying in 1 Corinthians 7:31: ". . . using this world as if not using it to the full; for the visible form of this world is passing away." What is being advocated is "non-attachment"—which has a significantly different shade of meaning from the more familiar word "detachment." To be detached suggests having broken free, perhaps violently, from something to which one is now opposed, with the possibility of

43

a corresponding increase of ego-consciousness expressed in aversion. For it must be kept in mind that aversions, distastes, hatreds, though negative in name, are as much forms of craving, in terms of self-regard, as their opposites. Nonattachment conveys the subtler notion, and one more rarely realized, of both enjoying an experience and not being involved in it. The doctrine of nonattachment will occupy us in a succeeding chapter.

Here we are concerned with another aspect of what has already been considered: which may be excusable, since it is the chief problem of human living and has many facets. To "have one's own way" is in certain respects a necessity for us. It is another name for the instinct to self-preservation. By it we defend ourselves against our enemies, promote our legitimate interests, play a distinctive and useful part in the community, and, in general, ensure our growth to maturity. And yet, considered from another standpoint, having one's own way, as has already been suggested, is the chief source of our troubles. Not only does it often bring in its train loneliness and a sense of guilt; it can lead to the complete or partial frustration of the effort to achieve those objectives on which our well-being depends.

In order to discuss intelligibly this situation, we must return to our distinction between the true self and the conscious ego— the outgoing, unself-conscious "I," and the self-regarding "me." Some light is thrown on the psychological division within our personalities by the theology of the Fall: we are more truly ourselves when "reborn" in grace than in our former unregenerate nature, as God-centered rather than self-centered. What our attention is now to be focused on is the conscious ego which, though not a separate being from the true self, tends to act as if it were and so take over and dominate the scene. One way to discuss the topic is in terms of original sin and its consequences, which would be both valid and relevant. But then we should have introduced the notion of *guilt,* a complex subject with many ramifications of its own. Besides, it is a sense of guilt which, often quite needlessly, aggravates human distress. Needlessly, because much, though by no means all, of our unhappiness is the product of ignorance rather than bad will. It may therefore be helpful to discourse calmly on the universal phenomenon of egocentricity, without any overtones of reproach, whether inner- or other-directed.

There is a fundamental aspect of this matter to which the Zen masters never tire of drawing our attention. They stress the immense difficulty of simply looking at things as they are. To dispose oneself to look directly at reality is, in fact, what Zen is all about. It is pointed out, for example, that we are to "consider the lilies of the field" (Matthew 6:28), not as flowers to be plucked, or as an object of poetic emotion, or even as examples of God's handiwork, but merely as themselves, "how they grow." What commonly happens is that we project on to the lilies, or whatever else we may be looking at, our desires or aversions, our nostalgic emotions, our utilitarian purposes, so that the object is not seen in itself, its "suchness," but as "sicklied o'er with the pale cast of thought."

There are times when it makes excellent sense, particularly if one happens to be a poet or an artist, to daydream a little, or to employ one's creative imagination on what one looks at. But it cannot make sense not to know when one is doing so, or not to be able to look at things in any other way. For then we should be unconsciously regarding external reality as a function of ourselves, as existing to serve "me," with consequences that must inevitably be disastrous. The conscious ego, instead of becoming more and more identified with the true self—the demanding "me" merging in the unself-conscious "I"—becomes increasingly inflated on its own account; it is engaged in substituting for the world as it is an imaginary world in which the conscious ego is supreme.

When this situation is transferred to the sphere of personal relations, its unrealities become even more painfully evident. Unless we can see another person as he or she is, we can neither know nor love. We may suppose that we do both, but what we know is our emotional reaction to the other, and what we love is an object that we have largely fashioned for ourselves. Our

failures here are what occasion such sound Zen advice as
"Wherever your attention alights, at this very point, *experience.*"[1] "Feel the consciousness of each person as your own consciousness. So, leaving aside concern for self, *become each
being.*"[2] Had we the grace and the responsiveness to follow
these counsels, we should be in no danger of the challenge:
"How is it that thou canst see the speck of dust which is in thy
brother's eye, and art not aware of the beam which is in thy
own? By what right wilt thou say to thy brother, Wait, let me
rid thy eye of that speck, when there is a beam all the while in
thy own?" (Matthew 7: 3-4).

All lies in sympathetic insight. If this is achieved, love may
be left to take care of itself; it will necessarily follow; or, rather,
it is already involved. Where there is no insight, love is replaced by that feeblest of substitutes—good intentions. Here it
should be stressed that what is called for is neither an acute
intelligence nor an exceptional mental equipment. These
might hinder rather than assist; though also, of course, they
could be an invaluable help. The basic requirement is what the
Christian masters of the spiritual life call "docility." This is not
an attitude of subservience, but an absence of prejudice, stub-
bornness, preconceived ideas, and opinionatedness. These defects prove, on examination, to be devices to bolster the threatened ego. Were we to shed, or sit lightly to, our opinions we
should feel, or so we imagine, uncertain of ourselves. So we
"cherish" our opinions irrespective of the evidence, until they
become convictions and even personal dogmas. Behind this te-
nacity of viewpoint may sometimes be discovered the unintelli-
gent traditionalism satirized by Sir Alan Herbert:

> As my poor father used to say
> In eighteen sixty three;
> And what my father used to say
> Is good enough for me.

[1] *Zen Flesh, Zen Bones*, p. 173.
[2] *Ibid.*, p. 171.

By way of commentary on these un-Zennish sentiments, the following story is worth recounting.

> Nan-in, a Japanese master during the Meiji era (1868-1912), received a university professor who came to enquire about Zen.
> Nan-in served tea. He poured his visitor's cup full, and then kept on pouring.
> The professor watched the overflow until he could no longer restrain himself. "It is overfull. No more will go in!"
> "Like this cup", Nan-in said, "you are full of your own opinions and speculations. How can I show you Zen unless you first empty your cup?"[3]

Egoism of the mind, revealing itself in a multiplicity of ways, is what accounts for our arbitrary views and willful actions. Were we truly "enlightened," our mental attitude would not be influenced by personal predilections, but solely by evidence —including, be it noted, the credibility of a competent authority, human or divine (as in the case of a Catholic's rationally grounded faith in God's revelation). Clinging blindly to one's opinions can be a more effective block to direct contact with reality, and therefore to union with God, than vice itself. This was the basic theme of the criticism leveled by our Lord against His enemies. They were not, the majority of them, "bad" men; they were right-thinking people; but they held uncritically to the accepted views about religion and consequently missed the point.

> Try not to seek after the true,
> Only cease to cherish opinions.[4]

Underlying this simple yet profound advice is the psychological fact that the earnest seeker after truth has usually decided in advance what kind of truth he is looking for. He is apt to discover, at the end of his researches, "what I had always thought." We bring back from the Indies, as Emerson remarks, what we

---

[3] *Ibid.*, p. 5.
[4] Seng-Ts'an, "On Believing in Mind," 9; quoted from *Buddhist Scriptures*, p. 172.

take to the Indies. It is the same predisposition of mind which
leads us to read the books and newspapers which reinforce
rather than challenge our views; the same that prompts us to
seek counsel not from an impartial critic, but from a like-
minded friend. No doubt it is all very human: that is the way
the world goes. Nevertheless it helps to explain why, even at
the business of facing reality at less than the ultimate level,
many are called but few are chosen. We are not chosen because
we don't choose to be chosen.

> The Great Way is calm and large-hearted,
> For it nothing is easy, nothing hard;
> Small views are irresolute, the more in haste, the tardier they go.
> Clinging is never kept within bounds,
> It is sure to go the wrong way;
> Quit it, and things follow their own courses,
> While the essence neither departs nor abides.
> Obey the nature of things, and you are in concord with
> The Way, calm, and easy, and free from annoyance;
> But when your thoughts are tied, you turn away from the truth,
> They grow heavier and duller, and are not at all sound.
> When they are not sound, the spirit is troubled;
> What is the use of being partial and one-sided then?[5]

In following the "Great Way"—we may call it the "Way of
Truth"—"nothing is easy, nothing hard." All we have to do is
to look and to listen. Really to look at another human being
does not imply the coldness and detachment of an impersonal
scrutiny. On the contrary, what is demanded is an amiable selflessness. Amiability is needed lest our communion in nature be
overlooked; selflessness, to prevent our conscious ego from
blocking the light. Too often we look at others through a cloud
of our own emotions. To see another person in his or her "suchness" means that we must be free from antipathy and aversion,
or, at the other extreme, from uncontrolled emotional attachment or infatuation. Not only such obviously hostile feelings as

[5] *Ibid.*, 15, 18, p. 173.

suspicion or resentment, but any mental preoccupation, to-gether with reactions arising from memories, anticipations, hopes, anxieties, fears, obscure our perception and effectively prevent us from *seeing* who it is that, at this particular place and time, happens to be our neighbor.

Similarly with listening, the ego all too frequently gets in the way. This explains why so many conversations are exercises in talking at, rather than with, one another. Not only do we prefer the sound of our own voice, we prefer also the procession of our own thoughts. We tend to be more interested in what we are going to say next than in what someone else is saying now. When this tendency gets out of hand the consequences are pain-fully familiar: we become bores, we look to others mainly to provide us with a cue for our own remarks. Having lost interest in drawing others out so that they speak their minds, we neither get to know nor learn anything from them.

This, of course, is to heighten and oversimplify the pic-ture. In daily life things are seldom quite so bad: the reason being that our true self is ever ready to step in and restore san-ity. But it may be allowed that here, roughly depicted, are the roots of egoistic conduct. These roots, unless something is done about them, grow and come to flower in a habitual self-center-edness, of which the signs are unmistakable. Among them are possessiveness, greed, a craving for power and prestige, ruth-lessness, and a tendency to treat others as if they existed for one's own purposes. Conditioning these disorders is an indefin-able restlessness and discontent from which, naturally enough, every attempt is made to escape. But the way of escape com-monly chosen only aggravates the condition and so leads us back, sadder but no wiser, to the point of departure. We seek to defend or enhance the conscious ego, already inflated through its craving for satisfaction, by *grasping*, refusing to let go.

> Clinging is never kept within bounds,
> It is sure to go the wrong way;
> Quit it, and things follow their own courses. . . .

Nor is it merely persons and things to which we cling; we strive to hold on, in memory at least, to pleasant experiences and gratifying emotional states. We recall the past and complain sorrowfully that times are not what they were. Or we try to live in the future: mentally we grasp at some enchanting prospect that lies just over the horizon. Life would be intolerable, we commonly tell ourselves, without something to look forward to. Again, it is part of the human pattern—which of us can claim exemption from these feelings and attitudes? But they help to explain why suffering is not something added to life's routine; suffering, so often the product of our own ignorance and inadequacy, is bound up with life itself.

There is obviously nothing particularly acute or profound about these remarks. They have only to be set down for their truth to be apparent. The cure for the situation indicated above can hardly be less evident, though we shall be at pains to consider it at length. A hint of what will be developed later is contained in an interesting remark by the novelist D. H. Lawrence, to which F. R. Leavis, the literary critic, has drawn attention. "Few people live on the spot where they are," said Lawrence; to which Leavis adds, truly enough, "which is equivalent to saying that few people really live." To live on the spot where one is is to live in the spirit of Zen, as can be seen from such typical Zen sayings as:

The Way is near, but men seek it afar. It is in easy things, but men seek for it in difficult things.[6]

The Way is like a great highroad; there is no difficulty whatever in recognizing it. What is wrong with us is that we do not really search for it. Just go home and plenty of people will point it out to you.[7]

Every day is a good day;
your every-day mind—that is the Way![8]

[6] Quoted from R. H. Blyth, *Zen in English Literature and Oriental Classics,* p. 20.
[7] *Ibid.,* pp. 20-21.
[8] *Ibid.,* p. 51.

It would be easy to parallel from Christian sources the higher simplicity of these sayings. The Way (*Tao*) here spoken of is the way of our true self, in other words, God's way for us, as distinct from the variety of paths that the unregenerate ego, grasping at this, that, or the other, would lead us along. Zen's uniqueness—if it has any, which, as we shall see, is doubtful!—lies in its insistence on the "every-day mind" as the key to the total situation. A mind dwelling on the past or the future, or even too intently on the present, is not sufficiently receptive. The aim is to become aware of immediate reality with nothing, not even a thought, intervening. Only then can our true, that is, the God-centered, self make the egoless response.

What adds to the difficulty of bringing our true self fully to life is that we not only have our obtrusive individual egos to deal with, we have the corporate ego of the group or groups to which we belong. The group may be a business company, a local community, a club or society, having some kind of juridical personality of its own. Corporate loyalty is thus apt to involve us in attitudes and lines of conduct which conflict with those dictated by our true self. The same could hold of the professions: the law, medicine, the Church, each imposing its code of behavior and demanding that its peculiar solidarity be recognized. Membership in these groupings, particularly the last named, can of course powerfully assist us in the process of "becoming what we are." But the fact remains that as they concretely exist, they are neither identical with us as individuals nor coextensive with humanity as a whole. Their requirements, therefore, bring added, though necessary, complexity to our lives.

It may be allowable, even appropriate, to say something about the Church, in terms of the clerical profession, because it is both the one I happen to be most familiar with and also closely related to the general line of suggestion pursued in these pages. The only point in this context that calls for consideration is the essential one. Zen implies "seeing into one's own nature," with a view to gaining the "enlightenment" without

which one cannot be one's true self. This self-examination need
not be restricted to one's private person; it can and should be
directed to one's public or professional function, whatever that
happens to be. Such an exercise might prove especially rewarding—though it could also be disturbing—when applied to the
clerical or priestly state, both for its own sake and because it enables us to see beyond the externals into the nature of the
Church itself.

Nothing emerges more clearly from the sources of the Christian revelation than that the priestly "nature" is to be a *mediator*. Jesus Christ is the one Mediator between God and man (1
Timothy 2:5), a doctrine that is illustrated at length, with reference to our Lord's function as the Great High Priest, in the
Epistle to the Hebrews (*e.g.*, 8:6, 9:15, 12:24). The unique
mediatorial role of Christ is ministered to by a merely human
priest, not on his personal initiative, but as an "instrument."
Alluding to the priest's authority, his office of "binding and
loosing," St. Thomas states that the priest acts "as the instrument and minister of God." Moreover a priest may properly
discharge his function only as moved by God so to do, and,
more specifically, as prompted by the Holy Spirit.

Now no instrument can act efficaciously except in so far as it is
moved by the principal agent. Accordingly, Dionysius says (*Hier.
Eccl.*, cap. ult.) that *priests should use their hierarchical power in the
measure that they are moved by God*. A sign of this is that before the
power of the keys was conferred on Peter (Matthew 16:19) mention is
made of the revelation of the Godhead granted to him; and the gift
of the Holy Spirit, whereby *the sons of God are led* (Romans 8:14), is
mentioned before power was given to the apostles to forgive sins.
Consequently if anyone were to presume to use his power against the
Divine motion, he would not realize the effect, as Dionysius states
(*ibid.*), and besides, he would be turned away from the Divine order,
and consequently would be guilty of sin.[9]

This familiar doctrine should bring home the importance of

[9] *Summa Theologica, Supplement*, question 18, article 4.

not obtruding on to the scene of priestly activity either the personal ego or one's professional status. Both may appropriately be lost sight of in a larger and more compelling thought—that one prove faithful as an effective instrument of God's grace. Have we of the Catholic priesthood anything to learn from the ideal of the unworldly man which underlies Buddhism? "No one, indeed, has a right to ask of a Hindu Sannyasi, *what* he was in the world, for he has become a nobody, like the Spirit of God that 'cometh not from anywhere, and has never become anyone.' "[10] The Church's hierarchic structure being what it is, status and even honors cannot of themselves cause a loss of sensitivity, a hardening of the heart. Where trouble must inevitably arise, however, is when positions of power and prestige become an object of craving if not yet attained, or, if attained, of clinging attachment, lest they be lost or insufficiently recognized. In this case there need be no hypocrisy, as with the scribes, but our Lord's warning about them may still have its point. We are to beware of desiring "to be saluted in the market place, and to sit in the first seats in the synagogues, and in places of honor at banquets" (Mark 12:39). The more a priest's genuine humanity reveals itself, the better—that is why he should never stand on his priestly dignity! But his inner desires and hopes and fears, emotions which tend to inflate the conscious ego, should yield place increasingly to the true self, or, better, to the truest "Self" of all: "I live—yet no longer I, but Christ lives in me" (Galatians 2:20).

Failure at this point may account for the pomposity and autocratic methods of which we priests are sometimes accused. As soon as we obtrude the ego, act out of pique or merely to assert authority, to show them who's the boss, we are in danger of harming both ourselves and others. Instead of "taking a strong line"—by way of duty, we tell ourselves, but sometimes also, it may be, as motived by wounded self-esteem—how much wiser

[10] Ananda K. Coomaraswamy, *The Religious Basis of the Forms of Indian Society* (a lithoprinted address published by Orientalia, New York, 1946), p. 10.

we should often have been to look dispassionately at the situation and act solely in the light of its requirements. Such weaknesses are at once apparent to the discerning observer, even though his sympathetic understanding enables him to remain loyal and perhaps friendly.

Professional pride is apt to make us overtouchy on the topic of anticlericalism. This can be of various kinds. When what is involved is an attack on the structure of the Church, or an attempt to discredit the shepherd in the eyes of his flock, then it should be exposed for what it is. But when it is basically constructive criticism, a reminder in the light of the relevant facts of the inevitable gap between what we profess to be and what we are, there may be no harm in our being a little self-critically anticlerical ourselves. Everyone tends to resent being seen through; and yet, in the deepest sense, it is our business to be seen through. Any minister of God should have an awareness of his own inadequacy; if we are not fully conscious of this, or seek to hide it from others, the result is likely to be pretentiousness.

Attention has recently been drawn to what could be one form of this particular failing: our common inability to speak and write about religion in a simple, straightforward way. Religion, the Zen masters, and the Christian masters also, point out is or should be our "every-day mind." Why, then, in addressing the public are we so often not directly on our subject, but below or above it, comical or solemn? It is some excuse for ourselves that to speak or write directly to a theme and in a way to hold attention requires careful preparation. Anyone who has had the opportunity to study the technique knows that an arrangement of words that sounds or reads agreeably, as if it came spontaneously and without effort, is normally the result of labor and skill. Such talents do not necessarily accompany a priestly vocation. Nevertheless, if we find ourselves, as a British critic has recently charged, falling into a "tortuous prolixity," or "the employment of the cliché not encountered in the field of politics," or guilty of "complex modes of expression which conceal

rather than reveal"[11] our meaning, then our choice of words
clearly merits more attention.

Those familiar with American religious literature should
weigh the validity of the following comment by the same critic.
"Though we are happily spared the worst excesses of Victorian
sentimentality, much religious writing is still marred by a de-
bilitating pietism. . . . When they approach religious subjects
too many writers still think it necessary to adopt a special and
rather affected and mawkish tone. They think they are putting
on their Sunday best, but they do a disservice to religion by
making it appear something apart from the lives of ordinary
men." Unreality in the use of words may indicate an unreality
in their author. Here as in other contexts one's personal or professional ego may be standing in the way of one's true self. Failure may be due to laziness, to not taking the trouble, to seeking
self-gratification in what is said, instead of concentrating on the
requirements of the subject and the needs of those addressed.
But again, through our limitations the genuine self is seeking
for "realization." Provided our minds are focused on something
worth saying, that we have someone we should say it to, and
that we are open to the grace of unself-consciousness, we shall
command the appropriate eloquence.

In this calling to mind of what the Catholic clergy already
knows, we find that these thoughts have an even wider application. They apply to the Church itself. The Church is in the
process of self-realization as Christ's mystical Body. This the
Church already is, but it is also moving forward, so to speak,
"unto the building up of the Body of Christ" (Ephesians 4:12).
We can help or hinder the progress toward Christ's "fulness."
One way in which we could hinder that progress is by an unconscious obtrusion of the corporate clerical ego. This need
have nothing to do with any desire to dominate the laity or to
"keep them in their place"; indeed, it could go together with

[11] "Ill Writ," an unsigned editorial on religious literature in the London
Times Literary Supplement, March 9, 1962.

an earnest effort to enlist the layman's co-operation in the service of the Church. What we clergy have to be on our guard
against, I submit, is a tendency to equate our professional preoccupations with religion itself, and so unwittingly to attempt,
in some modified form, a clericalization of the laity. Do we, for
example, estimate the worth of those we influence in terms of
their basic goodness and general integrity, or with reference to
the regularity of their attendance at Mass and frequentation of
the sacraments, to say nothing of their pecuniary contributions
to the Catholic cause? These two sets of criteria may be related,
but they do not necessarily coincide.

By observing the necessary distinctions here we may gain
some light on one of our commonest problems—that of adoles-
cents and young people in their twenties abandoning the practice of religion. We are apt to put this down to moral difficulties:
the backsliders have become such, we tell ourselves, because
they refuse to live up to the Church's ethical teaching. It could
be so; but it is worth while to carry our analysis somewhat further. Another reason, verified by considerable experience, is
that they feel themselves to have outgrown the routine business
of religion; they will tell you that they are seeking something
beyond ritual and ceremonial and catechism morality. This
being so, since their souls are still hungry, they turn elsewhere,
to Zen Buddhism, for instance, not realizing that they already
have, within their own religious tradition, what they are looking for. "Your every-day mind—that is the Way!"

We touch here, it seems to me, the point of maximum difficulty in getting Catholicism understood in its richness and
depth. A child's mind can grasp only the elements; but when
that mind has grown to maturity, how can it reintegrate those
elements at the adult level? We fear to scandalize the simple
people, the ordinary folk; yet is it a less offense to scandalize
the educated and thoughtful, who are equally God's children?
The Church has no esoteric teaching; nothing is kept back
from the generality to be disclosed to the select few. Again it is
the complex problem of how to do the simple thing; in this

case, of how we clergy can let the Church's true self be seen through our personal and professional limitations.

For us to co-operate with God in making known His Church's inner riches, we need to be fully aware of what we are about, at both the personal and the professional level. We note, for example, that as clergy we have, quite legitimately, a vested interest, not excluding an economic interest, in focusing attention on the Church's juridical structure and its ritual. Both these are of divine institution; they constitute, one might say, the Church's "ego," that by which it is distinguished from other societies and performs its public function. But as with ourselves, so with the Church, the self-conscious ego should become increasingly transparent to the inner self. "The structure of the Christian society," wrote Pope Pius XII, "proof though it is of the wisdom of the divine Architect, is nevertheless something of a completely lower order in comparison with the spiritual gifts which enrich it and give it life."[12]

Among those spiritual gifts are the sacraments. Their underlying theology cannot be too often recalled. St. Thomas, following his habitual practice of conducting the discussion at its basic level, asks "Whether God alone, or the minister also, works inwardly in producing the sacramental effect?"[13] He at once makes it clear, by a reference to the eighth chapter of the Epistle to the Romans, that he is concerned not simply with a religious ritual, but with the existential confrontation between the individual human being and God. The grace of the sacrament does not come from the person of its minister, but directly from God by His immediate presence, the minister being the external agent, a mere instrument.[14]

There are two ways of producing an effect; first, as a principal agent; secondly, as an instrument. In the former way the interior sacramental effect is the work of God alone: first, because God alone

[12] Encyclical Letter, *Mystici Corporis Christi*, June 29, 1943.
[13] *Summa Theologica*, III, 64, 1.
[14] "... *nam eadem ratio est ministri et instrumenti* ...," ibid.

can enter the soul wherein the sacramental effect takes place; and no agent can operate immediately where it is not: secondly, because grace which is an interior sacramental effect is from God alone, as was established in the Second Part (i.e., *Summa Theologica,* I-II, 112, 1); while the character which is the interior effect of certain sacraments, is an instrumental power which flows from the principal agent, which is God.

In the second way, however, the interior sacramental effect can be the work of man, in so far as he works as a minister. For a minister is of the nature of an instrument, since the action of both is applied to something extrinsic, while the interior effect is produced through the power of the principal agent, which is God.

Here is the Church's sacramental theology outlined in its classical simplicity; it is in striking contrast to certain later and more elaborate presentations, diffuse and overlaid with symbolism. St. Thomas's unfailing eye for the essential appears no less clearly in his exposition of his favorite sacrament, the Eucharist. He asks "Whether the Eucharist is necessary for salvation?"[15] and replies with a distinction. The reception of the sacrament in what we now call Holy Communion is not necessary, but something else is, namely, the *reality* of the sacrament (*res sacramenti*), which is "the unity of the mystical Body of Christ." This reality can be had simply by desiring to receive the sacrament. In other words, what should have first place in our thoughts about the Eucharist is the reciprocal love which, according to Christ's intention, binds together the members of the Church.[16]

All this is familiar enough to members of the Catholic clergy. How often do we preach it to the laity? They might be much helped were they to "see through" us, though in a sense different from what the phrase commonly implies, even more than they do. For them to perceive in the Eucharist, not only a rite

[15] *Ibid.*, III, 73, 3.
[16] For a more developed treatment of the doctrine of the Eucharist, see my *The Love of God* (New York: Doubleday & Company, Image Books edition, 1959), pp. 243-48.

that belongs to the sanctuary, but a reality touching in the most practical way their everyday personal relations may need a change of heart on their part. Equally, perhaps, for them to see us clergy as so transparently instruments of sacramental grace that nothing of the ego obscures from view the divine realities we serve may call also in some cases for a change of heart on our part. We complain on occasion of the lack of vocations to our seminaries and religious houses. Humanly enough, we seek a scapegoat; we blame the times, the allurements of "the world," the parents who fail to lead their children along the right path. Less often do we turn our eyes inward and raise the most pertinent question: To what degree do we ourselves exhibit a quality of living that would convince an idealistically minded young man that here, in substance, is the type of life to which Christ invited His disciples?

The Eastern religions have a spiritual preceptor known as a *guru*.[17] His authority is supposed to rest solely on his wisdom and experience; his personality and manner are such that they carry with them self-authenticating testimony that he is an "enlightened one." He does not seek a following; followers come to him for what he is and has. He does not "rule" or try to hold them; they are free to leave and go elsewhere when they choose. Here, of course, is an aspect of the Catholic priestly life, with its mediation of truth and wisdom to others. It is an aspect,

[17] The *guru* is now by no means unknown in the West. Readers of Evelyn Waugh's novel *The Loved One* will remember the advice given through correspondence by the Hollywood "Guru Brahmin," who was, in fact, "two gloomy men and a bright young secretary." A serious point may be drawn from this, namely, the possibilities of much harm arising from submitting oneself to an unknown *guru*—or, for that matter, to an inexperienced "spiritual director." "One should know a *guru* very well before blindly obeying any instructions he may give—know his character and motives especially, and if possible his effect on earlier students." The student should be ready to learn, but "care has to be taken not to be caught by teachers who are not conscientious, but who are merely setting up in this field to get rich quick, or to feel important. And he must beware, as the sage Ramakrishna said, of unripe *gurus*." Ernest Wood, *Yoga* (Harmondsworth, England: Penguin Books, 1959), p. 87.

however, which may deserve more attention than it commonly
receives among us. The priest is the minister of God's word as
well as of the sacraments, and God's word is not only or chiefly
in speech. Sometimes we help others best by leaving them
alone, standing, a friendly onlooker, in the background, so that
they can make independent personal choices, live in the light of
conscience, the witness to their own best selves. "A church or society," writes Coomaraswamy, "that does not provide a way of
escape from its own regimen, and will not let its people go, is
defeating its own ultimate purpose."[18] Catholicism is well able
to meet such a challenge; but we must look into the nature of
the Church, whose "soul" is the Holy Spirit, to see how this
is so.

The distinction between clergy and laity, when we consider
their common unity "in Christ Jesus," is relatively unimportant. The diversity of interest between "we" and "they" tends
to disappear. The laity, on equal terms with the clergy, have
God for their Father and Christ as their Brother. At this level,
priest and people alike find the exemplar of how the conflict
between the conscious ego, the separative self, the demanding
"me," and the inner, realistic "I," the unitive self as surrendered to God, can be resolved. If Siddhartha Gautama, after
long trial, achieved the supreme "enlightenment," so becoming
the Buddha, Jesus of Nazareth, the incarnate Son of God, according to Christian theology, was in His very person "the
Light of the world" (John 9:5). The nature He shares with us
was, at the outset, so caught up in God, His ultimate "Self," as
not to have a created personality, a human "self," at all. "I and
the Father are one" (John 10:30).

When the same Son of God told His disciples that, in order
to follow Him, they must deny themselves (Mark 8:34), there
is a sense in which this may be regarded as an ontological as

[18] *Hinduism and Buddhism*, p. 29. On the sentence quoted above, the author himself has the following note: "On Law and Liberty cf. St. Augustine,
De spiritu et littera. It is by the Spiritual Power that the Temporal power
is freed from bondage."

well as a practical requirement. Not until the conscious ego is "lost" (v. 35) can we be wholly in union with God. If we "deny" ourselves by a calculated personal effort, even for the highest motives, this could still be a subtler form of unregenerate human nature's having its own way. Only when we allow God to take over completely will the true self and the conscious ego, the "I" and the "me," act as one. "I live—yet no longer I, but Christ lives in me" (Galatians 2:20). In this condition we shall not be particularly anxious to have our own way. Accordingly, we may safely do what we please.

CHAPTER FOUR

THE IMPORTANCE
OF NOT BEING EARNEST

The title of this chapter is intended to be meaningful rather than facetious, though it may also indicate a taste for lightness of touch—as befits both Zen and mature Catholicism. A sense of humor about religion, like the anticlericalism with which it is often allied, may be of two kinds. It can stem from skeptical disillusionment and result in a scarcely concealed cynicism expressing itself, not in genuine humor, but in its dubious substitute, sardonic wit. Or the smile may be evoked—for it is a smile rather than laughter—by an eye for the realities of the situation: the contrast between the heavenly treasure and its earthly container, including us humans in general and oneself in particular. Whether this contrast is to be regarded as ludicrous or tragic will depend, no doubt, on one's cast of mind: but in either case, Aristotle's remark (quoting Georgias Leontinus) is to the point:

> Humour is the only test of gravity, and gravity of humour. For a subject which will not bear raillery is suspicious; and a jest which will not bear a serious examination is certainly false wit.[1]

A distinction, verified by experience and in common par-

[1] Quoted from R. H. Blyth, *Zen in English Literature and Oriental Classics*, p. 56.

lance, may be drawn between being "earnest" and being "in earnest." It is wholly in the spirit of Zen and, again, of Catholicism that one should be in earnest. "Whatever lies in thy power, do while do it thou canst" (Ecclesiastes 9:10). When there is a call for action from the true self, there can be no holding back. One's intelligence and practical energies, as each occasion requires, ought to be fully engaged. Absence of mind, where the mind should be present, has nothing to commend it. There are in fact many tasks of such urgency, responses to duty so demanding, as to make refinements on the concept of earnestness appear otiose.

Appearances, however, are sometimes deceptive. It is not in sophisticated circles only that the earnest approach, often regarded as mandatory in the advocacy of religion, is felt to be suspect. Allusion has already been made to the undesirability of attempting to foster devotion by the employment of emotive and highly charged language. The point may further be illustrated by a passing reference to such currently fashionable phrases as "commitment" and "ultimate concern," which commonly occur in discussions, not so much of Catholicism, as of the more up-to-date forms of Protestantism. These expressions are presumably intended to indicate the urgency and general impressiveness of the matter in hand. On inspection they appear, to one observer at least, to suggest a sense of strain, a stance almost of falseness. This could be due to the implied stress upon the will unenlightened by the intelligence, as if the act of faith were an attitude of blind trust into which one forced oneself in the teeth of the evidence.[2]

Now it is true that Christian faith is in things unseen, that it presupposes good will, that it involves both trust and deliberate choice; but the mental processes culminating in belief never disregard the testimony of reason. If the believer finds

[2] These remarks, and indeed this whole chapter, were written before I came across Walter Kaufmann's thought-provoking essay on "Commitment" in his *The Faith of a Heretic* (New York: Doubleday & Company, 1961). But see Postscript.

himself in darkness, it is from excess of light, in the manner of
Aristotle's owl gazing at the sun. Fundamentally, faith is a response to reality, and so an "enlightenment"; it is not a des-
perate plunge into the fog, as it is depicted, for example, by a
brilliant irrationalist like Kierkegaard. Jesus' recurring reproach to His disciples was not that they failed to "commit"
themselves, but that they were so slow to see the light. "Have I
been so long time with you, and dost thou not know me,
Philip?" (John 14:9).

Religious conviction is not strengthened, or made more persuasive to others, by adventitious emotion; earnestness may
therefore be left to take care of itself. When we act in accordance with the true self, our integrity and sincerity will be
evident. It is when we act egotistically that we are prone to be
inappropriately "earnest"; that is to say, to gain plausibility for
intrinsically dubious attitudes by emotional and moralistic
overtones. Man is a creature of emotions; his religion, therefore, cannot be purely intellectual or spiritual. But when religion becomes a field for emotional self-indulgence or senti-
mentalism—ultimately, as an Anglican Dean of St. Paul's has
called it, "the most merciless of all moods"—when, in other
words, what is being sought is not the God of consolation but
the consolations of God, then we are left with selfishness mas-
querading as piety.

Thus religion itself, misunderstood or understood superficially, instead of bringing relief can actually intensify, or at
least do nothing to mitigate, humanity's suffering. We are faced
once more with the root of the trouble—the restless craving for
or grasping at something we want or fear to lose. The object of
this craving may be tangible, like sensual pleasure, wealth, or
material security, or such intangibles as honors, prestige, power,
or even some spiritual "ideal" that we have formulated for ourselves. We are apt to cling to what gratifies or enhances the conscious ego, heedless of the still small voice of our true self,
prompting us to stand aside, relax, and let go. Being unwilling
or unable, so we persuade ourselves, to "let go," we hold on, be-

come *attached,* and so ever more deeply involved in the unending round of *karma,* described in the New Testament by the formula "whatsoever a man soweth, that shall he also reap" (Galatians 6:7).

Of all life's harsh facts here is perhaps the harshest: that the feelings and emotions which are a part of our being, through which we gain so much joy, are precisely what entangle us, unless we can find a way out, in an endless sequence of trouble, frustration, and suffering. This was the situation faced in all its painful reality by Gautama Buddha; it is a situation, as the masters of the spiritual life concur, from which there is only one path of release. *What then is the Holy Truth of the Stopping of Ill? It is the complete stopping of that craving, the withdrawal from it, the renouncing of it, throwing it back, liberation from it, nonattachment to it.* More summarily and in a somewhat different context, the message of Christianity is the same. "Whosoever shall seek to save his life shall lose it: and whosoever shall lose it shall preserve it" (Luke 17:33).

We may attempt to analyze a little more closely what is involved. Essentially our inner distress is caused by the tension between the two apparently conflicting psychological entities within us, which we have labeled (not very satisfactorily) the true self and the conscious ego—corresponding respectively, again by a rough verbal approximation, to the self as subject, the "I," and the self as object, the "me." These in reality are not two but one; we cannot, however, *realize* them as one until we attain "enlightenment"—which, in Christian terminology, is the actual experience of the truth that "the man who unites himself to the Lord becomes one spirit with Him" (1 Corinthians 6:17).

The true self is our being in its immediate dependence on the creative act of God, Who is the self-existent Being. The conscious ego is the created being, ontologically identical with the true self but psychologically distinct from it, in as much as the ego is affirming its individuality in contradistinction to other individuals. It should be noted that the ego's self-affirmation takes place both at the conscious level and also unconsciously (in the Freudian or modern sense of the "unconscious"). We act self-centeredly without being aware of it.

Before we proceed further let it be emphasized that the self-affirmation, which in fact constitutes the conscious ego, is inevitable; it is an aspect of the life process. Therefore one should not feel *guilty* about it. A rationally based sense of guilt has its place, despite a number of moderately plausible arguments that have been advanced to the contrary. But to introduce the concept of guilt at this point is to focus attention unduly on the conscious ego and so to make more difficult an understanding of the human situation. Such characteristically Zen admonitions as "Do not discuss right and wrong" and "Do not think good, do not think not-good" have here their relevance.[3] These are not counsels of immorality; they indicate that if the conscious ego is preoccupied with such questions, the true self will to that extent be eclipsed. Natural instinct is often a better guide to what is good than one's most carefully formulated thoughts on the subject.

The conscious ego has been well called the "separative self." When we become an object of our own thought, a "me," we feel our separateness from other people and from the world around us. Necessary as is self-awareness for the whole complex business of living, as soon as that awareness focuses on the ego as a separate entity, we are tempted to identify our total being with ego-consciousness. This is the temptation to which the existentialists have yielded—man is what he is in virtue of his separateness. The flattery thus administered to the ego effectively cloaks from its adherents the absurdity of their philosophical position. Existentialism has not, of course, per-

[3] Compare Jesus' brusque dismissal of any facile application of ethical categories: "Why dost thou come to me to ask of goodness? God is good, and He only" (Matthew 19:17); "Judge not, that you be not judged" (Matthew 7:1); "He that is without sin among you, let him first cast a stone at her" (John 8:7).

formed the impossible feat of getting rid of God; it has merely made a god of each existentialist.

Whatever heightens the ego's isolated consciousness provides an immediate reward in terms of a superficial "awareness"; we undergo a personal *experience;* but at a deeper level there is anxiety. To be confronted by something alien to self creates insecurity, none the less real for our being unconscious of it; from this we seek escape in some compensating reassurance. Seeking reassurance outside ourselves is what leads to restlessness and the fatal *craving:* the conscious ego, still unable to "realize" its identity with the true self, strives to maintain its supposed autonomy by grasping for support. Here it should be carefully noted that it is not nature's self-indulgence as such that causes trouble, or even a reasonable desire for such indulgence. There is sound psychology, even wisdom, behind the popular saying "A little of what you fancy does you good." Nature regenerated by grace does not cease to be nature; it still calls for fulfillment rather than frustration; therefore it should be moderately indulged. To deny nature its due is apt to make the individual more, rather than less, egoistic. Given the appropriate context, sensuous pleasure, wealth, power, and prestige, whatever we care to mention, can be enjoyed without any betrayal of one's true self. But because these are ego-enhancing experiences, they easily tempt us to excess and to an absorbing desire for them, that craving—the result, it may be remarked, of original sin—which, while it lasts, debars us from the saving "enlightenment."

What impedes true self-expression in us, as distinct from egoistic assertion, is the "identification," that is, the total absorption, of the ego in what is at odds with ourselves. For example, we become infatuated by someone; we get possessive, make exorbitant demands on others, our children, our friends, those we are responsible for; we harbor grudges, aversions, resentments, even hatreds. And here the sad truth must be stated that hatred and dislike bring greater short-term emotional rewards than love. The explanation is that hatred sharpens the opposition between the individual and its supposed enemy; this inflates the ego and gives it a sense of exultation—one gets a "kick" out of it!—which can be sustained or revived by resentful memories and reminiscences. Whereas love, arising from the depths of the true self, creates no emotional spasm, being in natural harmony with the emotions: the result is not ego-enhancing, but a long-term deeper satisfaction, the calmness of unself-conscious well-being.

Here is a Zen (it might also be a Christian) story, which illustrates the point that what counts is not so much what we do, whether this be conventional or unconventional, as the inner attitude toward our own conduct.

There is a story of two monks on a journey who came to a river with no bridge across it. As they were about to begin to ford it, a young woman came up. The first monk was just going to offer to carry her across, when the second said to her, "Get on my back and I'll carry you over." She did so and parted from them gracefully on the other side. After the two monks had walked on for a few miles, the first monk, unable to contain himself any longer, burst out, "What did you mean by carrying that girl across the river? You know monks are allowed to have nothing to do with women!" The other said, with a smile, "You must be tired, carrying that girl all this way. *I* put her down as soon as we got to the other side of the river."[4]

What is to be done about this ego-awareness, which is a necessity, since without it the individual can achieve little, yet which can torment him almost to the point of wishing for death? The first answer is that nothing can be done about it. If we consciously watch ourselves, strive directly to eliminate egocentric thoughts, the trouble increases, as it would by contemplating one's own unattractiveness in a mirror. The same could be true of a course of asceticism, by which we attempt a violent withdrawal from the objects of craving. Asceticism of itself does not eliminate ego-awareness, rather the reverse. Even prayer and devotion, though they can bring us nearer

[4] *Zen in English Literature and Oriental Classics*, pp. 277-78.

to the root of the matter, have not the power to provide a final solution.

In a sense there is no final solution. We cannot remove from the human condition what is an integral part of it. But we can, with God's grace (and here, in substance though not in modes of expression, Catholicism and Zen agree), make sense of our self-preoccupation, live with it, and eventually find beatitude through it. Expositors of Zen, at this point, make much of the virtue of following one's own nature, just relaxing and letting things be. What is forgotten by some, though not by all Zennists, is that for such counsels to be fruitful we must perform an inner task demanding a high degree of fidelity. This task essentially is to become aware, not merely in terms of ego-consciousness, but by the awakening of the true self, and to respond in attitude and action to this awareness. Eastern and Western religious tradition speaks with one voice: enlightenment or salvation depends on answering adequately the challenge "know thyself."

The self-understanding here indicated is not a conceptual, still less a verbal, knowledge, such as could be gained by studying human psychology and reading the appropriate books. These pursuits should help, though they could also conceivably hinder; but the perception now being touched on is quite other. Those to whom it has never come—that is, to judge by the present state of the world, the vast majority of the human race—are hardly in a position to describe it. Those who have received it, or think they have, do not normally attempt to give an account of their experience. Though here Zennists sometimes appear to want it both ways. Enlightenment, or *satori,* is held by definition to be ineffable, yet considerable eloquence is expended on its discussion. But this amiable inconsistency, if it be such, is shared with a number of Christian saints who, in their accounts of what seems to be a parallel experience, devote time and trouble to describing the indescribable.

Satori is a difficult and to some extent controversial subject.

I shall try to indicate what I think it means later.[5] It may be suggested to Zen enthusiasts, however, that the claim by any individual to have experienced *satori* can never carry much conviction. The more genuine the enlightenment, the less likely one is to speak of it. For this would necessarily be an affirmation of the conscious ego, the separative self, whereas *satori*, as I understand it, is the awareness, which cannot be verbalized, of the nonduality between the true self and the conscious ego, the "I" and the "me." More generally, *satori* bridges the gap between knowing subject and known object,[6] brings with it the metaphysical intuition of undifferentiated "being as such," and to this extent justifies the declaration *tat tvam asi:* "That art thou." *Satori* is the quintessence of Zen, whose spirit may be illustrated in so direct and spontaneous an action as merely raising one's hand. "When I raise my hand thus," says D. T. Suzuki, "there is Zen; but when I assert that I have raised my hand, Zen is no longer there." In other words, "Those who say do not know; those who know do not say." They do not say because what they know—or, rather, the manner in which they know it—is unsayable.

It is important to note that the metaphysical implications of *satori* are often presented by expositors of Zen as being incompatible with orthodox Christianity. This point has already been touched on with regard to the real distinction between creature and Creator—a doctrine fundamental to Catholicism, though a doctrine of considerable subtlety. "After the creation there are indeed more beings, but there is not *more being* or

---

[5] See pp. 127-134.

[6] The basic apprehension of "being" (*ens, esse*) is undifferentiated; that is to say, we know (provided our mind is unclouded by sense images and we are sufficiently conscious of what we know) being, before we know this or that particular being—"*Prius est esse quam esse tale.*" Being is what first comes to our minds: "*quod primo cadit in intellectu ens.*" St. Thomas, *Summa Theologica*, I, 11, 2, 4. The gap between knowing subject and known object is bridged, in the sense that the intellect becomes what it knows: "*intellectus in actu est intellectum in actu.*" *Ibid.*, I, 55, 1, 2. But see the further remarks on *satori*, pp. 130-131.

perfection, because whatever perfection there is in the effect, was existing in a higher mode of being in the first eternal Cause."[7] The first eternal Cause, needless to say, is the God in Whom "we live and move and have our being" (Acts 17:28) .

The experience of nonduality, just now alluded to, between the "I" and the "me," or, more generally, between the knowing subject and the known object, is normally interpreted by Zen Buddhists as being between the supposedly noncreated, only seemingly existent, individual human self and the ultimate Self, which is God. This position, as so stated, cannot be reconciled with Catholicism. But it is a position, as can without difficulty be shown, in no way demanded by the characteristic Zen insight. Moreover this doctrine, though it may be implicit in the Hinduism from which Buddhism arose, is not explicitly stated in the Buddha's Four Holy Truths, whatever Gautama himself may have thought on the point. Zen expositors, in evolving a philosophy somewhat remote from "the every-day mind" of Zen, have reached behind the Buddha to the Atman-Brahman nondualist antithesis, the original setting for the deeply impressive *tat tvam asi:* "That art thou" doctrine of Brahmanism.

These somewhat abstruse considerations need not detain us further. They serve to give substance to a thought that has emerged in the author's mind while this book was being written. It is possible that the Zen insight and style of life will eventually find their natural place in a Catholic context. The metaphysical tradition that culminated in Zen Buddhism touches the deep things of the spirit at a level not generally reached by popular Catholicism. But that level exists, within the Church, for anyone who seeks it to find. A Zen saying is that "Tao may be transmitted only to him who already has

[7] "*Propterea communiter theologi dicunt: post creationem sunt quidem plura entia, non vero est* plus entis *seu plus perfectionis, quia quidquid perfectionis est in effectu praeexistebat eminentiori modo in prima Causa aeterna.*" Reginaldus Garrigou-Lagrange, O.P., *De Deo Uno* (Paris: Desclée de Brouwer, 1938) , p. 167.

it." This should be pondered by devotees of Zen, whether
cerebral, aesthetic, beat, or square, and perhaps most of all
by one or two notable Western Zen pundits, clinging precari-
ously to their intellectual respectability while swinging a loose
leg. The student may discover that Catholics, potentially at
least, not only have the "Tao," but that Catholicism offers a
more fruitful field for its cultivation in the Western world than
can be found elsewhere.

However this may be, Catholicism and Zen agree on two
essential points. First, the way of escape from what the Church
calls *concupiscence*—that is, disordered desire, for anything
whatever, not merely sensuous enjoyment—and the Buddhist
tradition describes as *craving* or *grasping* cannot be had by
the ego's conscious efforts to find release; it depends on the
ego's "rebirth" as the true self under God's direct illumination.
Secondly, this rebirth or change of heart, though it cannot be
achieved by the ego, nevertheless demands that the ego fulfill
an inner task. We have by constant watchfulness to correspond
with the movement of God's grace, ever striving to bring our
true self into being. Corresponding with grace depends
on keeping the eye of our mind, according to its natural powers and as further enlightened by faith, open and clear. In the
resulting state of clarity the conscious ego will imperceptibly
recede into the background, becoming aware of what it is already, the true self.

One sign that this process is taking place is the disinclina-
tion to think—though, of course, we must necessarily talk (in
moderation!) —in terms of the first person singular. It is not
what *I* do or suffer, but, at most, what seems to be happening
through me. " 'I did it', an infantile idea," writes Coomaraswamy;[8] and, quoting Walt Whitman, "These are really the
thoughts of all men in all ages and lands, they are not original
with me. If they are not yours as much as mine, they are nothing, or next to nothing."[9] Which, in substance, seems to be

[8] *Hinduism and Buddhism*, p. 76.
[9] *Am I My Brother's Keeper?*, p. 78.

the same point as that made by St. François de Sales: "We all know that our good works are better to the degree that there is less of self in them. The *I, me* and *mine* render worthless over half that we do. They are like an ugly cobweb clinging to a beehive and spoiling all the honey."[10]

The key to liberation, the truth that makes us free, lies in nonattachment to whatever enhances our separative self. For every attachment there arises a corresponding fear, the fear of losing what we cling to. This fear in its turn intensifies ego-consciousness, which may then seek to sustain itself by another attachment—and so the process of entanglement can go on endlessly. The nature of this distress and the means to its relief have never been noted more carefully than by the author of perhaps the most perceptive discussion of the spiritual life written in English, the fourteenth-century anonymous treatise *The Cloud of Unknowing*. The author equates the conscious ego, the separative self, which he calls simply "yourself," with sin, considered not as guilt but as self-centeredness. He says that this situation must first be accepted, that is, a man should find "his awareness held and filled with the filthy and nauseating lump of himself," which stands between him and God.[11]

For if you will take the trouble to test it, you will find that when all other things and activities have been forgotten (even your own) there still remains between you and God the stark awareness of your own existence. And this awareness, too, must go, before you experience contemplation in its perfection.

You will ask me how to destroy this stark awareness of your own existence. For you are thinking that if it were destroyed all other

[10] Jean Pierre Camus, *The Spirit of St. François de Sales,* edited and newly translated and with an introduction by C. F. Kelley (New York: Longmans, Green & Co., 1953) , p. 44.

[11] Sin so considered is complete alienation from God, which is the perfect description of "hell." St. Thomas points to the theological roots of the matter: "God loves sinners in so far as they are existing natures; for they have existence and have it from Him. In so far as they are sinners, they have no existence at all, but fall short of it; and this in them is not from God." *Summa Theologica,* I, 20, 2, 4.

difficulties would vanish too. And you would be right. All the same my answer must be that without God's very special and freely given grace, and your own complete and willing readiness to receive it, this stark awareness of yourself cannot possibly be destroyed. And this readiness is nothing else than a strong, deep sorrow of spirit.

But in this sorrow you need to exercise discretion: you must beware of imposing undue strain on your body or soul at this time. Rather, sit quite still, mute as if asleep, absorbed and sunk in sorrow. This is true sorrow, perfect sorrow, and all will go well if you can achieve sorrow to this degree. Everyone has something to sorrow over, but none more than he who knows and feels that he is (i.e., that he exists over and against God). All other sorrow in comparison with this is a travesty of the real thing. For he experiences true sorrow, who knows and feels not only what he is, but that he is. Let him who has never felt this sorrow be sorry indeed, for he has not yet known what perfect sorrow is. Such sorrow, when we have it, cleanses the soul not only of sin, but also of the suffering its sin has deserved. And it makes the soul ready to receive that joy which is such that it takes from a man all awareness of his own existence.[12]

Several points are of special interest in this remarkable passage, not least its modern "existential" character. Most noteworthy is it that the implied directive to attain a state corresponding to Buddhist recollectedness is placed within the Catholic context of "God's very special and freely given grace, and your own complete and willing readiness to receive it." Secondly we observe the counsel to discretion, not to impose undue strain on body or soul. Physical austerity is not mentioned, for that could intensify ego-consciousness and so defeat the end in view, which is the enlightenment arising from being no longer burdened by self-preoccupation—"that joy which is such that it takes from a man all awareness of his own existence." There must be no straining of the spirit either, since this likewise could be a form of craving or grasping, which must on all counts be avoided. The essential thing is to "real-

[12] *The Cloud of Unknowing*, translated into modern English with an introduction by Clifton Wolters (Harmondsworth, England: Penguin Books, 1961) , Chapters 43 and 44, pp. 103-04.

ize," to become fully aware. that simply *to be* apart from God, which is the very condition of creaturehood, is a sorrow.

Here we are brought to the root cause of our congenital distress, by whatever name we call it: *angst,* dread, fear, anxiety, depression, melancholy, which can become so acute as to give rise to the question whether life, all things considered, is worth living. To be reconciled to this, the human condition, is a necessary preliminary to becoming our true selves. To refuse to attune oneself to "the still sad music of humanity," or to distract oneself from it by an unending round of diversions, is to make the situation worse. "Let him who has never felt this sorrow be sorry indeed." Suffering is never unbearable once it is understood—understood, not merely rationally, but as absorbed into our being; for then it is accepted as part of the pattern of things. We can be mellowed, humanized, cleansed of our pretensions by it. Suffering only becomes frustrating when it is refused. The "dark night," through which in one form or another all must pass, "makes the soul ready to receive that joy which is such that it takes from a man all awareness of his own existence." Notice that it is not claimed that this joy cancels suffering, only that the joy is of such quality as to eliminate the egocentric awareness which can make suffering intolerable.

What lends an added touch of modernity to this exposition is its psychosomatic emphasis: soul and body work together.

For the love of God beware of illness as much as you can, so that as far as possible your self is not the cause of any weakness. I tell you the truth when I say that this work demands great serenity, an integrated and pure disposition, in soul and in body. So for the love of God control your body and soul alike with great care, and keep as fit as you can. Should illness come in spite of everything, have patience and wait humbly for God's mercy.[18]

No particular stress is laid on asceticism; holy indifference, fortified by common sense, is much to be preferred.

[18] *Ibid.,* Chapter 41, p. 101.

You will ask me, perhaps, how you are to control yourself with due care in the matter of food and drink and sleep and so on. My answer is brief: 'Take what comes!' Do this thing without ceasing and without care day by day, and you will know well enough, with a real discretion, when to begin and when to stop in everything else. I cannot believe that a soul who goes on in this work with complete abandon, day and night, will make mistakes in mundane matters. If he does, he is, I think, the type who always will get things wrong.

Therefore, if I am able to give a vital and wholehearted attention to this spiritual activity within my soul, I can then view my eating and drinking, my sleep and conversation and so on with comparative indifference. I would rather acquire a right discretion in these matters by such indifference, than by giving them my close attention and weighing carefully all the pros and cons.[14]

A passing phrase in the first of the three excerpts quoted above from *The Cloud of Unknowing,* an allusion to one's physical posture during recollection, is of particular interest— "sit quite still." Those who know something of Zen will here feel themselves on familiar ground. *Zazen,* sitting meditation, is Zen Buddhism's characteristic practice. Images of the Buddha, not kneeling, but sitting cross-legged, in either the "lotus" (*padmāsana*) or "adept's" (*siddhāsana*) position, are familiar to all even in the West. A disciplined yet pliant physique as an aid to recollectedness, which is axiomatic in the religions stemming from India, is deservedly being given increasing attention by Christians. What is in question is not merely St. Teresa's well-known advice, that while at prayer one should be comfortable, but that centuries of tradition appear to have established a nexus between certain bodily postures and the "attention without tension" of deep recollectedness and mental clarity. Some further remarks will be made on this topic.[15] For the moment it may suffice to recall that kneeling is the traditional and appropriate attitude for Christians before the transcendent God, Creator of the universe. For recalling the presence of the same God within the human spirit, who would

---

[14] *Ibid.,* Chapter 42, pp. 101-02.
[15] See Supplementary Discussion I, On Yoga, pp. 163-170.

presume to improve on the posture of the Compassionate
Buddha?

Before passing on, a brief additional passage may be cited
from *The Cloud*. Its direct application is to Christians eager
to find a short cut to the spiritual heights; but with hardly
a change of phrase, what follows can provide a timely and incisive warning to Western dilettantes who take up the cult
of Yoga, Buddhism, or Zen on the grounds that it is rather
"chic." To dabble in the world's oldest metaphysical and religious tradition—perhaps to confuse it, as is often done, with
occultism, magic, and the gateway to some superhuman condition—opens up endless possibilities of trouble.

> A young man or woman, just starting in the school of devotion
> hears someone read or speak about this sorrow and longing: how a
> man shall lift up his heart to God, and continually long to feel his
> love. And immediately in their silly minds they understand these
> words not in the intended spiritual sense, but in a physical and ma-
> terial, and they strain their natural hearts outrageously in their
> breasts! And because they are without grace, and are proud and spir-
> itually inquisitive they strain their whole nervous system in untu-
> tored, animal ways, and thus they quickly get tired with a sort of
> physical and spiritual torpor. This causes them to turn from the life
> which is within and seek empty, false and physical comforts from
> outside, ostensibly for the recreation of body and soul. . . . Or, again,
> they experience a spurious warmth, engendered by the fiend, their
> spiritual enemy, through their pride, and materialism, and spiritual
> dabbling. . . . For I tell you truly that the devil has his contemplatives
> as God has His. These beguiling, false experiences and this false
> knowledge have as many different and surprising varieties as there
> are temperaments and states to be deceived.[16]

The moral of all this is that before entering on the path
that leads to ultimate self-knowledge, one should profit by the
experience of others. More specifically, those of European or
American antecedents, before turning for a dubious salvation
to India or Japan, should examine the chief formative tradi-

[16] *The Cloud of Unknowing*, Chapter 45, pp. 105-06.

tion of their own culture, namely Catholicism, where the practice of nonattachment is cultivated and well understood. A
shrewd observation by an authority on Zen applies in this
context. "No one can stand outside tradition, outside Christianity or Buddhism, without falling into these aberrations and
eccentricities of thought and feeling."[17] Nonattachment requires that we be not taken in by the world and its ways, not
that we physically renounce them. But because we have a tendency to be taken in, almost literally, by what attracts us, dealing with the situation calls for exceptional clarity of mind.
The need for insight must be stressed. A forceful will is no
substitute; unenlightened, it could be a hindrance. The technique of the stiff upper lip is not to be despised; here as elsewhere there can be no achievement without a measure of
courage. Since what is called for, however, is sensitive awareness,
the lip, so to speak, should be quite relaxed. Fidelity to our
perceptions will bring the necessary control. Actuated by God's
grace, the true self tends to replace the conscious ego, and ac-
companying this process are at least the beginnings of a liberation from craving for what we have not and from clinging to
what we have.

The difficulty, stated in its simplest terms, is not to hold on!
Not to hold on to the fleeting years, for example. People at
seventy tell themselves that they are as old as they feel they
are, and therefore that they're still young. Whereas the true
self tells us to "be our age," or, more profoundly, that *now,*
since it is the only point at which we make contact with God,
is the best age for us to be. Clinging to the past or longing for
the future involve us alike in unreality. Again, with what fond-
ness the individual cherishes the conscious ego, holds on to his
self-regarding thoughts. So he explains and justifies and vin-
dicates himself, while all the while the still small voice of his
genuine self is telling him to be quiet and say nothing, so that
the same self may become manifest. Then the broodings, resentments, jealousies, the daydreams of which the dreamer is

the hero, the complacent reminiscences; or the wallowing in guilt and misery, the vengeful thoughts, the inner urge to pull down and destroy, the violence directed against others, perhaps even against oneself. They are all, positively or negatively, part of the same pattern: the thrust of the conscious ego to preserve its illusory independence and autonomy.

Examples of what holds us in bondage, preventing liberation, could be multiplied indefinitely. The whole situation was perfectly understood by St. François de Sales; he points to the only remedy. "I have hardly any desires, but if I were to be born again I should have none at all. We should ask nothing and refuse nothing, but leave ourselves in the arms of divine Providence without wasting time in any desire, except to will what God wills of us."[18]

From what has been said it should be clear that for the true self to emerge, so to speak, into the light of day the mind must not be busy with thoughts. Irrelevant thoughts are not only distractions in themselves; they generate desires and so bind us more firmly to the wheel of clinging and craving. The mind must "let go," lose its superficial life filled with preoccupations, in order to gain its deeper life of unimpeded, unself-conscious looking at reality. Once more there is unanimity among those qualified to instruct us: the Buddhist "emptiness," the Zen "no-mind," the "void" of St. John of the Cross,[19] the "cloud of unknowing," are various descriptions of the same prerequisite: to see things in their "suchness"—above all, to bring the mind into contact with the ultimate Source of all things—one must keep one's own thoughts out of the way.

But now you will ask me, 'How am I to think of God himself, and what is He?' and I cannot answer you except to say 'I do not know!' For with this question you have brought me into the same darkness,

[18] Quoted from Aldous Huxley, *The Perennial Philosophy*, p. 221. Mr. Huxley adds the characteristic comment: "But meanwhile the third clause of the Lord's Prayer is repeated daily by millions, who have not the slightest intention of letting any will be done, except their own."

[19] On this may be recommended the Rev. Leonard A. McCann, C.S.B., *The Doctrine of the Void* (Toronto: Basilian Press, 1955).

the same cloud of unknowing where I want you to be! For though
we through the grace of God can know fully about all other matters,
and think about them—yes, even the very words of God himself—
yet of God himself can no man think. Therefore I will leave on one
side everything I can think, and choose for my love the thing which
I cannot think! Why? Because He may well be loved, but not thought.
By love He can be caught and held, but by thinking never.[20]

In this passage two points should be observed. First, the devout agnosticism expressed by our author does not invalidate
human thinking about God, such as has resulted in the Church
creeds and doctrinal statements generally. The mental concepts
verbalized in theological propositions are of their nature inadequate, but they are not worthless; they help to focus our
minds at the level of rational thought. For it should be remembered that, although God's self-disclosure is received by
man's intelligence as the supernatural gift of faith, faith's content is signified to us through words or ideas that are purely
human and natural. What is reached beyond the "cloud of
unknowing" is the kind of nescience alluded to by St. Thomas,
when he speaks of an "imperfect" vision, "whereby, though we
see not what God is, yet we see what He is not; and whereby
the more perfectly we know God in this life, the more we understand that He surpasses all that the mind comprehends."[21]

The second point bears on the fact that God can be reached
by love though not by knowledge. "By love He can be caught
and held, but by thinking never." Catholic theologians are
apt to discourse at length on the interplay of knowledge and
love. What concerns us here, however, is that thought about
God does not establish immediate contact with Him, but love
does. "The idea of the thing understood is in the one who understands," says Aquinas,[22] "while the act of the will consists
in this—that the will is inclined to the thing itself as existing
in itself." For this reason St. Thomas holds that, though the

[20] *The Cloud of Unknowing,* Chapter 6, pp. 59-60.
[21] *Summa Theologica,* II-II, 8, 7.
[22] *Ibid.,* I, 82, 3.

intellect in itself is more important (*nobilior*) than the will, short of the Beatific Vision, since love is a function of the will, "the love of God is better than the knowledge of God."

It is interesting to note that St. Thomas's position here is endorsed by an authority on Zen. "In some way or other the abstract exists, no doubt, but the point is that the mind does not desire the abstract, it desires the thing. So in the *Summa Theologica*, Aquinas says, 'He who is drawn to something desirable does not desire to have it as a thought but as a thing.' "[23] The desire here mentioned should not be understood, needless to say, as an egocentric craving, but as the sense of nonfulfillment described by the author of *The Cloud*, the "sorrow" of existing independently of Him who alone *is* Existence. Accordingly the most pregnant expression of man's love for God omits all mention of the creaturely ego—"*Thy* kingdom come, *Thy* will be done." Of which the inescapable corollary is—*my* kingdom must go, *my* will be effaced!

It is thus that the would-be independent ego discovers its identity, no longer as the separative, but as the unitive, self, totally correspondent to Reality. The inner task, by which we remove impediments to such enlightenment, is essentially to "Be still, and know that I am God" (Psalm 46:10). Being good, it is sometimes forgotten, is the only effective basis for doing good. Action, fortunately, will always be required of us, not seldom to a degree and with an intensity that demonstrate we are very much in earnest. But beneath the surface, at the core of our being, we could be uninvolved. Within the true self, if we would have it so, there can be light and a certain calm.

[23] R. H. Blyth, *Zen in English Literature and Oriental Classics*, p. 89.

CHAPTER FIVE

WITH FIRMNESS IN
THE RIGHT

The qualification which modifies the phrase "with firmness in the right," from the most celebrated of Second Inaugural Addresses, should never be overlooked: "as God gives us to see the right." We are not helped by being egoistically in the right. For reasons that should now be clear, we need a surer guide to what is the appropriate thing to do than is normally provided by earnest personal conviction. Not the least of Abraham Lincoln's great qualities was that amid the passions aroused by a life-and-death struggle his perceptions remained "slow, cold, clear and exact," so that he could assess at its true worth the partisan's all-too-familiar boast that his cause is a "crusade," that God is on his side. "What I am most tired of, Joshua," the President once said to a close friend, "is righteousness and rant." Would he have been any less fatigued had he been on the scene a century later?

Equally to be guarded against, as a sufficient sanction for one's conduct, is an unverified "inner light." The vagaries of illuminism are many, and one need not be unduly moralistic in finding a number of them questionable. Does the "direct pointing" of Zen, as exemplified by some of its devotees, have a merely self-authenticating, and therefore socially irresponsible, character? Zen exponents are understandably defensive at the frequently made charge that their ethic, where it exists, is quietistic and amoral. To a Western mind it might appear that here is Zen's Achilles' heel, the weakness inherent in an attitude to life which brings intellectual and aesthetic satisfaction, but has no beneficial effect upon conduct. The point, at any rate, is worth examining.

Zennists have much to tell us, though in a somewhat deprecating way, about "thought," but they are notably silent on what Martin Heidegger has called a more dominating factor in man's make-up, the "ought." Examining the index to the most recent anthology of D. T. Suzuki's prolific writings on Zen, I find only one entry against "morality of Zen"; and this is not a reference to Suzuki but to his editor. Here is a relevant passage:

> There is only one way to be moral and that is to have transcended the dualism of rules and no rules and to do the right thing at the right time in the right way, and this calls for an act of creation in the living context. It is neither something that can be antecedently specified nor is it something to be extemporized out of sheer spontaneity. Creative morality, that is Zen, is beyond rules and no rules, and one comes to it only when one gives up trying to cope with life from the outside. The enlightened man who has entered into union with life resolves the dualism of conformity vs. antinomianism, and only he can say with Confucius: "I can do whatever my heart desires without contravening principles."[1]

One must be allowed to consider this rather simple-minded. With its imprecision and ecstatic tone, it exemplifies the approach of too much writing about Zen. To those looking for an escape from life's obligations, "creative morality" will have an obvious appeal. The more thoughtful, persuaded that duty exists and that unpleasant facts should be faced and not evaded, are likely to be confused. The "dualism of rules and no rules," Buddhism and Catholicism may agree, can sometimes be transcended, but the degree of enlightenment that this implies is

[1] *The Essentials of Zen Buddhism,* p. xxix.

only to be reached by the faithful observance of nonattachment, along the lines indicated in the last chapter. Moral cre-
ativeness, with its strong flavor of the ego, is a poor substitute
for the egoless response to the needs of each situation, the "self-
naughting" through which the true self comes into being. Confucius may possibly have anticipated St. Augustine's *"ama et
fac quod vis"*—"love and do as you please"; but one does not
attain the insight of a Confucius or an Augustine by supposing
that there is a simple recipe for doing "the right thing at the
right time in the right way." One follows instead the Buddha's
Holy Truths or the pattern of Christ-like selflessness and compassionate love.

These remarks do perhaps raise the whole question of what
is to be the ultimate fate of Zen in the Western world. Zen may
finally emerge as no more than a passing fashion, a modish cult
among avant-garde intellectuals and aesthetes. This would indeed be a pity: to observe one of the most fruitful intuitions
of the human spirit come to nothing, largely as a result of too
much advocacy and too little criticism. Zen itself is, by definition, outside the range of critical analysis. The existential realities of selflessness, simplicity, and unself-consciousness do
not lend themselves to conceptualist probing; but the same
cannot be said of the literary presentations of, for example, D.
T. Suzuki, abounding as they are in information, though to a
mind with a taste for rational discourse, at times naïvely ram-
bling and diffuse.

It remains to be seen whether the distillation of a centuries-
old Chinese and Japanese tradition can find a permanent habitat in Europe or America. What needs to be noted is that in
China and Japan a code of morality could be maintained,
thanks to the influence of Buddhism and Confucianism, without the sanctions of a revealed religion as this is understood
in the West. Even so, it is worth recalling, with Dr. Conze,[2] that
the *Ch'an* (= Zen) sect, by cultivating a moral indifference,

[2] *Buddhism: Its Essence and Development,* p. 204.

lent itself to the purposes of Japanese militarism. René Guénon has pointed out that "apart from foreign importations that can never have had a very deep or extended influence, the religious point of view is as unknown to the Japanese as to the Chinese; in fact this is one of the few traits in common to be observed in the characters of these two peoples."[3]

Implicit in the full development of Zen, at least as I see it, is the inner task and code of conduct demanded by Mahayana Buddhism, itself a practical expression of the profound psychology of the Indian wisdom (*prajna*) doctrine of the Vedanta. Can one pluck the flower, which is Zen, and transplant it, rootless, to an alien soil? It seems improbable. The attempt to do so may account for some of the oddities, not to say frivolities, attending the current interest in Zen:

> I believe in fundamentals:
> Wearing sandals, eating lentils. . . .

One of the suggestions that might be gathered from these pages is that Zen's appropriate context, in Europe and America, is in a Western wisdom tradition parallel to, and in some respects identical with, that from which Zen arose. Such a tradition runs, it must be confessed, not as an open river, but rather as a hidden stream, in Catholic Christianity. Could there be here possibilities of cross-fertilization—Zen finding in Catholicism a fecund soil in which to take root; Catholicism, with renewed insight, flowering more evidently before the world as its true self? Who knows?

To return from this digression. *"What then is the Holy Truth of the steps which lead to the stopping of Ill? It is this holy eight-fold Path, which consists of right views, right intentions, right speech, right conduct, right livelihood, right effort, right mindfulness, right concentration."* The holy eight-fold path comprises the Buddhist "code" of ethics. This being said, it must at once be emphasized that we are not here dealing with

[3] René Guénon, *Introduction to the Study of the Hindu Doctrines* (London: Luzac & Co., 1945), p. 102.

any systematic body of law. A comparison with the Ten Commandments would be quite out of place. Even the translation
"right"—as applied to "views," "intentions," etc.—could be
misleading if it suggested some fixed external norm to which
conformity was demanded. For this reason some scholars prefer
to render the Sanskrit *samyak* (Pali, *samma*) by "complete"
rather than "right"; though this also presents difficulties, which
need not be discussed here.

It will be noticed that the first two sections of the eight-fold
path concern thought, both theoretical and practical; the next
four apply to external action; and the final two bring us back
to the mind, embracing recollectedness and one-pointed awareness—"one-pointed," not as implying effortful concentration,
but rather undistractedness: the power to "awaken the mind
without fixing it anywhere." A rough order of progression may
be discerned in the eight-fold path: there is a movement from
an elementary stage of thought, through activity to full enlightenment. What is seen at the end, however, is not something different from what one began with; only it is seen
differently. The difference lies in the fact that our untutored
view of things is apt to be in terms of what they mean to us,
as colored by our likes and dislikes, our attractions and aversions. By the enlightened view things are seen in their "suchness," without reference to our personal tastes—*sine ratione
boni vel delectabilis,* as the mediaeval schoolmen expressed the
same truth, "not considering whether the thing is good or bad,
pleasant or unpleasant." But to look at things, and people
especially, as they are requires that we be unself-conscious, that
our conscious ego does not obtrude. The "I," provided it be
nonattached, free from prejudices and preconceptions, can look
at things objectively, but as soon as the "me" comes into our
thoughts, objectivity is lost.

The aim and object of wise living is that the "I" in each
man, his true self, attain realization. Catholicism expresses this
fulfillment in terms of God being glorified. But so far as the
individual is concerned, he gives glory to God by removing the

impediments to God's self-manifestation within the human spirit: a process which necessarily brings with it the emergence of the true created self. The more we are under God's dominion, the more we are ourselves. Christian thought on this topic is more usually expressed in terms of God's transcendence. The "remoteness" of God provides the context for a law being given from on high, a law to which creatures are subject. Moses on Mount Sinai is the historic exemplar of this aspect of the Creator-creature relationship. Rulership is most easily visualized as coming from "above." Moreover, an axiom of Catholicism, as we have seen, is the existence of a real distinction between God and man: so that a morality conceived in terms of a divinely given code of conduct *ab extra* is supported by the highest sanction.

But this is not the whole story by any means. An ethical code imposed from without can lead to a merely legalistic system of morality, an adherence to the letter of the law at the expense of its spirit. These possibilities were well understood by the Hebrew prophets. The greatest of them foresaw a time when men would no longer be obeying God's law as in compliance to directives from above; that law would not even have to be told them by others; it would be known by men looking into their own hearts. "A time is coming, the Lord says, when I mean to ratify a new covenant with the people of Israel and with the people of Juda. . . . I will implant my law in their inmost thoughts, engrave it in their hearts. . . . There will be no need for neighbor to teach neighbor, or brother to teach brother, the knowledge of the Lord" (Jeremiah 31: 31, 33, 34; cf. Hebrews 8:8-11).

The message of the New Testament points to a fulfillment of this promise. There is no encouragement to an antinomian irresponsibility; what is indicated is an "interiorization" of God's law, with particular reference to the indwelling of the Holy Spirit. "The Spirit of Truth, whom the world cannot receive, because it seeth Him not, nor knoweth Him. But you shall know Him; because He shall abide with you and shall be in you" (John 14:17). The "world"—that is to say, the separative self, the conscious ego, entangled in its craving to preserve a spurious identity in opposition to God—cannot know the spirit within. But as soon as we yield to the continual pressure of God's grace, urging us to "be ourselves," we can realize His self-manifestation. "And he that loveth Me shall be loved by my Father: and I will love him and manifest myself to him. . . . If anyone love Me, he will keep my word: and We will come to him and make our abode with him" (John 14:21, 23). The Spirit's presence declares itself by the Spirit's "fruits," not merely by dictating action. The Holy Spirit affects conduct at its source: modifying character by such qualities as love, peace, joy, long suffering, kindness, goodness, faithfulness, meekness, self-control. These being present, an external "law" would be superfluous (Galatians 5:22-23; cf. Ephesians 5:9).

To live with such fidelity to the Holy Spirit as is here implied, it need hardly be said, is exceedingly rare among Christians—as rare, one would guess, as is living a life of full "enlightenment" among Buddhists. Accordingly human weakness has had to be fortified by ethical props, emphasis again being placed on such an external, more or less tangible, code as the Ten Commandments. On this basis prescriptions for conduct have been worked out in minute detail. Because the mass of men lacked time, opportunity, or perhaps the innate capacity to acquire the degree of recollectedness needful for them to be left safely to their own consciences, such a development was inevitable. *"Casuistry"* is an ill-sounding word, but what it signifies can make excellent sense—as a particular instance of how a given moral problem has been solved, so serving as a guide in parallel cases. Provided it be kept in mind that about concrete moral particularities our judgments may not always be certain, that modifying circumstances are often too complex to evaluate, and that each individual's conscience is inviolable, it is merely doctrinaire to inveigh against casuistry.

Nevertheless it is of some importance to recall that at the

formative period of Catholic systematic theology, ethical discussions proceeded on rather different lines. St. Thomas's exhaustive treatment of Christian morality was based on his concept of the "good life"; that is to say, the life of virtue, having the vision of God as its final end. What must further be emphasized, with particular reference to the Zen doctrine of living according to one's nature, is that this is not necessarily alien—despite what certain Western Zen apologists would have us believe—to the Catholic concept of the virtuous life. Aquinas, who follows Aristotle here and not the Book of Exodus, states the matter as follows:

> One who has virtue is thereby well disposed according to his nature. Hence Aristotle says (*Phys.*, vii, text 17) that 'virtue is a disposition of a perfect thing to that which is best; and by perfect I mean that which is disposed according to its nature'. Consequently virtue implies a kind of goodness; because the goodness of a thing consists in its being well disposed according to its nature.[4]

St. Thomas applies this doctrine likewise to the infused theological virtues, since he will not allow that nature has been radically vitiated by sin. Ignorance and an enfeebled will, the two chief natural defects following man's fall from grace, though they underlie what the Buddha called "the Holy Truth of the Origination of Ill," still leave intact humanity's essential goodness. St. Thomas's confidence that human nature is basically good, combined with his undeviating principle that grace perfects and does not destroy nature, leads him to take the position that, even apart from grace, men naturally "love God before themselves and with a greater love." If this were not so, "it would follow that natural love would be perverse, and that it would not be perfected but destroyed by charity."[5]

Virtuous living, it may therefore be said, is natural living. Confusion arises on this point, particularly among professional Zennists, from supposing that the self-discipline implied in ac-

[4] *Summa Theologica*, I-II, 71, 1.
[5] *Ibid.*, I, 60, 5.

quiring the virtues, let us say, of prudence, justice, courage, and moderation, is contrary to nature. Which is like arguing that the effort required to master grammar and syntax must make verbal communication "unnatural." To affirm, with Buddhism and mature Catholicism, that the ultimate "enlightenment" is, in the deepest sense, a self-realization is one thing. To imply that we have thus a sanction for uninhibited self-indulgence, at least in its more refined forms, is quite another. The point has been well made:

This makes very clear the difference from that Western cult of an instinct and of spontaneity, which have their roots below in a substratum which we may well call sub-personal. He who thinks that he can find in Zen the confirmation of a form of ethics which should be tantamount to freedom, but which is instead only intolerance of all inner discipline, of all command emanating from the higher parts of one's own being, will be greatly deceived. The spontaneous character of Zen, the freedom which can even go "beyond good and evil," presupposes an actual "second birth," an event of which Western immanent and vitalistic theories have not even a suspicion. Now we greatly fear that this very misunderstanding is one of the principal reasons of the suggestion which Zen can exercise on certain Western minds.[6]

There appears to be a fundamental harmony of view between the tradition underlying Buddhism and the natural foundations of Catholicism with respect to man's relationship to God's law. This has been pointed out by Coomaraswamy, referring to the two basic principles: "The one is the universal pattern and law of all order under the Sun; the other is the share of this Law for which every man is made responsible by his physical and mental constitution." Then he adds:

It will serve to illustrate the "massive agreement" of the common tradition that has been all men's heritage if we point out that it is in the same way that in Scholastic philosophy the distinction is made of Eternal from Natural Law. In the words of St. Thomas Aquinas,

[6] From Julius Evolva's essay "Zen and the West," *Anthology of Zen*, pp. 209-10.

"all things under Providence are regulated and measured by the Eternal Law, but those of the individual, who participates in the Law, by the Natural Law: not that these are two different Laws, but only the universal and the particular aspects of the same Law." In either sense, the participation determines the part that the creature "ought" to play in the world.[7]

Again, the opportunity occurs to invite the authorities on Zen, whether oriental or occidental, to give us their account of the content of the word *"ought"*!

Aquinas, it is relevant to note, thinks of our participation in the Divine law as an "enlightenment" directly by God. God's law is "not distinct from Himself";[8] and He makes that law known to us by "the light" of His countenance (Psalm 4:6) — "thus implying that the light of natural reason, whereby we discern what is good and what is evil, which is the function of the natural law, is nothing else than an imprint on us of the Divine light. It is therefore evident that the natural law is nothing else than the rational creature's participation of the eternal law."[9]

All this has its application, it should be noted, apart from God's revealing Himself to us by the gift of faith. When we come to the "New Law" of the Gospel, we observe that its chief element is "the grace of the Holy Spirit bestowed inwardly."[10] Even here, St. Thomas is careful to maintain firm links with the natural law. He points out that the New Law, "in the teaching of Christ and the apostles, added very few precepts to those of the natural law." He concedes, however, that "afterwards some precepts were added, through being instituted by the holy Fathers."[11] On the matter of these additional precepts, St. Thomas makes his own a caustic comment

[7] *The Religious Basis of the Forms of Indian Society*, p. 19.
[8] *Summa Theologica*, I-II, 91, 1, 3.
[9] *Ibid.*, I-II, 91, 2.
[10] *Ibid.*, I-II, 106, 2.
[11] *Ibid.*, I-II, 107, 4.

from St. Augustine, which may still be pondered by any whom it might concern.

In such precepts also, as Augustine says, moderation should be observed, lest good conduct become a burden to the faithful. For he says in reply to the queries of Januarius (*Ep.*, lv) that, 'whereas God in His mercy wished religion to be a free service rendered by the public solemnization of a small number of most manifest sacraments, certain persons make it a slave's burden; so much so that the state of the Jews who were subject to the sacraments of the Law, and not to the presumptuous devices of man, was more tolerable.'

It should now be clear that the central Catholic tradition, without being committed to a dispiriting moralism, stresses the importance of ought as well as thought. The Church's ethic is the counterpart of the Church's metaphysic: the will is not forced into action by something alien to itself, it responds naturally to the light of the intellect. From which it follows that if the intellect's light is defective, the will's action will be inappropriate. But equally, if an intuition of the real is not followed by a corresponding volition, one's adjustment to reality necessarily remains one-sided and incomplete. This is not to say that to see necessitates to do: no action may in fact be called for. What is implied, however, is that understanding generates compassion, a loving attitude toward one's fellow beings. This, at any rate, is what should happen, if the troublesome ego did not, as occurs so often, stand in the way of the true self. "I see and approve the better, but follow the worse." The time-honored saying is verified for the simple reason that a clear head does not of itself guarantee a good heart, still less the kind of conduct that a good heart might prompt us to.

The solution to the problem of our moral energies lagging behind the intelligence, of disobedience to the heavenly vision, cannot be found in the will itself. Strength of will does not lie in the will's spontaneous energy, but in its clear motivation. What is needed, then, is not a more penetrating intelligence, but a total insight, such as invites a response from the self at its deepest level. Without this enlightenment the restless activity of the separative self, the conscious ego, remains unsubdued, with the inevitable result that much of our conduct is willful where it should be wise. We notice that we most frequently go wrong, not by failing to act, but by precipitate action, by commission rather than omission, or by acts for which, had we reflected, we should have substituted others. Obeying the self within, moved by God's grace, we learn restraint, how to be silent, how to forbear.

Socrates is the classical example of one who, out of his respect for virtue, was able to see life steadily and see it whole; his vision remained unclouded, since he always heeded the voice holding him back from any excess. "It began in my early childhood—a sort of voice which comes to me; and when it comes it always dissuades me from what I am proposing to do, and never urges me on. . . ."[12] ". . . the prophetic voice to which I have become accustomed has always been my constant companion, opposing me even in quite trivial things if I was going to take a wrong course."[13] This is in the great tradition of "enlightenment." It would be reassuring to find it more clearly expressed in contemporary Zen.

That morality must have as its final sanction, not an external rule, but one's own inner being is a sound human instinct. There are, however, at least three ways of understanding this proposition. First, one may think of oneself as an autonomous individual whose only rule is what happens to be the personal inclination at the moment. *"Hoc volo, sic iubeo, sit pro ratione voluntas."*[14] Of this the logical result is moral anarchy. Secondly, and here is the possibility inherent in Zen, one may think of oneself in "nonduality" with the ultimate Self, as a result of the satori (= "enlightenment") experience. Given a high level of moral integrity and social responsibility—though

[12] Plato, *The Apology*, 31 D, translation by Hugh Tredennick (Harmondsworth, England: Penguin Books, 1959).

[13] *Ibid.*, 40 A.

[14] "I will it, I insist on it! Let my will stand instead of reason." Juvenal's *Satires*.

Zennists themselves do not appear particularly interested in such data!—this could work out, despite its unsatisfactory theoretical basis, as something closely akin to holiness. But where the mind, inflated by a so-called "cosmic consciousness," is supported only by an ethic based on untutored natural instincts, the results, in terms of willful and even arrogant conduct, can easily be predicted.

There is, however, another way in which one can become freed from an alien law. To be at one with God, aware of His near presence, is to find any sense of constraint or servitude removed; for there is no bondage to a Lord, "Whose service is perfect freedom." Love has cast out fear; the creature is no longer a servant, but a friend of the divine Spirit. This is the Spirit of Wisdom which, as the Church indicates by its prayer at the climax of the Pentecostal season, God gives interiorly to our human spirit. "We beseech Thee, O Lord, mercifully pour into our minds [*mentibus nostris*] the Holy Spirit, by whose wisdom we were created and by whose providence we are governed."[15]

The Church's concern for wisdom, enlarged on at length by Aquinas, recalls a similar preoccupation in Buddhism. For wisdom (*prajna*), the attempt to penetrate to the actual reality of things as they are in themselves, is the crown of all Buddhist endeavor.

> Homage to Thee, Perfect Wisdom,
> Boundless, and transcending thought!
> All Thy limbs are without blemish,
> Faultless those who Thee discern. . . .
>
> As the drops of dew in contact
> With the sun's rays disappear,
> So all theorizings vanish,
> Once one has obtainèd Thee. . . .[16]

15 First collect for the Saturday after Pentecost.
16 Rahulabhadra, "Hymn to Perfect Wisdom," 1, 10, quoted from *Buddhist Scriptures*, pp. 168, 169.

From this one may pass, with scarcely a change of emphasis, to the *Summa Theologica*. Within the space of a single article (II-II, 45, 2) St. Thomas makes the following points: first, wisdom denotes right judgment "according to the Eternal Law"; secondly, wisdom, as a gift of the Holy Spirit, judges what it deals with, not in a detached, rational, abstract way, but existentially, by a kinship of nature (*connaturalitas*) — which might be rendered: *tat tvam asi:* "that art thou"; thirdly, this kinship or sympathy with the object arises from the fact that the wise man has not merely learned about God, but is consciously experiencing the Divine (*patiens divina*); finally, this enlightenment—no single word could be more apt—is the direct result of God's love, whereby the Divine Enlightener and he who is so "joined to the Lord" are "one spirit" (1 Corinthians 6:17).

When this point has been reached, though the distinction between Creator and creature remains, no room is left for any sense of separation between man and God. When one is directly under the prompting of the Holy Spirit, no other law applies; only the Spirit's guidance may be followed. It should not be overlooked, however, that to conform to reasonable laws at lower levels is also what the Spirit prompts us to. "The law of the Holy Spirit is above all law framed by man: and therefore spiritual men, in so far as they are led by the law of the Holy Spirit, are not subject to the law in those matters that are inconsistent with the guidance of the Holy Spirit. Nevertheless the fact that spiritual men are subject to human laws is itself due to the leading of the Holy Spirit."[17]

Given that the created self is "one spirit" with the Lord, "Then only when the victory is His, can we recognize Him as our friend, then only are we liberated from the Law, being identified with it, and so 'crowned and mitred above ourselves', and so become a 'law unto ourselves', in the sense that 'Christ was all virtue, because He acted from impulse and not from

[17] *Summa Theologica*, I-II, 96, 5, 2.

rules.' "[18] The impulse, in this case, being that of the Holy Spirit to Christ's human nature (see, for example, Luke 4:1); the same impulse, be it noted, that led to His self-humiliation and obedience unto death (Philippians 2:8). Jesus, like the rest of us, learned what obedience to His Father's will was "by the things which He suffered" (Hebrews 5:8). Even though, as it can likewise be for the rest of us, He endure His sufferings in all patience, "for the joy that was set before Him" (12:2).

[18] *The Religious Basis of the Forms of Indian Society,* p. 9.

CHAPTER SIX

"SEEMS, MADAM?
NAY, IT IS"

The problem of conduct, for the vast majority of us, has been neatly summarized as follows: "How to get through the petty annoyances of life and undergo the major operations of marriage and death. How can we establish a harmony between ourselves and the outside world full of misunderstandings, deceit, and the suffering and death of those we love, when all the while we ourselves are full of that same stupidity, insincerity, cruelty and sloth?"[1] The solution to this problem, Buddhism and Christianity agree, lies in the grace of an enlightened compassion. Enlightenment is needed, so that our human nature be no longer a mystery to us, that our failings give us no shock of surprise; compassion, in order that by being nonattached to the conscious ego, the separative self, the individual can realize his kinship with his own suffering nature, wherever it may be found.

Chief among the obstacles to this fundamental enlightenment is the situation indicated by Hamlet's words, *"Seems,* madam? nay, it is; I know not *seems."* Shakespeare, the incomparable psychologist, portrays in this scene (Act 1, Scene ii) an omnipresent human conflict—the conflict between accepted convention and the realities of the case as seen by direct in-

[1] R. H. Blyth, *Zen in English Literature and Oriental Classics,* p. 95.

sight. Queen Gertrude, her own heart heavy with guilt, is pleading with Hamlet her son to keep the mourning for his dead father within customary bounds. Hamlet, his grief compounded by revulsion at his mother's second marriage, replies that he knows all about the appropriate customs, but, in this case, "I know not *seems.*"

QUEEN
> Good Hamlet, cast thy nighted colour off,
> And let thine eye look like a friend on Denmark.
> Do not for ever with thy vailed lids
> Seek for thy noble father in the dust.
> Thou know'st 'tis common; all that lives must die,
> Passing through nature to eternity.

HAMLET
> Ay, madam, it is common.

QUEEN
>   If it be,
> Why seems it so particular with thee?

HAMLET
> *Seems,* madam? nay, it is; I know not *seems.*
> 'Tis not alone my inky cloak, good mother,
> Nor customary suits of solemn black,
> Nor windy suspiration of forced breath,
> No, nor the fruitful river in the eye,
> Nor the dejected haviour of the visage,
> Together with all forms, modes, shapes of grief,
> That can denote me truly; these indeed *seem,*
> For they are actions that a man might play;
> But I have that within which passeth show;
> These, but the trappings and the suits of woe.

How much of our conduct, how many of our attitudes, stem from the true self responding appropriately to the needs of the situation? How many, if carefully examined, would prove to be no more than postures, thoughtlessly or calculatedly adopted —"actions that a man might play"? Conventions are often well grounded; there is no particular virtue, there could be a good deal of vice, in being "unconventional." But conventions are to be recognized for what they are; they should be "seen through," not equated with a law of nature. No difficulties arise with such obvious conventions as, for example, driving a car on the right rather than the left side of the road; or the custom of a green light for safety, red for danger. These arrangements could just as well be the other way round without anyone being the worse off. When we come to the area of social and political relations, however, and still more of religion, the situation at once becomes complex. In politics, are right and left merely "conventional" attitudes, or do they reach to the root of the matter? In religion, is the form of worship no more than a form, changeable at will? These are matters on which prejudices run deep and emotions high. Here we are apt to be asked and are ready, often much too ready, to ask others—"Why seems it so particular with thee?"

That a distinction exists between seeming and being, appearance and reality, is recognized by thoughtful people everywhere. But the ensuing problems seldom receive the attention they deserve. For the tradition of thought which lies behind Zen Buddhism, the danger of illusion from failing to notice that things are not always what they seem is fully appreciated. The result of "enlightenment" is to free one from, among other things, the hazards of *maya*.

Maya is a Sanskrit word often translated as "illusion"; but it is important that this be not confused with "delusion." A delusion implies that we are totally deceived, whereas *maya* does not exclude the notion that what we see is really there, but suggests that we see it through a veil, or incompletely, or out of focus, or as shrouded in mist, and moreover that—because of our clouded minds or distaste for facing facts—there is some danger of our mistaking the mist for what it hides. As Mr. Alan W. Watts has pointed out,[2] from the same root as *maya* come such words as "mensuration" (Latin, *mensura*), "mental"

[2] *The Way of Zen*, p. 42.

(*mens*), "dimension," and "month" (*mensis*). We shall not pursue the applications of the *maya* doctrine in Hinduism and Buddhism. All that need be noted is that *maya*, of which no single word conveys the exact meaning, has nothing specifically Indian about it; it is as universal and up to date as are the possibilities of self-deception. What should be observed, however, is that *maya* is a necessity: it is the medium through which we measure, classify, and arrange phenomena so that we can understand and deal with them. Being a practical necessity, *maya* is helpful to us, provided that we do not mistake it for reality. Thus Hamlet's "forms, modes, shapes of grief" are *maya;* they are the conventions of mourning, appropriate especially to public funerals—where they are meant to be, and no doubt usually are, seen through. "*Maya* is not illusion," writes Coomaraswamy, "but rather the maternal measure and means essential to the manifestation of a quantitative, and in this sense 'material', world of appearances, by which we may be either enlightened or deluded according to the degree of our own maturity."[3]

Maya enables us to organize and articulate life as experienced into convenient groupings and instrumentalities, to impose upon reality our ideas and the words by which those ideas are expressed. So long as we know what we are about and do not, for example, mistake words and ideas for the realities themselves, we are helped immeasurably. It we could not in this way bring things into line, so to speak, adjusting them to our measure, we should be swamped by the waves of unorganized nature surrounding and bearing in upon us. At the same time, we are wearied and frustrated by this activity: we must do it to survive, yet it misleads and confuses us. Moreover our tidy little arrangements dissatisfy; they block the vision of what lies beyond and often distract and dissipate our mental energies. This situation, with specific reference to religion, has been described characteristically by Cardinal Newman.

[3] *Hinduism and Buddhism,* p. 3.

The unprofitableness and feebleness of the things of this world are forced upon our minds; they promise but cannot perform, they disappoint us. Or if they do perform what they promise, still (so it is) they do not satisfy us. We still crave for something, we do not well know what; but we are sure it is something which the world has not given us. And then its changes are so many, so sudden, so silent, so continual. It never leaves changing; it goes on to change, till we are quite sick at heart:- then it is that our reliance on it is broken. It is plain we cannot depend upon it, unless we keep pace with it, and go on changing too; but this we cannot do. We feel that, while it changes, we are one and the same; and thus, under God's blessing, we come to have some glimpse of the meaning of our independence of things temporal, and our immortality. And should it so happen that misfortunes come upon us (as they often do), then still more are we led to understand the nothingness of this world; then still more are we led to distrust it, and are weaned from the love of it, till at length it floats before our eyes merely as some idle veil, which, not-withstanding its many tints, cannot hide the view of what is beyond it:- and we begin, by degrees, to perceive that there are but two be-ings in the whole universe, our own soul, and the God who made it.[4]

After this memorable passage, one of the most moving that even he ever wrote, Newman comments immediately: "Sub-lime, unlooked-for doctrine, yet most true!" It is a Christian statement of the doctrine of *maya*. Nevertheless, the "idle veil" which impairs our vision cannot be ruthlessly torn aside, still less should it be turned away from in disgust; it must be ac-cepted as a limiting factor, and quietly seen through. Mental concepts, the spoken and written word, restrict the range of our understanding, but they also focus it. By a concept the mind apprehends intuitively what it contemplates; through words we communicate the concept to others, and, at the same time, often clarify our own thought. This being understood, we may then agree with the verses from Saraha's "Treasury of Songs":

[4] John Henry Newman, "The Immortality of the Soul," *Parochial and Plain Sermons* (London: Rivingtons, 1870), pp. 19-20.

> The whole world is tormented by words
> And there is no one who does without words.
> But in so far as one is free from words
> Does one really understand words.[5]

Here some tentative thoughts may be offered with regard to the presentation of the Church's teaching, bound up as it is with the use of words. This is a delicate topic and therefore one not often openly discussed; but the underlying theology could not be clearer, and Catholicism's appeal should be enhanced rather than otherwise by a candid facing the facts. There is some need for it; the experience of many educators points to a failure in this area being responsible for the immaturity of much Catholic thinking and even a widespread abandonment of religion. The question that arises is this: How can an educated and thoughtful Catholic grow in the understanding of his Faith when his mind is largely restricted to the Church's creeds and dogmatic formulas, as presented through the catechism and books of doctrinal instruction?

This, roughly speaking, was the question tackled, with noteworthy ineptitude, by the Modernists in the first decades of the present century. Their lack of success, understandably enough, may account for the problems they felt to be so urgent being swept, so to speak, under the ecclesiastical rug and left to take care of themselves. Men like Loisy and Tyrrell, for all their brilliance, did not understand the nature of Catholicism; they were insufficiently grounded in its philosophy, as well as being unaware of the functions and insensitive to the difficulties of the Church's hierarchy. The Modernists adopted a procedure the reverse of what was called for: instead of trying to adapt the Catholic intelligence to a better understanding of its age-long heritage, they embarked on an attempt to reformulate the Church's teaching in accordance with the supposed requirements of the modern mind. The solid traditions of Christian belief, together with its philosophical foundations,

[5] *Buddhist Scriptures*, p. 177.

were in danger of being dissipated in a vague, esoteric symbolism. It was inevitable that these efforts should meet with con-
demnation.

No one, except the enemies of the Church, could conceivably
be helped by the Catholic creeds and dogmas being emptied
of their content. Where everyone might benefit, however, is
by attention being focused more directly on the content, rather
than on its, necessarily inadequate, verbal expression. The
formularies of belief have the highest sanction behind them
as focal points for the mind. Thus the Church's doctrinal
propositions may never be disregarded; but they are intended,
like every form of words, to be "seen through"—in the sense
indicated by St. Thomas. "The believer's act of faith does not
terminate in a proposition [*enuntiabile*], but in a thing. For
as in science we do not form propositions, except in order to
have through them knowledge of things, so it is in faith."[6]
Aquinas, it will be noticed, is here, in effect, making a correct
application of the *maya* doctrine just touched on. The only
way to escape "illusion," even in matters of faith, is to get
beyond the verbal propositions to the reality they signify. In
the passage just quoted from the *Summa,* which is an answer
to an imaginary objector, St. Thomas is in fact agreeing with
the objection: "The exposition of faith is contained in the
Symbol (= Creed). Now in the Symbol we do not find [*non
ponuntur*] propositions but things. For it is not stated there
that God is almighty, but *I believe in God . . . almighty.* Therefore the object of faith is not a proposition but a thing."

Elementary as all this is, its significance can hardly be exaggerated. Yet it could be obscured, unintentionally, by those
who fail to appreciate the importance of allowing the believer,
both to accept a proposition of faith, and at the same time to
feel its inadequacy. This should in fact be pointed out to him.
A mind habituated to the verbal and juridical entities of canon
law, for example, might itself unconsciously fail to notice that

[6] *Summa Theologica,* II-II, 1, 2, 2.

the kind of clarity to be looked for in legal matters is, happily, not forthcoming in the Church's doctrinal statements; happily, because the gaps between the article of faith and the reality referred to, on the one hand, and between the same article and the mode of its reception in the mind of each individual believer, on the other, constitute the areas of greatest interest. The range of thought thus given scope to is boundless, while the always-to-be-treasured privacy of the conscience in making its response to God's revelation remains uninvaded.

In matters of belief, so runs a theological aphorism, no one should require of anyone what the Church does not require of everyone. The most vital thing in the Church is the life-giving Spirit which is the Church's "soul." It is God himself, as First Truth, who is the formal object of every individual's act of faith. The Church's part in proposing certain articles of belief does not touch the object of faith so considered; that is to say, what moves the believer to believe is not the Church but God Himself. The Church's teaching authority, though a *condition* of our knowing what is to be believed, does not directly influence the mind and heart; this only God can do.[7] When, further, it is recalled that the Supreme Object of faith is "ineffable,"[8] there is every reason to respect each individual believer's liberty of spirit. If Aquinas felt that we are reduced to "stammering as best we may"[9] about the things of God, the rest of us can afford to speak tentatively.

The reader will have noticed that the relationship of the Church's teaching to the content of God's revelation is somewhat parallel to the way in which the sacramental signs, in-

[7] "Propositio Ecclesiae nullo modo pertinet ad formale motivum fidei, sed *est solum conditio. Nam haec propositio non formaliter influit* in intellectum et voluntatem credentis, *sed solum nobis applicat Revelationem* iam existentem, et id quod movet credentem est unice auctoritas Dei actu revelantis." R. Garrigou-Lagrange, O.P., *De Revelatione per Ecclesiam Catholicam proposita* (Paris: Lethielluex, 1926), p. 239. Italics in the original.

[8] Henricus Denzinger, *Enchiridion Symbolorum* (Barcelona: Herder, 1948), p. 428.

[9] *Summa Theologica*, I, 4, 1, 1.

cluding their effective (*ex opere operato*) instrumentality, are related to the grace that is signified (*res sacramenti*). In each case we are intended to penetrate the outward to reach the inward. Whatever tends to arrest the mind at the external forms, be they words or material things, preventing a deeper insight, is detrimental to the purpose for which the words and things exist. From which the conclusion may be suggested that the Catholic faithful might be helped by being offered, and learning to appreciate in their religion, fewness and precision of words, with a corresponding ceremonial simplicity in liturgical worship and the administration of the sacraments.

Let us beware of extremes, however. Almost all blessings come our way through words and material things; it is good for us so to be hedged around. To name a thing, to give it a label, is to limit, in a way to spoil it; but our mind receives its needed focus, we gain in knowledge. Creeds and dogmas, and with greater elaboration, sacramental symbolism, are a divinely sanctioned form of naming. Naming pinpoints what otherwise would remain vague and elusive. What is described or defined is undoubtedly limited in the process, but without description or definition, how can truth be generally communicated? All this is well understood, and put into effective practice, by the Church in conveying its message to the world. Nevertheless, at a time when contemporary culture is submitting the whole process of linguistics and symbolism to close scrutiny, awareness of the problems confronting the educated laity is needed. The man in the street may dismiss as merely academic or amusing such a query as What is the meaning of meaning? But it can easily be shown to be thought-provoking, with particular reference to the general proclamation of Catholicism. Take, for example, two typical pronouncements by that remarkable philosopher Wittgenstein, with which any intelligent student is likely to be confronted in the course of his college career.

My statements are illuminating in this way: in that he who understands me finally realizes that they are nonsensical when he has used them as steps by means of which he has climbed beyond them.[10]

Or, again, consider the philosophical profundity, as it is nowadays claimed, which lies beneath the apparent triviality of Wittgenstein's last aphorism: "What can be said at all can be said clearly; and whereof one cannot speak, thereon one must be silent." Wittgenstein, it is worth remarking, was born of a Catholic mother and baptized into the Church. He did not in any way criticize traditional religious beliefs. What he did do, however, was to raise the kind of questions that cannot be disregarded by those who wish to preserve religious belief in a skeptical world. Of any verbal proposition, he held, we must always ask *how the key terms are used and how we acquired their use.* A reasonable requirement, surely, with no ill intent! Yet what would be the results if this test were applied consistently to the work of theologians and devotional writers? If they are merely repeating formulas from the past, not thinking them through in terms of the present, the results—a lifeless, routine, unchallenging presentation of the Faith—can easily be predicted. Wittgenstein's comment appears apt: "The questions that concern us originate, as it were, when language idles, not when it works."

Another convention of thought and imagination, which can help but also hinder our efforts to reach beyond Newman's "idle veil" to ultimate Reality, is the use of symbols. The language of signs plays an enormous part in the Church's liturgy and sacramental theology: words relate to material things and these to spiritual realities. As the symbolism in these contexts is restrained and its application clear, the devotion of the faithful, passing through the visible to the invisible, can be greatly stimulated. Moderation, however, in all things. It may be doubted whether the extensive use of what is called "typology," favored by certain contemporary Catholic scholars and theolo-

[10] Quoted from Erik Stenius, *Wittgenstein's Tractatus: A Critical Exposition of Its Main Lines of Thought* (Ithaca, N. Y.: Cornell University Press, 1960) , p. 2.

gians, is as illuminating as it is unquestionably intended to be. To exchange one set of metaphors for another does not necessarily clarify a discussion; it may leave the essential point more obscure than it was at the outset. Thus in reverting to what is in substance the allegorical method of some of the early Church Fathers, even though utilizing the resources of modern Scripture scholarship and psychology, one is on highly debatable ground. It could be argued that here, theologically speaking, is regression rather than progress.

On this, if not on every topic, Dr. Walter Kaufmann makes excellent sense. He notes that *"there is no nonsense whatever which may not be said to be symbolically true,* especially if its symbolic meaning is not stated."[11] And he adds, "To show that religious propositions are true when understood symbolically, one must do three things: specify what each proposition symbolizes; show that the meaning one finds is not arbitrary but warranted by the proposition; and show that other interpretations are not just as plausible."

In fairness it must be admitted that there are at least two sides to this question. A recent writer has remarked on "Christian theologians who have little regard for those confreres who revel in symbolism that grows vaguer and vaguer," and adds that this may be a case of "French clarity versus German obscurity (in matters metaphysical)" . . . "an instance of the mighty struggle, now centuries old, between old Greek and modern German schools, between thought focused and thought moving with apparent joy in a vast cloud of unknowing."[12] There can be little doubt on which side Aquinas stood in this debate; it is here precisely that he indicates his preference for the rational clarity of Aristotle, by contrast with Plato's poetic imagery. St. Thomas stigmatizes Plato's use of language as a

[11] Walter Kaufmann, *Critique of Religion and Philosophy* (New York: Harper & Brothers, 1958; Doubleday & Company, Anchor Book edition, 1961) , p. 189 of latter. Italics in the original. But see Postscript.

[12] "Symbols and Faith," an unsigned article in the London *Times Literary Supplement,* March 23, 1962, p. 204.

"poor method of instruction" (*malum modum docendi*). "For
he teaches all things figuratively and by symbols, meaning by
the words something else than the words themselves mean, as
when he said that the soul is a circle."[13] Whether this is altogether fair to Plato, of whom his critic's direct knowledge was
extremely limited, may be questioned; but at least we are made
to understand St. Thomas's concern with accurate language.

If Catholic thinkers need to acquire greater sensitivity to the
mental climate in which they live, the same applies to the expositors of Zen. They often appear blithely unaware of the
critical weakness inherent in a number of Zen's key positions.
The point may be illustrated with reference to one of the bet-
ter-known Zen aphorisms.

> Before a man studies Zen, to him mountains are mountains and
> waters are waters; after he gets an insight into the truth of Zen
> through the instruction of a good master, mountains to him are not
> mountains and waters are not waters; but after this when he really
> attains to the abode of rest, mountains are once more mountains and
> waters are waters.[14]

Now this may be satisfactorily interpreted; it makes good sense
according to the central philosophical tradition of the West.
One starts with a direct, matter-of-fact view of life for which
the mountains and waters "out there" are just what they appear to be. Then, learning from reflection on experience that
things are not always what they seem, one is forced to conclude
that what one apprehends is not so much out there as, mentally
speaking, "in here." This can be a bit confusing. Finally, one
discovers that such reflection does not invalidate, it merely
subtilizes, the findings of common sense—mountains are mountains and waters are waters, after all. Let us note, however,
Suzuki's own interpretation: "The reason I can see the mountains as mountains and the waters as waters is because I am

[13] St. Thomas, *Aristotelis Librum de Anima commentarium*, I, VIII, 107.
[14] Quoted from D. T. Suzuki, *Zen Buddhism: Being Selected Writings*, edited by William Barrett (New York: Doubleday & Company, Anchor Book
edition, 1956), p. 14.

in them and they are in me; that is, *tat tvam asi.* If not for this identity, there would be no Nature as *pour-soi.* 'The primary face' or 'my nose' is to be taken hold of here and nowhere else.' "[15]

This passage has a whimsical quality to which a stolid Western mind has some difficulty in adjusting. Leaving aside "my nose," to say nothing of "the primary face," why should we be obliged to take the position that "there would be no Nature as *pour soi*" if it were not for "this identity"—the identity, that is to say, of the "I" and the "mountains and waters"? Suzuki declares that "I am in them and they are in me." Now it is intelligible to hold, with Aristotle, that the mountains and waters are in me, in the sense that they actualize my powers of knowing so that I perceive them. But what conceivable grounds have I for saying that I am in the mountains and waters? Only the mountains and waters would be in a position to know this, if it were true. Suzuki, bemused by the pathetic fallacy, is indulging in an almost childish looseness of language. Even if it be allowed that the impression of mountains and waters is as vivid as it is claimed to be, it may still be said that he suffers confusion of mind and, here as elsewhere, misrepresents the facts. For it should be noted—as is indicated by such terms as "reason" and "because"—that Suzuki is attempting to give an *account,* not just a description, of the Zen experience. We may agree with Zen expositors that "those who say do not know and those who know do not say"; since, once they start to say, they make it only too clear that—in respect of logic and a consistent epistemology—they do not know.

Logic and a consistent epistemology, admittedly, are not everything, but they are not to be dismissed, least of all by those who would commend Zen to the West. The discoveries that have proved most valuable to the human spirit fulfill, rather than destroy, the tradition in which they are destined to take root. The thought processes by which European civili-

[15] *Ibid.*, p. 240.

zation has been laboriously built up have their limitations; they also have a validity which the "direct pointing" of Zen may complement but cannot replace. The same may be said of the tendency among Zennists to reduce the conduct necessary for achieving "enlightenment" (= satori), or "salvation," to "voluntarily assumed rules of expediency." This viewpoint does not pay sufficient regard to the fact that the central tradition of Christian morality, against which Western exponents of Zen appear to be in more or less open rebellion, is based on deep ontological foundations. "Why drag in right and wrong?" Zen writers are fond of asking. To which the reply might take the form of another question: Why drag in truth and nontruth? The answer in both cases could be the same: These notions are not dragged in, they are there as part of the given. The sense of *ought,* as has already been remarked, is as much a factor in the human situation as is the capacity for thought.

This is a crucial point which must be lingered on, since it indicates the area of widest divergence between Catholicism and one of the best-known Western presentations of Zen. Mr. Alan W. Watts speaks, with a note of enthusiasm, of the Zen experience being "profoundly inconsequential,"[16] and though not professedly antinomian, he seems to advocate an ethic of spontaneity, "without stopping to deliberate and 'choose.' " "The response to the situation must follow with the immediacy of sound issuing from the hands when they are clapped, or sparks from a flint when struck." Within this general context, Mr. Watts remarks,

This is only [*sic!*] to say that Zen lies beyond the ethical standpoint, whose sanctions must be found, not in reality itself, but in the mutual agreement of human beings. When we attempt to universalize or absolutize it, the ethical standpoint makes it impossible to exist, for we cannot live for a day without destroying the life of some other creature.[17]

[16] *The Way of Zen*, p. 148.
[17] *Ibid.,* pp. 147-48.

At first sight this would appear to render the specific Zen insight irrelevant to Catholicism. One might add also that Zen seems to have been uprooted from its historical setting in the Buddhist tradition. When more closely inspected, however, these views exhibit the same type of loose thinking that has been remarked in Dr. Suzuki. Why, for example, should one oppose "reality itself" to the "mutual agreement of human beings," as if this were necessarily arbitrary and unreal? It may be suggested that the Buddha's "eight-fold path" and the not dissimilar Christian ethic based on the cardinal virtues of prudence, justice, fortitude, and temperance command the mutual agreement of millions of human beings precisely because of moral sanctions that are seen to lie "in reality itself." The fact that "we cannot live for a day without destroying the life of some other creature" may be true, but why, if true, should it make the ethical standpoint invalid? We need not attempt to "universalize or absolutize . . . the ethical standpoint," whatever this process may be held to mean, since ethical conduct arises from the response of an individual conscience to the requirements of a particular situation.

The legitimate point, if I understand it correctly, that Mr. Watts wishes to make is that a good deal of so-called "morality" is merely a matter of artificial convention; and that if it is not seen to be such it constitutes or can produce "illusion" (*maya*). Illusion breeds unreality thinking, and to think unreally about conduct, more than about anything else, frustrates, rather than liberates, one's true self. All this may be conceded; but left as a general principle, it does not carry us very far. Everything depends on the application.

The uncertainty of the moral judgment in any given case is understood and allowed for in Catholicism, though the consequences of this psychological fact are perhaps insufficiently considered. The possibility of action conceived as a service to God and yet being fatally wrong is clearly indicated in the New Testament (John 16:2). To distinguish between the letter that kills and the spirit which gives life (2 Corinthians 3:6) is a task incumbent, one would think, on every moralist. But the insight and discretion that are here implied are not to be had for the asking. The theme that has been recurring throughout these pages reappears in this context: the separative self, the conscious ego, which tends to hasty and even arrogant judgment of others, must yield to the objective estimate attainable only by one's true, God-centered self. We must beware of imposing a subjective, personal, or merely localized standard of moral judgment on what comes before us. We should occasionally reflect to what extent the standards and customs of the age, or the place where we live, represent immutable law, or merely long-ingrained habits of thought, or no more than passing fashion. Into which, if any, of these categories, for example, would the persecution of heretics in the Middle Ages, or the theory that the sun moves round the earth in Galileo's day, have fallen?

Whatever the theories propounded, now as always the relevant question appears to be: How are the key terms used and how did we acquire their use? It may be permissible, even helpful, to let one's thought run along these lines with regard to such a contemporary problem as the moral aspects of the so-called "population explosion." One can well imagine the pressure brought to bear, not least by an inquisitive press, on Catholic moralists to give their opinion on so complex a topic. When comment is being persistently sought, snap judgments are apt to be made. If, moreover, the faithful are seeking anxiously for guidance, advice cannot easily be postponed pending exhaustive research. Provided it is made clear that what is offered in response to such enquiries is no more than an individual's interpretation of Catholic principles, being subject to authoritative revision by the Pope and the Bishops, this could well be the only available course. Some time in the future, however, the Church's magisterium may have to make some far-reaching decisions on the matter. The thought occurs that constructive work could be done by historians and theologians, with due regard to the Catholic "rule of faith," to pre-

pare the ground and provide the material on which final judgment is to be passed. With respect to the Catholic teaching on
sex and marriage, many of us would be grateful, not so much
for a reference to well-known principles, as for an objective,
detached, and scholarly study on how the key terms are used
and, particularly, how they acquired their use.

When, precisely, and in what historical context was the
Church's basically unchanging doctrine formulated? To what
extent, if any, did St. Paul's antifeminism, or St. Augustine's
early Manichaeism, or St. Thomas's Aristotelian teleology enter
into the terminology used? Do the terms used allow a full understanding of what should be the role of Christian charity and
compassion in the application of the Church's teaching on sex?
Do the terms used cover all the relevant data, physiological,
psychological, and sociological? An obvious question which exponents of Catholicism must often ask themselves may be repeated here. "Do we face the facts of modern life with sufficient
honesty? Do we tend, perhaps, to meet the complex problems
of today with a peremptory *non possumus;* because we lack the
knowledge, or the ability, or, it may even be, the courage, to
think creatively: to discover how, without detriment to the
Church's age-long dogmatic positions, new applications of
Catholic principles may meet the emergence of hitherto undis-
closed facts?"[18]

There are other ways, besides challenging its authority, of
being disloyal to the Church. The attempt to close questions
which the Church universal chooses to leave open, or to claim
the Catholic name for a personal viewpoint—or, at best, the
viewpoint of a group or school of thought within the Church—
or to give a blanket approval or disapproval where the mind
of the Church is to discriminate and weigh the pros and cons,
are so many ways of impeding the Holy Spirit's action and thus
harming Christ's mystical Body. Let it be stressed that there
is nothing tendentious about the foregoing queries. They are

[18] Aelred Graham, "Towards a Catholic Concept of Education in a Democracy," *Harvard Educational Review,* Fall, 1961, p. 405.

raised in passing to illustrate the desirability, here as elsewhere,
of looking through words and phrases to the underlying realities. True doctrinal development in the matter of sex need
not lie in any marked modification of the Church's present
standpoint, but in a heightening of Catholic awareness, a general deepening of insight, so that sex can with less difficulty
be sublimated in the light of a clearer understanding of the
goal of human existence. It should be noted also that Buddhism and Catholicism do not differ in regarding a preoccupation with the sex instinct as perhaps the strongest form of that
craving whose indulgence bars the way to final liberation.

One way of expressing the goal of human existence, to keep
it within this-worldly terms, is to attain a state of enlightenment such that whatever one does will be "for the glory of
God" (1 Corinthians 10:31). "Glory" in this context means
making God known in a way that leads to His being praised;
"clara notitia cum laude."[19] It is in this sense that Jesus speaks
of our giving glory to God. "Let your light shine before men,
so that they may see your good works, and give glory to your
Father who is in heaven" (Matthew 5:16). It will be noticed
that there is nothing narrowly "religious" about this requirement; it is not a case of bringing "gifts" to God or of "offering"
oneself to Him. What is implied is that there will be such clarity in one's character, such integrity and appropriateness in
one's conduct, that both character and conduct will be seen
to reflect conformity to that ultimate Reality which is God.
"After saying: Sacrifices and oblations and burnt offerings and
sin offerings pleased Thee not . . . He then said, 'Behold I come
to do Thy will'" (Hebrews 10:8, 9). The reference here is not
to well-meaning intentions but to objective conformity to God's
will, so that one becomes its instrument.

Again, our attention is focused on the need for enlightened
awareness. God makes Himself known to us, not through the
conscious ego, but as the still small voice of the true self. To

[19] St. Thomas, *Summa Theologica*, I-II, 2, 3.

hear that voice we must know how to be recollected even amid
the activity of the workaday world. This in its turn implies
that we "see through" mental concepts and words and conventions of behavior to their underlying truth. What makes possible this mental attention, however, is not insight alone, but
a rightly adjusted will, expressing itself in love. The reason for
this is that, while knowledge brings what we know into our
own minds, love takes us to reality itself. "Why, love may reach
up to God himself even in this life—but not knowledge."[20]

Love so understood is not, as it were, a possessive taking hold
of God, but a yielding, a surrendering of the separative self,
the conscious ego, with the result that, "I live, yet no longer I,
but Christ lives in me" (Galatians 2:20). In this condition the
true self's characteristic prayer is of extreme simplicity—"Thy
will be done" . . . "Not my will but Thine be done."[21] In this
condition we are on the way toward penetrating Newman's
"idle veil," the necessary "conventions" of *maya*, to the realities beyond. "Faith gives and communicates to us God Himself,
but covered with the silver of faith," writes St. John of the
Cross.[22] "For that same substance which now we believe,
clothed and covered with the silver of faith, we shall behold
and enjoy in the life to come, fully revealed, with the gold of the
faith laid bare."[23] It "seems" is even now giving place to the
ultimate "*It Is.*" "And if we pray with intention for the ac-
quiring of goodness, let us pray, in word or thought or desire,
no other word than 'God'. For in God is all good, for He is its
beginning and its being."[24]

[20] *The Cloud of Unknowing*, Chapter 8, p. 65.
[21] Despite the antinomian possibilities in Zen, and the aberrations of some
of its exponents, its basic intuition may still perhaps justify the comment:
" 'Thy will be done on Earth as it is in Heaven; is the heart of Zen.' " R. H.
Blyth, *Zen in English Literature and Oriental Classics*, p. 85 n.
[22] Commentary on the *Spiritual Canticle*, stanza xii, translated by E. Allison
Peers, *The Complete Works of Saint John of the Cross* (London: Burns,
Oates & Washbourne, 1934-35) , Vol. 2, p. 247.
[23] *Ibid.*, p. 246.
[24] *The Cloud of Unknowing*, Chapter 39, p. 98.

CHAPTER SEVEN

PLAYING GOD
OR LETTING GOD PLAY?

One can discover a whole philosophy behind some of our most commonly accepted sayings. They gain currency, strike us as apt, because of their underlying, if crudely expressed, wisdom. "Be yourself," someone may have the courage to tell us. "Stop playing God." What admirable, if disconcerting, advice it is! Why should it so often be necessary? And all the more necessary when, as is usually the case, the need for it is not recognized: when one is unaware that one is acting out a part, a part which belongs properly to God.

How does this self-deception come about? The answer is that it is bound up with the human condition, in which we tend to behave, whatever our theoretical beliefs, as if we were on our own, autonomous individuals, instead of giving practical recognition to the fact that our task is not to initiate but to respond. To see the situation as it really is we need to be "saved," "enlightened," "liberated"—whatever word we prefer for that *rebirth* which alone can lift us out of our habitual egocentricity. In Christian terminology, we look for a continual infusion of God's grace, to eliminate the results of original sin.

Consider some of the ways in which we tend to play God. In general, we do it whenever the conscious, self-regarding ego, as distinguished from the true self, provides the springboard for action. To behave arbitrarily, gratifying a whim or personal preference, to the disregard of obligations dictated by the matter in hand, is to presume beyond our state. Here it should be noted, parenthetically, that there is a hint of unintentional blasphemy in the phrase "playing God." It suggests that God acts as He pleases, without reference to any consideration but His free unmotivated choices. Whereas, according to the much more satisfying view of Catholic theology, God, though uniquely free, acts always in accordance with the divine wisdom. There is thus nothing arbitrary in what He does. We, contrariwise, are apt to assume God's freedom to choose, acting not with final wisdom, but on our own limited knowledge, or even willfully disregarding such knowledge as we have.

It cannot be too carefully noted that egocentricity reveals itself in thought before proceeding to speech and action. Opinionatedness, for example, is one of the commonest forms of mental self-assertion. We should face the sobering fact that there are vast areas of knowledge and experience on which, in all probability, we have no right to any opinion at all. One man's opinion is by no means as good as another's; the value of his opinion is to be measured by his mastery of the relevant material and the soundness of his judgment. Mental egocentricity can reveal itself also in unsuspected ways; for example, in those preconceived notions which we like to call our "ideals." Ideals considered as broad and flexible patterns of expectation or behavior are clearly desirable, as providing the necessary stimulus to action. But when ideals are stubbornly clung to in doctrinaire fashion, so hardening into a limited set of images to be realized or projects to be executed with little reference to the world as it actually is, mental growth is impeded and the ego is in danger of being stabilized in immaturity.

Parents who are more anxious for their children to conform to parental notions of what is best for them than to flower as distinctive personalities, young men on the lookout for the ideal wife, girls in search of the dream husband, someone, that is to say, not to be looked at and loved, but to provide a wish-

fulfillment for the ego, are indulging alike in unreality thinking, and so inevitably preparing unhappiness both for themselves and those they profess to "love." In politics, the egoism
of the "left," deriding established traditions in the name of
freedom, and of the "right," contemptuous of dissent as an
offense against order, find almost equal scope. On the ultimately important issue, the vital question "God and man being
what they are, what is the appropriate response?" is reduced
to a personal triviality—"What does religion mean to me?"
Such are the confusions arising, the troubles we bring upon
ourselves, from our incapacity to follow the simple advice:

> Try not to seek after the true,
> Only cease to cherish opinions.[1]

A word may here be said about the need to keep the self-
regarding ego out of any exercise of authority. Official respon-
sibilities, operating at the external, juridical level, should be
discharged impersonally and according to law. This is not to
eliminate the human touch—the principle that the Sabbath
was made for man, not man for the Sabbath, must always be
kept in mind—but to make the obvious point that to obtrude
personal relationships into matters affecting the welfare of a
community or social group is to introduce confusion and often
embarrassment. One of the many benefits of the reasonable
customs and conventions of life—which, as has been suggested,
ought to be both recognized and "seen through"—is that they
cushion the impact of personality on personality. In other
words, they curtail the opportunities for indulgence in individual egoism. To be insensitive to the exigencies of official
status, or to be incapable of conducting intrapersonal relations
in the relatively impersonal terms dictated by custom, is a sign
of defective insight, or, what amounts to the same thing, of
an ego seeking to deal with every situation on its own terms.
    When it comes to the more delicate areas of personal influ-

[1] Seng-Ts'an, "On Believing in Mind," 9, quoted from *Buddhist Scriptures,*
p. 172.

ence and guidance, the need to guard against any tendency to self-assertion is paramount. The most effective help given to others in this context is by what one is, not what one says or does. The best we can do is to dispose those we would guide to see for themselves. The imperative mood is almost always out of place. God alone directly influences the human soul, because He only can directly enlighten the mind and move the will while leaving the individual's freedom intact. Any impulse to assume the role of guide to other people's consciences should be, if not promptly resisted, most carefully scrutinized. Spiritual direction is in place when it is sought for, seldom when it is offered. Similarly, the motives for seeking spiritual direction should be examined, lest they contain elements which prove to be self-defeating. Is it true guidance that is being looked for, or a corroboration of one's own views and projects? If the latter, then what is being sought is an intensifying of the very ego-consciousness that God's Spirit directs one to lose. How gratifying can be the cachet of being known to have, or possessing a soul so complex as to need, a spiritual director! In any case, the aim of a good director is not so much to organize another's life as to make himself superfluous, like a nurse teaching a child to walk by itself. His function is to inform and clarify his protégé's mind so that, learning to trust the light of his conscience, he can make sound and independent decisions on his own. He is then in a position to respond fruitfully to the ultimately reliable interior direction, that of God's Holy Spirit.

As recorded in Matthew 7:1-5, Jesus explicitly warns us against any tendency to "play God." "Judge not, that you be not judged." What we have always to take account of is the instinct of the self-regarding ego to project itself into every situation. "Don't judge others by yourself" is almost always a timely theme for one's mental soliloquy. Positively or negatively, in approval or disapproval, we are apt to read ourselves into others. As with things and situations, so with people, we should know how to observe without drawing conclusions. As

soon as we have passed judgment, be it noted, we have committed our ego; personal pride is to that extent involved.

> The perfect way knows no difficulties
> Except that it refuses to make preferences;
> Only when freed from hate and love
> It reveals itself fully and without disguise. . . .
> If you wish to see it before your own eyes
> Have no fixed thoughts either for or against it.
> To set up what you like against what you dislike—
> That is the disease of the mind:
> When the deep meaning (of the Way) is not understood,
> Peace of mind is disturbed to no purpose.[2]

The "disease of the mind" is not the actual presence within
us of likes and dislikes, but deliberately to harbor them, "to set
up what you like against what you dislike"; because this causes
craving and aversion, so enhancing the separative ego and
eclipsing the true self, God's voice within us. We need to be
liberated not only from hate but from possessive love. To hate
evil and love good is natural; but if we *cling* to the hate, we
become embittered or self-righteous, and if to the love, it becomes *amour-propre* or an infatuation. Whereas our attitude
should reflect the loving-kindness of our heavenly Father,
"Who makes His sun rise equally on the evil and on the good,
His rain fall on the just and equally on the unjust" (Matthew
5:45).

Attachment to a particular form of "good works," or to the
fruits of our labors, can be as injurious as some of the more
obvious forms of self-indulgence. We have to identify ourselves
with God's cause, not God's cause with ourselves. St. François
de Sales used often to illustrate the importance of nonattachment to the fruit of one's work by the following story about St.
Ignatius Loyola.

It is well known that Bl. Ignatius of Loyola, having with such
pains founded the Company of Jesus, realized that it not only had

[2] Seng-Ts'an, "On Believing in Mind," 1, 2, quoted from *Buddhist Scriptures*, p. 171.

produced many fair fruits, but many more would ripen from it in the future. Nevertheless, he had the nobleness of soul to resolve that, though he should see it dissolved (which would be the bitterest pain which could strike him), within half an hour afterwards, he would be firm and at peace in the will of God.[3]

Another form of religious activity, the practice of which needs to be carefully watched, is that of asceticism. Discipline of mind and body, the central tradition of both East and West agree, is an essential prerequisite of nonattachment, itself a condition of gaining insight into the Truth that makes us free. The quite different implications of the two words, however, *asceticism* and *discipline,* are worth considering. "Ascetic" has the same origins and associations as "athletic." What is involved is a deliberately chosen form of "exercise," usually painful and sometimes competitive. Both these aspects of asceticism are illustrated in the not always edifying legends of the Fathers of the Egyptian desert. Little benefit is to be derived from ascetical practices which, even though offered to God, have the effect of concentrating attention on the ego. Calculated self-denial, unfortunately, is at times hard to distinguish from a more or less thinly disguised form of self-concern.

What may have added to the possibilities of confusion on this matter is the Vulgate rendering of such a text as Matthew 3:2—"Repent, he said, the kingdom of heaven is at hand" (Knox translation).[4] In subsequent usage, the phrase (cf. Matthew 4:17; Mark 1:15, 6:12; Luke 13:3, etc.) acquired penal overtones and came to be regarded as a sanction for physical austerities. All this could have been legitimate enough, but the evidence suggests that the New Testament emphasis had been modified. What was originally being inculcated—from the

[3] *The Spirit of St. François de Sales,* p. 130.
[4] Rendered by the Douai translators: "Do penance: for the kingdom of heaven is at hand." A note on this text in the Douai version indicates, though not fully, the difficulty: "*Do penance. Poenitentiam agite, μετανοεῖτε.* Which word, according to the use of the scriptures and the holy fathers, does not only signify repentance and amendment of life, but also punishing past sins by fasting and such like penitential exercises."

Greek *metanoia*—was not physical mortification, but something at once deeper and more difficult. The challenge to Christ's first disciples was not to abandon an easy, luxurious mode of life; that would have had little meaning, since they were, for the most part, poor hard-living people to whom luxuries came rarely. The call, then as now, was to a change of heart, to be converted, to turn away from their prejudices and preconceptions and to learn from Him how to do God's will.

It is often forgotten that Jesus of Nazareth was not Himself an ascetic, nor did He teach asceticism in the commonly accepted meaning of the term. The form of self-denial He demanded was more exacting. He undertook a fast, when directly prompted by the Holy Spirit to do so (Luke 4:1-2); but, unlike John the Baptist, His regular diet was not locusts and wild honey. "The Son of Man came eating and drinking" (Matthew 11:19); He could bear the charge of being "a glutton and a winebibber." This point is being emphasized, not as giving countenance to any excess in food and drink, but as drawing attention to the deeper implications of Christ's mission, with its weight of suffering. The suffering was not sought out; it came upon Him, inevitably, in the execution of His duty. By living up to the light given to His human mind, being faithful to His unique vocation, He involved Himself, the circumstances being what they were, in crucifixion and death. To take up one's cross and follow Christ is in parallel fashion to act in accordance with one's lights, to be faithful to the true self; it is to carry out the will of God, enduring patiently the trials that this must necessarily involve. These are the terms in which our Lord's passion and death are expressed in their most authoritative formulation. He "accepted an obedience which brought Him to death, death on a cross" (Philippians 2:8).

Thus, from the relatively superficial notion of "asceticism," we are brought back to the fundamental concept of "discipline." The word is basically the same as "disciple"—one who learns. Jesus learned what was to be done from His Father; and we learn, if we know how to attend, from the Holy Spirit. To respond faithfully to the Spirit calls for a high degree of alertness and pliancy. To achieve this, body and soul must needs work together; and it is possible that Catholics could be helped to a more fruitful application of the Church's own teaching by giving some attention to the mental and physical disciplines developed many centuries ago in India. Anyone who has felt prompted to adapt these to a Christian context,[5] in however modest a way, will probably testify to their effectiveness. They induce a sense of calm and physical well-being, together with increased powers of "attention without tension," which it is difficult not to consider wholly for the good. The Christian reader may care to be reminded that the word translated *yoke* in Matthew 11:29, 30—"Take my yoke upon you . . . my yoke is easy and my burden light"—is etymologically the same as *yoga*. Which is a relevant thought in a number of respects: it emphasizes the primacy of the spiritual; it indicates the reality of discipline, in the sense of something to be learned; there is a burden, but since, as with all God's acts, it accords with and does not frustrate nature, the burden is light and the yoke easy. Thus the externally imposed austerities of asceticism are replaced by an inwardly directed withdrawal from excess.

Yoga is a harmony. Not for him who eats too much, or for him who eats too little; not for him who sleeps too little, or for him who sleeps too much.

A harmony in eating and resting, in sleeping and keeping awake: a perfection in whatever one does. This is the Yoga that gives peace from all pain.

When the mind of the Yogi is in harmony and finds rest in the Spirit within, all restless desires gone, then he is . . . one in God. Then his soul is a lamp whose light is steady, for it burns in a place where no winds come.[6]

[5] Well worth reading is *Christian Yoga* by J.-M. Déchanet, O.S.B. (New York: Harper & Brothers, 1960) . But see Supplementary Discussion I, "On Yoga," pp. 163-170.

[6] *The Bhagavad Gita*, 6:16-19, translated from the Sanskrit, and with an introduction, by Juan Mascaró (Harmondsworth, England: Penguin Books, 1962) , p. 70. *Note:* The translator points out, in his introduction (p. 27) ,

Having lingered on the obvious point, that we should not
attempt to "play God," or, for that matter, indulge in any form
of "one-upmanship," we may find it worth while to consider
briefly the idea of play itself. It is a pity that we do not find
the whole matter of "relaxation" discussed more fully by those
qualified to instruct us on the difficult business of getting
through life. From a glance at the index to the *Summa Theologica* it is clear that St. Thomas, in his careful way, devoted
considerable thought to the subject of *ludus,* "playfulness." He
decides that it is a remedy against physical fatigue and that
play quietens and so delights the soul. His general view, as we
should expect, is balanced and sober: there can be "devout"
play, which is praiseworthy, and even recreational play, though
this should be indulged in only moderately by those sorrow-
ing for their sins. To be lacking in playfulness can be a fault,
though not as grave as the opposing excess. To indulge in recreational play in a disorderly manner indicates softness (*mol-
lities*).

Really to play, as distinct from entering into highly competitive or professional games, indicates that one does not take
oneself—the separative, egotistical self—too seriously. So considered, the benefits of play can hardly be overestimated. Rec-
reation is a form of escape; but an escape, so it could be, from
a certain artificiality and false constraint to the reality of nature. "The great man," says one of the Zen masters, "is he who
does not lose his childlike heart." A similar thought is expressed by Rôshi (Lao-tse), speaking of the man who follows
the Way: "He is like a child alone, careless, unattached, devoid
of ambition."[7] Playfulness in maturer years lies, perhaps, more
in an attitude than in the pursuit of any elaborate diversions.
The level at which everyday life appears pretty nonsensical,

---

that directly or indirectly, in part at least, the *Bhagavad Gita* was known to
St. Teresa of Avila. She comments characteristically: "Whoever said this no
doubt understood what he was talking about."
[7] Quoted from R. H. Blyth, *Zen in English Literature and Oriental Classics,*
p. 352.

especially when we humans are at our most solemn, may not be that of ultimate truth but it could be close to it; though it is a level on which we can safely take our stand only when we regard our own posture as the most amusing aspect of all.

Someone has remarked that any occupation is suspect which requires a man to dress up or put on a uniform. This appears a little extreme; but it may surely be said that to feel more insecure and uncertain of oneself when off than when on "parade" is a disturbing sign. Not to be able to enjoy, for example, should one feel so drawn, "the virtue of the sun and the spirit of the air" by bodily contact, without a sensation of embarrassment or guilt, could argue too great a concern with an "image" of ourselves. A sense of the appropriate is part of the art of life; but so also is casualness, since this is one aspect of the nonattachment to the ego which marks the emergence of the true self. Really to relax, both in mind and body, is to intermit the conventions of ideality, sentimentality, and sophistry which inhibit a part of most people's lives, and be ourselves. This explains why we often benefit others, and are benefited by them, more on impromptu than on carefully prepared occasions.

> They that in play can do the thing they would,
> Having an instinct throned in reason's place,
> —And every perfect action hath the grace
> Of indolence or thoughtless hardihood—
> These are the best. . . .[8]

From this point it should be easy to make the transition to the thought that creatures are, as Plato expressed it, the playthings of God. "As regards the best in us, we are really God's toys."[9] The idea is not often explicitly developed among Catholics, lest it be misconceived as imputing irresponsibility or ruthlessness to God, but in itself it is part of the Christian revelation. That God does what He pleases with His own is the

[8] Robert Bridges, "The Growth of Love," *Poetical Works* (London and New York: Oxford University Press, 1913) , p. 187.
[9] Quoted from Ananda K. Coomaraswamy, *Am I My Brother's Keeper?*, p. 83.

theme of the Book of Job, is the teaching of the Hebrew prophets (*e.g.*, Isaiah 45:9), is embodied in the Pauline theology
(Romans 9:18 ff.), and was later articulated in Catholicism
through the Augustinian-Thomistic synthesis on grace and free
will. Aspects of this have already been touched on; here all
that need be emphasized is that everywhere and always "we are
in God's hands, thank God!" As the Book of Proverbs reminds
us, alluding to the creative Wisdom, according to which God
patterned the world: "I was at His side, a master-workman, my
delight increasing with each day, as I made play before Him
all the while; made play in this world of dust, with the sons
of Adam for my play-fellows" (8:30-31. Knox Version). The
doctrine of God's universal sovereignity, the fact that He dis-
poses of us at His pleasure, is disturbing, it could even be ter-
rifying, to our individualistic ego, the separative self; for this
is the human personality considered as being on its own, potentially in opposition to God. But the true self—which is not
fulfilled until it can say: "I live, yet no longer I, but Christ
lives in me" (Galatians 2:20)—finds no difficulty; in fact, the
opposite, since it feels safer in God's hands than in its own.
From this point of view, nothing could be more satisfactory
than that the Spirit, like the wind, should breathe where it
pleases (John 3:8), or that grace be given not by merit but
according to Christ's gift (Ephesians 4:7). The thought of being disposed of according to God's pleasure may create difficulty as a doctrinal proposition; as an experience, if we are to
listen to those who have been "enlightened," it is beatitude.

How wisely, it seems to me, are we reminded that "We who
play the game of life so desperately for temporal stakes might
be playing at love with God for higher stakes—our selves, and
his. We play against one another for possessions, who might
be playing with the King who stakes his throne and what is his
against our lives and all we are: a game in which the more is
lost, the more is won."[10] Read sympathetically, this may be

[10] *Hinduism and Buddhism*, p. 14.

understood in a thoroughly Catholic sense; as also can the appended note:

> Thou didst contrive this "I" and "we" in order that
> Thou mightest play the game of worship with Thyself,
> That all "I's" and "thou's" should become one life.
> Rūmī, *Mathnawī I.* 1787.

With this we may compare our Lord's words addressed to God His Father, in reference to the disciples: ". . . for they are Thine: and all things that are mine are Thine, and Thine are mine: and I am glorified in them" (John 17:10). All "I's" and "thou's" should become "one life," as branches in the parent "Vine" (John 15:1 ff.), as members of one "Body" (1 Corinthians 12:12; Ephesians 5:30, etc.).

"What is man?" asks the Cardinal de Bérulle. "An angel, an animal, a void, a world, a nothing surrounded by God, indigent of God, capable of God, filled with God, if it so desires."[11] But supposing he does so desire and his desire is granted, what happens in terms of individual consciousness? Here it should be acknowledged that the claim to some kind of direct experience of God—the Ultimate Reality, Brahman, the Summum Bonum, or whatever term is used to name the Unnameable—underlies both the Buddhist and the Catholic traditions, to say nothing of philosophers of the Neoplatonic school communing "alone with the Alone," or romantic poets in contact with Nature, at the level of Wordsworth's "something far more deeply interfused." What appears to be substantially the same claim, though with the minimum of religious overtones, is made by Zen with respect to the well-known—or, to be more accurate, much-talked-about—*satori* experience. This, if I understand what the authorities say, is a down-to-earth version of the Buddhist "enlightenment."

For Dr. Suzuki, satori is Zen's *raison d'être;* though he seems to hold, unaccountably, that the experience he attempts to describe is peculiar to Zen. As usual, there is controversy among

[11] Quoted from Aldous Huxley, *The Perennial Philosophy,* p. 39.

Zen experts. Should satori be earnestly sought after? Suzuki says Yes; Hubert Benoit, a much more persuasive expositor to at least one Western mind, says No! Does meditation (*dhyāna*) have an important preliminary part to play? Suzuki says No in one place[12] and Yes in another.[13] Benoit speaks, more soberly, of an inner task comparable to that required by St. John of the Cross.[14] Are there many *satoris*? Once enlightenment (= satori) comes, does it stay? It is hard to find a consistent answer to these questions.

The contemporary interest in Zen and its climactic intuition focuses attention on something of great importance; but Zen enthusiasts are inclined to harbor the illusion that what is new to them is, in some general sense, a unique and original "discovery." There are many parallels to the central Zen experience, as has been pointed out by a distinguished Buddhist scholar with specific reference to satori. In Plato, *Epistle* 7: "Suddenly a light, as from a leaping fire, will be enkindled in the soul"; in Plutarch, *De Iside*, c. 77: "the principle of knowledge, that is conceptual, pure, and simple, flashes through the soul like lightning and offers itself in a single moment's experience to apprehension and vision"; in the Biblical Book of Numbers, 12:4: "And the Lord spake suddenly unto Moses . . ."; in Acts of Apostles, 22:6: "suddenly there shone from heaven a great light."[15]

There are at least three elements which seem to be common

[12] ". . . Zen is not a system of *dhyāna* . . . ," *The Essentials of Zen Buddhism*, p. 158.

[13] "This seeking or quest is generally done in the form of meditation which is less intellectual . . . than concentrative (*dhyāna*) ," *ibid.*, p. 186.

[14] "To the Night succeeds what St. John of the Cross calls the theopathic state, that which Zen calls Satori." *The Supreme Doctrine*, p. 220.

[15] Ananda K. Coomaraswamy, *Time and Eternity* (Ascona, Switzerland: Artibus Asiae Publishers, 1947) , p. 14. After giving the above references in a footnote, Coomaraswamy remarks that "the Full Awakening of a Buddha is 'single-instantaneous,' " and adds, "see E. Obermiller in *Acta Orientalia* 11. 81, 82, and Index, s.v. Cf. Zen *satori*. The event is truly 'momentous'. Many other parallels could be cited."

to all types of intuitive experience such as satori. The first is its cognitive character, as evidenced by a powerful heightening of consciousness; secondly, there takes place a fusion of subject and object, with the result that the knower, during the experience, cannot differentiate himself from the known; thirdly, the experience is pleasant, often to the point of a kind of intoxication: even in its more modest form it has 'a beatifying effect, "such sober certainty of waking bliss."

Before attempting a brief account of what I take satori to be, three further remarks should be made. First, because satori is essentially a cognitive experience, it will be modified in each case by the mentality of the recipient. Professional Zennists, untroubled by any urge to self-criticism or the requirements of a consistent epistemology, may be unwilling to acknowledge the validity of the principle, that what is known is in the knowing mind according to the measure of that mind, but thoughtful Westerners are likely to continue probing at this point. Secondly, because satori is not only a mental but a personal experience, its effects will differ according to the degree of integration previously attained by the recipient as a person. The more he has been responsive to reality at every level and under all its aspects, the more satisfying the satori. Again, the professionals should take note: if one's interests are mainly intellectual and aesthetic, with little concern for ethical obligations or social responsibility, then this imbalance will be accentuated, not redressed, by satori. One whose character, let us say, was amoral or nihilistic could receive the Zen "enlightenment" and no one, including himself, be substantially the better for it. He might, in fact, be considerably worse off—compounding his other limitations by the illusion that he is now, somewhat exceptionally, in the know. Thirdly, satori is one thing, the account given of it by the recipient quite another. Because the experience is one that defies translation into words, the language employed is likely to reflect only indirectly the experience, and directly the preconceptions and general mental furniture of the recipient. From this point of view the enigmatic, paradoxical aphorisms of the Zen masters are no more satisfactory than the often high-flown and theologically inaccurate language of the Christian mystics.

With these provisos, I shall now try to state what the satori experience seems to me essentially to be. This particular "suggestion" is based on the validity of the distinction which has underlain much of our discussion so far. We can distinguish ourselves as the subject thinking and the object thought, or, more simply, as "I" and "me." Whenever we act or think, it is I who act or think; but whenever we think of ourselves acting or thinking, the subject of our thought is "me"—even though, be it noted, we may speak of ourselves and often (without sufficient analysis) think of ourselves as "I." The "I" and "me" are substantially identical, but cognitively, at the normal level of knowledge, they are distinct. This might be expressed by adopting a term from Buddhist psychology, the I and me exist in "nonduality." Put another way: whenever I think or act unself-consciously, it is *I;* whenever I think or act self-consciously, it is *me.*

This distinction without a difference, the reader will have noticed, has been the basis of the recurring terminology employed in this essay: self, true self, unitive self being various ways of referring to the unself-conscious *I;* the ego, the self-conscious or self-regarding ego, the separative self, referring to the self-conscious *me.* It has been noted throughout that the "self-conscious me" is a necessity of thought; our self-education would be impossible without it; we could not "organize" ourselves in relation to other people and the world around us. Yet bound up with this very fact, the self-conscious me is the focus of our distress: it separates us from our neighbors, from nature, and, though again a necessity of religious thought, from God.

Now satori, I submit, is the disappearance of the self-conscious me before the full *realization* of the unself-conscious I. One does not, let it be stressed, become newly aware of the I, since that would transform it into the me which has dropped from consciousness. Instead one becomes aware of the "is-ness," in which the I is included, though without differentiation. The mind is thus confronted with *esse, being* without restriction. Accordingly one's sense of separateness—from others, from nature, from God, from one's own happier self—is lost: and one "identifies" totally with the basic element in all that one knows —being, existence, reality. Now as direct knowledge of reality is pleasurable, and the more abiding the reality the greater the pleasure, it follows that the immediate awareness of apparently unlimited *existence*—which results in what has been called "cosmic consciousness"—has a deeply beatifying effect. I say "apparently unlimited," not because the *being* experienced in satori is necessarily unlimited, but because a sense of limitation cannot enter into the intuitive experience of being as such.

This brings us to a point of great importance overlooked by the Buddhist tradition generally. To identify the "I" or the "self," which is included in the experience of "enlightenment" (= satori), with God, the Supreme Spirit (Brahman), is an understandable, though quite gratuitous, assumption. It is understandable because a creature's experience of apparent "infinity" leads naturally to the thought that here must be Ultimate Reality. Nevertheless the assumption is gratuitous, because in order to affirm of one's experience "This is God," one would have to be a *comprehensor Dei,* a "comprehender of God." Unless this could be shown to be true, the affirmation "This is God" would beg the question, that is, assume what needs to be established. Behind this assumption lie two other assumptions equally undemonstrable. First, that there is no real distinction between God and man; secondly, that there is no dependent subordination of creature to Creator. A case has been argued for these positions; but, as we have seen, they are incompatible with Catholic Christianity. Moreover, they are not, I think, implicit in the Buddhist psychology, even though taken for granted by many Buddhists; nor are they required by the essential Zen intuition. Granted the reality of creation, for which a much stronger case may be argued, St. Thomas's conclusion is hard to resist.

> Since therefore the created light of glory received into any created intellect cannot be infinite, it is clearly impossible for any created intellect to know God to an infinite degree. Hence it is impossible for the created intellect to comprehend God.[16]

As has already been said, the account given of satori by one who has experienced it is likely to reflect only indirectly what is, by definition, an ineffable experience, and directly the pre-conceptions and general mental furniture of the recipient. St. Paul speaks of having been "caught up into Paradise," but adds that God only knows what happened to him (2 Corinthians 12:3); St. Augustine relates his experience in terms of the Neo-platonic contact with "eternal Wisdom" (*Confessions,* ix, 10); St. Bernard prefers the erotic phrases of Solomon's *Song of Songs;* St. Thomas Aquinas, following the Zen dictum that those who know don't speak and those who speak don't know, chose to say nothing, except that his satori experience left the *Summa Theologica* looking like so much "straw."

To a Western mind, the Zen attempts to describe satori are apt to appear either enigmatic or overdrawn. More illuminating are the accounts given of the *koan* system favored by the Rinzai school of Zen. The *koan* exercise was developed, among other reasons, it is interesting and relevant to note, "To save Zen from being buried alive in the darkness of quietism."[17] Does Dr. Suzuki's comment in this context still need to be taken to heart by Western practitioners of Zen? "The rampant growth of Zen quietism since the beginning of Zen history most dangerously threatened the living experience of Zen." Essentially the *koan* system consists in meditation on a series of conundrums. Well-known examples are: What is the sound of one hand? Is there Buddha-nature in a dog? Questions like these are to be puzzled over until the flash of insight comes;

[16] *Summa Theologica,* I, 12, 7.
[17] *Zen Buddhism,* p. 149.

then one pierces through words and the futilities of mere reason to a direct perception of reality. For instance, to the query "What is the meaning of the first patriarch's visit to China?" the inspired reply apparently was, "The cypress tree in the front courtyard." This type of answer is much admired in Zen circles.

It would be presumptuous for a rational-minded critic from a different tradition to cavil at a much-respected discipline; though he may be allowed the conjecture that the results of the *koan* system, where it is not indigenous, are likely to be meager. Many of the recorded *koan* dialogues exhibit such an arbitrary, even whimsical, character that one questions the quality of enlightenment to which they lead. It may be suggested that the purpose of the *koan* is not unlike that of the New Testament parables—a question is posed in a manner that obliges the listener to reach mentally beyond normal conventions of thought and conduct to basic reality. By this comparison the average *koan* falls decidedly flat. One looks in vain among the Zen examples for so existential or soul-searching a question as: "Which of these three, thinkest thou, proved neighbor to him who fell among the robbers?" (Luke 10:36).

Nevertheless, satori has about it "the light of common day" which distinguishes it, not necessarily to its disadvantage, from the less approachable "enlightenment" of Indian spirituality, as expressed in the *Bhagavad Gita*. Zen writers do, however, speak of attaining "cosmic consciousness"—a condition arising, I have suggested, not from omniscience but from not feeling any bounds to one's awareness. Here is a record by St. John of the Cross of his own experience:

Mine are the heavens and mine is the earth; mine are the people, the righteous are mine and mine are the sinners; the angels are mine and the Mother of God, and all things are mine; and God Himself is mine and for me, for Christ is mine and all for me. What, then, dost thou ask for and seek, my soul? Thine is all this, and it is all for thee.[18]

[18] "A prayer of the soul enkindled with love," translated by E. Allison Peers, *The Complete Works of Saint John of the Cross*, Vol. 3, p. 244.

Though verbalized in terms of ego-consciousness, as what is happening to "me," we have here an "identification," through the cognitive experience of a living faith, with what has long been the object of contemplation. It is a merging of the separative self in what it sees, the "I live, yet no longer I, but Christ lives in me" (Galatians 2:20). The whole might well be described as the Catholic satori. By comparison the Zen experience may be thought to look a little thin.

Still, it could be that the Zen and generally Buddhist insight, with its stress on living in the present, has a providentially constructive part to play in the Western world. Catholicism is fully aware of the distinction between time and eternity, the *nunc fluens* and the *nunc stans,* but it may be that Catholics, like the majority of other people, have still to "realize" that the only moment at which we can actually live and receive God's grace is *now.* The past has gone, the future is not here; "now" is the one acceptable time. To live in the present should not be confused with a world-renouncing attempt to live in God's eternity; the extent to which we do that depends on God's initiative, not ours. Living in the present is to keep one's mind like a mirror, unsmudged by hopes or fears, anticipations or regrets, so that one sees precisely what one looks at and judges only what one sees. Thus we may avoid what is perhaps the most prevalent and harmful form of "playing God"—the secret judgment of our neighbor's motives. This form of self-indulgence, more even than thoughts of sensuality, makes "purity of mind" impossible. The reason is that judging others stirs up such sentiments as hatred, contempt, envy, resentment, and self-complacency; all of which enhance the separative self, the "me,"[19] placing it in opposition to one's neighbor, and so to God. St. Catherine of Siena, in the light of her own satori experience, was well qualified to make the point:

[19] " 'He abused me, he defeated me, he robbed me'—in those who harbor such thoughts hatred will never cease." From an article by David Ben-Gurion, New York *Times Magazine,* April 29, 1962.

She said, moreover, that if one would attain to purity of mind it was necessary to abstain altogether from any judgment of one's neighbour and from all empty talk about his conduct. In creatures one should always seek only for the will of God. With great force she said: "For no reason whatever should one judge the actions of creatures or their motives. Even when we see that it is an actual sin, we ought not to pass judgment on it, but have holy and sincere compassion and offer it up to God with humble and devout prayer."[20]

It was the same saint who recalled God's revealing to her: "Thou (the human being) art that which is not. I am that I am. If thou perceivest this truth in thy soul, never shall the enemy deceive thee; thou shalt escape all his snares."[21] Securely, then, we may let God have His way with us. We are safer in His hands than ever we could be in our own.

Because the Holy Ghost over the bent
    World broods with warm breast and with ah! bright wings.[22]

---

[20] "From the Testament of St Catherine of Siena, written down by Tom maso di Petra"; quoted from Aldous Huxley, *The Perennial Philosophy*, p. 145.
[21] *Ibid.*, p. 163.
[22] Gerard Manley Hopkins, *God's Grandeur*, quoted from W. H. Gardner's edition (Harmondsworth, England: Penguin Books, 1953).

CHAPTER EIGHT

ANY SEASON
A GOOD SEASON

> In spring, hundreds of flowers;
> In autumn, a harvest moon;
> In summer, a refreshing breeze;
> In winter, snow will accompany you.
> If useless things do not hang in your mind,
> Any season is a good season to you.[1]

These lines express the attractiveness of Zen, its immediacy, and its truth. "Every day is a good day," said Unmon, a Zen worthy. Could we but realize it, for us, every day is the best day, every moment is the best moment, and so,

> Your every-day mind—that is the Way!

All of which may be interpreted in the light of St. François de Sales's saying: "Every moment comes to us pregnant with a command from God, only to pass on and plunge into eternity, there to remain for ever what we have made of it." The implication is not that we are merely recipients of a series of Divine imperatives demanding blind obedience. Rather, what is called for is that we should be spiritually wide awake, mentally alert, in terms of ought as well as thought, so that we respond appropriately to each situation as it arises. Deviousness is the anti-

[1] Quoted from *Anthology of Zen*, p. 79-80.

thesis of Zen, as of genuine holiness. Says Unmon, again, with memorable simplicity: "If you walk, just walk. If you sit, just sit; but whatever you do, don't wobble."

One aim of any satisfying religious philosophy is to teach us how to adjust to the inevitable. "Things and actions are what they are," said Bishop Joseph Butler, "and the consequences of them will be what they will be: why then should we desire to be deceived?" Why indeed? Unfortunately unregenerate human nature often does desire to be deceived, as Gautama Buddha and our Lord Himself were made painfully aware. When closely examined, there is a salutary fatalism about the Catholic doctrine of grace and free will, which it is helpful rather than otherwise to keep in mind. The depressing thing would be if we really were, in any ultimate sense, masters of our fate and captains of our soul. To attain religious maturity is to have learned that such apparent self-mastery as one has functions best when it is surrendered to God. The most obvious remark, we are apt not to notice, is often the wisest. To be able to say, happily, at whatever comes our way, that that is how things are, would mean, I suppose, that we had achieved "enlightenment," Buddhahood, or, in Christian terms, the gift of being confirmed in God's grace.

Before developing further this line of thought, we may attempt a general evaluation of Zen with respect to Catholicism. Zen has been summed up by certain Christian missionaries in Japan as an Eastern "existentialism." This may be fair comment on Zen practice by given individuals, and even the theory, as commonly presented in the West, gives plenty of scope to the egoistic and arbitrary ethics associated with existentialism. But Zen, as we have seen, has much more substantial antecedents than a line of European thinkers from Kierkegaard to Jean-Paul Sartre. Zen starts from the oldest psychology known to us, and continues, though in a different form, the original Hindu tradition that the true light of the mind will declare itself when greed and lust and craving have passed away. What is here implied is something much weightier than a cult of spontaneity and the free play of the spirit. Catholicism shows a better understanding than Zen of the prerequisites of liberty. "For who loves that," as Milton remarked, "must first be wise and good."[2]

The claims of Zen Buddhism are often summarized in what are called *The Four Statements:*

> A special transmission outside the Scripture;
> No dependence on words or letters;
> Direct pointing at the Mind of man;
> Seeing into one's Nature and the
>   attainment of Buddhahood.[3]

The first two statements, it would appear, throw the onus of authenticity on to a Zen master, or guru, who has presumably attained satori. Unqualified reliance on a "director," however expert, commends itself less to the Western than to the Eastern mind. An impersonal rather than an individual sanction, when dealing with man's relation to ultimate Truth, has much to be said for it. This, at any rate, is the Catholic emphasis; where also we find a special transmission outside the Scripture, and in virtue of the gift of faith, no slavish dependence on words or letters. The realism of *direct pointing*—"Behold the lilies of the field, how they grow"—and the degree of calm awareness implied in seeing into one's own nature deserve more attention from Catholics than they commonly receive. According to the great tradition of the West, as well as of the East, an honest fac-

[2] Though R. H. Blyth, who quotes this, has an interesting general comment on Milton. "Of all the poets, Milton seems the farthest from Zen: religion without pantheism, poetry without mysticism, interest in mankind but none in men, seeing Nature as a picture, but no real love of it as alive. This lack of Zen is connected closely with his want of Christian charity, notorious unsatisfactoriness as a husband and father, intolerant politics, and above all, his pride, not to say arrogance. He never forgets himself, except perhaps at the organ, where even his hard heart was 'dissolved into ecstasies'. God he seems to meet as an equal, as if he realised that his poetry would reflect glory on the Creator. He has the impudence to attempt (and fail) 'to justify the ways of God to man.'" *Zen in English Literature and Oriental Classics*, pp. 263-64.

[3] Quoted from *The Essentials of Zen Buddhism*, p. 1.

ing of facts together with unclouded self-knowledge, are pre-
conditions of attaining Buddhahood, or, in the more familiar
language of Christianity, the Beatifying Vision.

One conclusion has been suggesting itself strongly to the author's mind while writing this book. If Zen, as it well may have,
has a message for the West, that message will fail of its effect
unless embodied in an existing Western tradition. We are far
as yet from anything approaching "one world," and the notion
that Westerners can suddenly adopt a Japanese tradition, or
that such a tradition may be transplanted to Europe and America without harm to Western values of great importance, argues
considerable naïveté. Of this simple-mindedness Zen's best-
known exponent, it is regrettable to have to state, appears
markedly a victim. Professor D. T. Suzuki's authoritativeness
on Zen as it is understood and practiced in Japan need not be
challenged; but the same cannot be said of his understanding
of Western religious and philosophical tradition. This, in its
turn, raises the more serious question of the wisdom of conducting what may be called a Zen apostolate to the Western world.
At least those who are so engaged should ask themselves
whether they are really throwing light into dark places, or
whether, perhaps, they are unwittingly making confusion worse
confounded by promoting an apostasy among Westerners from
their own best, though nowadays largely unexamined, traditions.

It is pleasant not to be the first to raise such questions about
Dr. Suzuki. Julius Evolva alludes to the Zen theory—"according to which we must follow our own nature alone, that all evil
and unhappiness come to man from that which intellect and
will build up artificially, neutralizing and inhibiting the original spontaneity of our own being"[4]—and speaks, correctly
enough, of its "seducing" quality. He adds, "Suzuki does not
realize the misunderstanding which he brings about when, perhaps with a view to making himself better understood by his

[4] "Zen and the West," an essay in *Anthology of Zen*, p. 208.

Western readers, he speaks in this connection of 'Life', and nearly brings Zen into the frame of an irrationalistic philosophy of Life."

One wonders what company Dr. Suzuki has been keeping when discussing Western religious tradition. There are the well-known extracts from Eckhart, lending themselves to a pantheistic interpretation. St. Francis of Assisi, as presented by Paul Sabatier, receives honorable mention, as one would expect. But it is noteworthy, and perhaps significant, that Suzuki makes several allusions to two notable personalities, Pascal and Simone Weil, both of whom, though remarkable witnesses on their own account, were at odds with the elements in Catholicism which have the closest affinity to Buddhism. Suzuki partly recognizes this, with regard to Simone Weil, but the fact remains that his knowledge of the central Christian tradition is demonstrably superficial. Moreover, to a Western mind, he appears to empty Buddhism of its more serious content. The concept of suffering as an inescapable element in life is but lightly touched on, with the implication that provided we become sufficiently Zennish, all will be sweetness and light.

Dr. Suzuki is an anti-intellectual. Or at least, being unacquainted with the familiar Aristotelean-Thomistic distinction between the discursive reason (*ratio*) and the intuitive intellect (*intellectus*), he expends much time and eloquence in explaining what Western thinkers have taken for granted since they broke their first philosophical teeth. "This revelation will never come to us as long as we are bound up by the chain of logical reasonableness. God will never reveal Himself in minds stuffed with rationalistic ideas; it is not that He dislikes them, but that He is simply beyond them."[5] Stated with greater precision and less emotion, this might have been Aquinas at his more elementary. The essay from which the foregoing quotation is taken is entitled "The Essence of Buddhism"; yet it contains no discussion of Gautama's Four Holy Truths, which

[5] *The Essentials of Zen Buddhism*, p. 398.

include the ethic of the eight-fold noble path, together comprising the heart of the matter according to all schools of Buddhism. Perhaps Suzuki is here faithfully reflecting the Zen emphasis—*satori,* in noetic and aesthetic terms—rather than the Buddhist "enlightenment" as it affects the personality as a whole. This conjecture may be confirmed by his reminder of the Buddha's "supreme affirmation," which is reached by "going through with all kind of suffering, including intellectual and moral contradictions." The concluding sentence of the essay is distinctively Zen: "The supreme affirmation is: When hot we perspire, when cold we shiver."[6]

What is here, I think, being illustrated is that "the Way" is one's everyday mind; which is a truth that cannot be too much emphasized. Could Zen's function in the West be to heal the breach between religion and daily life? We are apt to forget that to regard the things of the spirit as lofty and sublime is to put them at a distance, and so provide ourselves with an excuse for not attending to them. Religion might well be thought of as matter-of-factness, since it deals with the supreme Fact. But to see it so we need to be aware that God is not only "in heaven," but within us and all about us. Our sense of God in His height needs as its complement a feeling for God in His fullness, a recognition that "the world is charged with the grandeur of God"; and not only with His grandeur, but with His lowliness. For we are often nearer to reality when we stoop than when we aspire to the heights.

The whole process of nature is God's immediate handiwork. The growth of trees and flowers, the warmth of the sun and the

[6] *Ibid.,* p. 414. *Note:* Lest, here or elsewhere, I should have been inadvertently unfair to Dr. Suzuki, it is pleasant to cite a tribute to him from a fellow Buddhist scholar, Dr. Edward Conze: "I must single out Daisetz Teitaro Suzuki, because to him I owe a debt of gratitude which can never be repaid. When, like others before me, in the middle of my journey through life I had strayed away from the right road, it was he who re-opened my eyes to the splendour of the Buddha's message." From the Introduction to *Buddhist Scriptures,* p. 16.

downpouring of rain, the ebb and flow of the tides, are as much the result of the Divine action as the bringing to a "new birth," the "enlightening," of each human being. And not only what is positively there, but what is absent, what appears to us as if it should be there, this, too, has God's immediate sanction. Destruction and death, calamities minute or monumental, sickness, sin, and misery, all have their place, as light eclipsed by darkness, sunshine by shadow, in the Divinely ordered pattern of things.

We have already reminded ourselves[7] that God is not subject to human ethical standards. From this standpoint (see Isaiah 55:8, 9), God may be regarded as "beyond good and evil." Thus, when St. Thomas discusses the Divine perfection[8] and goodness,[9] he does so in ontological and not strictly ethical terms. In other words, God is good because he has all the *being* proper to Him, that is, being without limit, and not because He acts in accordance with a humanly conceived moral code.

The lesson indicated by these considerations is, of course, not any countenance to immorality, but that we should lay ourselves open to being made sharers in the Divine goodness. More important than doing good is being good—and being good, so far as possible, in the way that God is good. "Be ye perfect as your heavenly Father is perfect" (Matthew 5:48) ; on which the parallel passage in Luke (6:36) provides the gloss: "Be ye merciful even as your Father is merciful." Thus to be self-righteously good is not really to be good at all; it is merely to impose one's own ethical standards on others. God's goodness shows itself by pouring existence into things, by God's giving Himself creatively, at a multiplicity of levels, in the line both of nature and of grace. But God's goodness shows itself also when, in given cases and various circumstances, He withholds perfection

[7] See pp. 34-37.
[8] *Summa Theologica,* I, 4, 1.
[9] *Ibid.,* I, 6, 1.

from things, with the inevitable result that what we call "evil" arises. Taking account of these possibilities, we learn to be tolerant of, to coexist with, a great deal of imperfection. We recognize, too, that evil exists within ourselves; and if we are growing in wisdom, we begin to see that the indignation we feel toward the evil, real or supposed, in others is a symptom of our own defects.

> When a mind is not disturbed,
> The ten thousand things offer no offence.[10]

In order for the mind not to be disturbed, it has to be freed from its self-regarding prejudices and consequent tendency to pass moral judgments. Good is good and bad is bad, but both— and, as is usually the case, a more or less subtle combination of each—have their place, like the entire range of colors in the visible spectrum, in God's scheme of things. Again, for the mind not to be disturbed it needs to be anchored within itself, and so capable of focusing its attention steadily on what is presented to it. It may be that the West has something to learn from the East on the importance of "mindfulness," that is, bringing one's mind completely to bear on whatever confronts it. What is called for is not intense concentration, with a knitting of the brows, but, rather, the opposite, an awakening of the mind without fixing it anywhere, the quietness of pure attention. Bare attention, a Buddhist writer points out, means "bare of labels."

Bare attention consists in a bare and exact registering of the object. This is not as easy a task as it may appear, since it is not what we normally do, except when engaged in disinterested investigation. Normally man is not concerned with disinterested knowledge of "things as they truly are", but with "handling" and judging them from the view point of his self-interest, which may be wide or narrow, noble or low. He tacks labels to the things which form his physical and mental universe, and these labels mostly show clearly the

[10] Seng-Ts'an, "On Believing in Mind," 11, quoted from *Buddhist Scriptures*, p. 172.

impress of his self-interest and his limited vision. It is such an assemblage of labels in which he generally lives and which determines his actions and reactions."[11]

These labels, which we have discussed earlier in relation to the veiling of reality brought about by *maya,* are what we must be able to "see through." Christians are disposed to think of the mental activities of meditation and contemplation as almost exclusively "religious," being directed to God and the saints. This is too narrow a view; it is also a view that could lead to illusions and unreality thinking. God and the saints as envisaged in personal meditation are partly the product of our own thought, with the attendant dangers of unconsciously placing before ourselves a God according to our image and likeness. Hence the warning of the *Doctor mysticus* of the Church, St. John of the Cross: "Wherefore, in order to come to this essential union of love in God, the soul must have a care not to lean upon imaginary visions, nor upon forms or figures or particular objects of the understanding; for these cannot serve it as a proportionate and proximate means to such an end; rather they would disturb it, and for this reason the soul must renounce them and strive not to have them."[12] What we may need to learn is that merely to look at things as they are, with bare attention, can be a religious act. We are thus enabled to apprehend God's creation as it is, our minds unclouded by egoistical emotions, and so made more aware of God Himself.

The chief impediment to this "attention without tension" is what is commonly called wishful thinking. We see what we want to see, or, negatively, what we fear to see; we do not see what is there. Our unconscious clinging (or it may be quite conscious) to certain contents of the mind—in the form of prejudices, desires, consolations, supports, ego-gratifying hatreds

[11] Nyanaponika Thera, *The Heart of Buddhist Meditation* (London: Rider & Company, 1962), p. 32.
[12] *Ascent of Mount Carmel,* II, 16, 10, translated by E. Allison Peers, in *Complete Works of Saint John of the Cross,* Vol. 1, p. 134.

and resentments—prevents us from "letting go" and examining with what has been called the *peeled eye* the thing before us. In analyzing this problem, Zen, and the long tradition of mental discipline behind it, offers its basic contribution. It will be remembered that the word "zen" is a modification of the Sanskrit word for meditation (*dhyāna*), which became *ch'an* in China and *zazen*, "to sit and meditate," in Japan.

Zen meditation, it should be carefully noted, is an exercise neither of the discursive reason nor of the creative imagination. Accordingly the word "meditation" here connotes something different from the points, reflections, compositions of place, resolutions, and the rest which form the machinery of meditation in certain modern Catholic books of devotion. The Christian counterpart of the Zen insight can be found more easily in an earlier age: in the New Testament, of course, but also in St. Thomas Aquinas, the author of *The Cloud of Unknowing*, and St. John of the Cross. Indeed the latter complains of misguided spiritual directors "laying their coarse hands where God is working," because they have not themselves "learned what it means to leave behind the discursive reasoning of meditations." "And therefore they disturb and impede the peace of this quiet and hushed contemplation which God has been giving the penitents by His own power, and they cause them to follow the road of meditation and imaginative reasoning and make them perform interior acts, wherein the aforementioned souls find great repugnance, aridity and distraction, since they would fain remain in their holy rest and their quiet and peaceful state of recollection."[13]

Inevitably, allowance must be made for the native background and personal dedication of the Carmelite friar, but St. John of the Cross is here making a point of universal validity; he indicates what the condition of the human mind must be as it opens itself to ultimate Reality. Zen meditation is instantane-

[13] St. John of the Cross, *Living Flame of Love*, III, 54, translated by E. Allison Peers, in *Complete Works of Saint John of the Cross*, Vol. 3, p. 190.

ously contemplative; it has been described as "seeing without desire." There is nothing occult, mysterious, or essentially difficult about it. It is the most natural thing for the mind to do, were not the mind clouded by clinging and craving. If we could disentangle ourselves from these, and keep fully aware without thinking of anything, we should perceive all that we see in its "suchness"; that is to say, within human limits, as God sees it.

To see things from God's viewpoint—*sub ratione Deitatis,* as the theologians express it—means that we are functioning not egoistically, but as our true selves. And our true self, as has been recalled, is the habitat of God—where, by faith and through His grace, "I live, yet no longer I, but Christ lives in me" (Galatians 2:20). So considered, meditation merges into contemplation as understood by the central Catholic tradition. "There are those who think that this matter of contemplation is so difficult and frightening that it cannot be accomplished without a great deal of very hard work beforehand, and that it only happens occasionally," writes the author of *The Cloud of Unknowing.*

> . . . Let me answer these people as well as I can; it depends entirely on the will and good pleasure of God, and whether they are spiritually able to receive this grace of contemplation, and the working of the Spirit . . . there are some who by grace are so sensitive spiritually and so at home with God in this grace of contemplation that they may have it when they like and under normal spiritual working conditions, whether they are sitting, walking, standing, kneeling. And at these times they are in full control of their faculties, both physical and spiritual, and can use them if they wish. . . .[14]

What interested Catholics should explore, I suggest, is whether contemplation has not a much more generalized and nonprofessional character than is often supposed. The notion that the contemplative state is an exclusive preoccupation with God is misleading, since God excludes nothing. Of possible relevance is the famous triune formula to be found in the early

[14] *The Cloud of Unknowing,* Chapter 71, p. 138.

tradition behind Zen Buddhism—*Sat-Cit-Ananda:* Being-Knowledge-Bliss, which is predicated of Ultimate Reality. This hardly corresponds to the revealed doctrine of the Holy Trinity, but it has its analogies in the metaphysic of Catholicism. The evidence suggests that St. Thomas would have been happy with it—since for him material *being* reaches a higher state of actualization by becoming an object of *knowledge,* and knowledge of things in their causes, which is wisdom, constitutes *bliss.* It may therefore be submitted that the contemplative state, when realized in an individual, reproduces at the created level, the *Sat-Cit-Ananda:* a Catholic contemplative would then enjoy, as already touched on, his satori: "the sober certainty of waking bliss." In precisely this context we find Juan Mascaró referring to "the greatest spiritual poems of all time," those of St. John of the Cross, and adding: "In his aphorisms he says: 'In order to be All, do not desire to be anything. In order to know All, do not desire to know anything. In order to find the joy of All, do not desire to enjoy anything'. 'To be', 'to know', and 'to find joy' correspond to the SAT, CIT, ANANDA, 'Being, Consciousness, and Joy' of the *Upanishads.*"[15]

In this condition the individual would have, though still through the veil of faith, the highest degree of awareness of God. But this awareness would not lead to the futile attempt, born of anthropomorphic conceptions of the Deity, at a possessive taking hold of God, since possessiveness and the desire to take hold are what "enlightenment" liberates one from. Rather, the individual would find himself more and more receptive to the Divine impulse (*patiens divina*), in a habitual state of "Not my will but Thine be done." He would thus become a channel of God's love (*agape*) for the world; he would be a mediator of the reality expressed in "God so loved the world as to give His only begotten Son" (John 3:16), and so become, as it were, an *alter Christus,* another Christ. It is of this

[15] Juan Mascaró, introduction to his translation of *The Bhagavad Gita,* p. 29.

mediation of God's love, we should note, that St. Paul speaks
in the memorable hymn to *agape* in 1 Corinthians 13. His
theme is not directly man's love for God, but what should be
man's Christ-like love for his neighbor. "Love is long suffering,
is kind; love envies not" (v. 4).

The parallel to this, in the tradition behind Zen Buddhism,
is *karunā*, compassion. " 'I do not ask the wounded person how
he feels,' " writes Coomaraswamy, quoting Walt Whitman, " 'I
myself become the wounded person'. That is *karunā*."[16]

> I understand the large hearts of heroes,
> The courage of present times and all times . . .
> I am the man, I suffered, I was there. . . .

To love someone is to love his whole personality. We are aware
that he, like ourselves, has his defects; but we don't make a
mental list of pros and cons, so giving him a nicely blended
mixture of approval and disapproval.

> As soon as you have good and evil
> Confusion follows and the mind is lost . . .
> The enlightened have no likes or dislikes. . . .[17]

Or, in Christian terminology, "Judge not, that ye be not
judged" (Matthew 7:1).

Christianity in its historical, eschatological dimension lays
much stress on death. Understandably so, since here, literally, is
the great moment of *crisis*. Viewed, however, from the standpoint of the "eternal now," death appears less daunting. Physi-
ologists tell us that, with regard to our bodies, we are both living and dying all the time. "We do not live, we do not die, we
live-die."[18] Preoccupation with the thought of one's death
occurs when the conscious ego, as it is constantly apt to do,
overwhelms, so to speak, the true self. For the true self lives and

[16] *Buddha and the Gospel of Buddhism*, p. 134.
[17] Quoted from Hubert Benoit, *The Supreme Doctrine*, p. 214.
[18] R. H. Blyth, *Zen in English Literature and Oriental Classics*, p. 235.

loves in the present, at least half consciously aware that the only death that counts is to be separated from ultimate Reality, which is God. As Robert Southwell wrote, "Not where I breathe, but where I love, I live." From this point of view we are more concerned about other people's deaths than our own. Here, understandably, is the most difficult field for the practice of nonattachment. We cling, grasp at, the lives and well-being of others, until we learn that these, too, are in better hands than our own.

In order to be able to live in the present, which is *the* secret of happiness, we must turn a realistic eye on the commonest of all forms of concern about death—clinging to youth and refusing to acknowledge old age. The colloquialism "Be your age" might be regarded as both a Zen and a Christian saying. And yet there is some truth in the often heard, if slightly pathetic, remark that one is as old as one feels oneself to be. From the viewpoint to which a thousand years are but as yesterday (Psalm 90:4), no one lives too long or dies too young. To the death of each, given appropriateness in living, Ben Jonson's exquisite lines might apply.

> It is not growing like a tree
> In bulke, doth make man better bee;
> Or standing long an Oake, three hundred yeare,
> To fall a logge at last, dry, bald, and seare:
> A Lillie of a Day
> Is fairer, farre, in May,
> Although it fall, and die that night;
> It was the Plant, and flowre of light.
> In small proportions, we just beautie see:
> And in short measures, life may perfect bee.

To live in the present we do not have to ignore the reality of time. For the Christian, time is an important category, since the origins of his religion, unlike those of Buddhism, are bound up with historical events. The veracity of the legends surrounding the life and work of Siddhartha Gautama is of little moment to the educated Buddhist; what matters to him is the whole process by which one may oneself become a Buddha, an "enlightened one." Christianity, on the other hand, is inseparably linked with the person and lifework of Jesus of Nazareth. The Judaeo-Christian tradition sees the time sequence as being itself a manifestation of God's purpose. To a Hindu who is sympathetic to Christianity, as Professor Mircea Eliade points out, "the most striking innovation (apart from the message and the divinity of Christ) is its valorization of Time—in the final reckoning, its *redemption* of Time and History."[19]

A vivid sense of history is one characteristic of Catholicism. The Church stands or falls by the validity of its claim to have been constituted, with Peter as its first pope, by our Lord Jesus Christ during His life on earth. The Church has grown in the understanding of itself as age succeeds age. We are as yet, it may well be, "early Christians"—two thousand years being a short period compared with, say, a million years. The Church, like its individual members, will advance in self-knowledge until it at length achieves its complete stature, the "fulness of Christ" (Ephesians 4:13). The recurring cycle of the Church's liturgy and the whole sacramental system are further indications of the reality of time. We may make contact with what is eternal; but the normal preliminaries are that account be taken of the Divinely ordained temporal instruments through which God's grace comes to us.

We should observe, however, that what makes for us any day a good day, any season a good season, is that the days and seasons can be, through an enlightened faith, focused upon the God who is timeless and eternal. "Time becomes a value, insofar as God manifests Himself through it, filling it with transhistorical meaning and a soteriological intention."[20] God's saving purpose, to express the last phrase more simply, is executed, with respect to the justification of the individual and the infu-

[19] Mircea Eliade, *Images and Symbols* (London: Harvill Press, 1961), p. 169.
[20] Mircea Eliade, *loc. cit.*

sion of Divine grace, not in history's time sequence but according to the timeless action of God, "instantly, without any succession in time."[21] Thus while Catholicism has its vitally important temporal aspects, its *raison d'être* is beyond time. "While we look not at the things which are seen, but at the things which are not seen. For the things which are seen are temporal: but the things which are not seen, are eternal" (2 Corinthians 4:18).

Our Lord Jesus Christ, according to His humanity, was involved like the rest of us in the time sequence; but according to His divinity He was one with the timeless God. "Before Abraham was, I am" (John 8:58). We ourselves can, through faith, make contact with the timeless God even in this life. Not that we can stand fully outside the time series, but given God's grace and our co-operation, we can live in a continuous present. This, it will have been noted, is what Zen Buddhism is aiming at. This, with greater possibilities of success, is the goal of Catholic spirituality. The days, the seasons, each one of them, become "good"—not in any lighthearted, irresponsible sense; not because our problems and sufferings suddenly vanish—but by the fact that we are rooted in Reality, fixed at the Center, seeing into our own nature and so perceiving its intimate relationship to God. We become more, rather than less, sensitive to "the still, sad music of humanity"; but we listen to it for its own sake, so to speak, and not as ego-regarding individuals troubled by an essentially personal distress. Thus the wide sympathy so generated coexists with the peace that passes understanding, which, provided he be unentangled by desire and craving, lies in the heart of every man.

Catholics, it seems, need more often to be reminded that the Church's concept of the spiritual life, as it affects each individual, has the evident psychological depth and power which are commonly associated with the Hindu-Buddhist-Zen tradition. St. Thomas Aquinas points out that human thought is, to

[21] St. Thomas, *Summa Theologica*, I-II, 113, 7.

some extent, a timeless activity, as it "abstracts from the here
and now."[22] He takes the position also that "nothing exists of
time except *now*."[23] No less significantly St. Thomas asserts that
we can, in some measure, apprehend timeless eternity and,
moreover, that God communicates to individuals a participation in the Divine eternity.

> The *now* that stands still *(nunc stans)* is said to make eternity ac-
> cording to our apprehension. As the apprehension of time is caused
> in us by the fact that we apprehend the flow of the now; so the ap-
> prehension of eternity is caused by our apprehending the *now* stand-
> ing still. When Augustine says that *God is the author of eternity*, this
> is to be understood of a participated eternity. For God communi-
> cates His eternity to some in the same way as He communicates His
> immutability.[24]

No forced interpretation is needed to discover here an echo of
the New Testament theology. "Eternal life" both consists essentially in *knowledge* (John 17:3) and is a reality, not just
hopefully to be looked forward to, but already given (1 John
5:11, 13) ; we have it *now*.

The theory of all this is apt to become abstruse, but the practice could hardly be simpler. We have to become "children of
time present"—living in the present being the childlike quality
par excellence. Not in this case, however, the "animal" present
in which infants live; but a present of which we are so conscious that it is hardly distinguishable from eternity. For eternity, be it noted, is not everlastingness, as if it were time going
on and on; eternity is a point of awareness to which the category of time, a sequence of before and after, simply does not
apply. This is what gives such significance to the New Testament message that eternal life is *now*. "Behold, now is the acceptable time; . . . now is the day of salvation" (2 Corinthians

[22] *Summa Theologica*, I, 107, 4.

[23] *Ibid.*, I, 46, 3, 3.

[24] *Ibid.*, I, 10, 2, 1. See also, as relevant to this context, St. Thomas's argument that human *delight* has a timeless quality, *ibid.*, I-II, 31, 2.

6:2) . The Catholic masters of the spiritual life never tire of repeating the simple theme. "Do what you are doing now, suffer
what you are suffering now," writes J. P. de Caussade. "To do
all this with holiness, nothing need be changed but your hearts.
Sanctity consists in *willing* what happens to us by God's
order."[25]

The willing here referred to must not be confused with an
attitude of grim determination. Rather, it is a quiet yielding to
the evident signs of what God wants from us, a calm acquies-
cence in the inevitable. Not forcefulness, but a certain emptiness of both mind and will is what is called for. The "doors of
perception," in Blake's phrase, need to be cleansed, so that we
can face reality as it is. We should cherish the thoughts that,
paradoxically, dwell on nothing at all; not so as to preserve a
mental vacuity, which has no merit, but to have the mind fully
receptive now on the spot where we are. "I cannot see that anyone can claim fellowship in this matter with Jesus or His
righteous Mother, His angels or His saints," writes the author
of *The Cloud of Unknowing,* "unless he is doing everything in
his power, with the help of grace, to attend to each moment of
time." "So pay great attention to this marvellous work of grace
within your soul. It is always a sudden impulse and comes
without warning, springing up to God like some spark from the
fire. An incredible number of such impulses arise in one brief
hour in the soul who has a will to this work!"[26]

These deeper, at once more exacting and more heartening,
aspects of Catholicism are here being stressed because they are,
I think, somewhat neglected in our day. If there is to be no salvation outside the Church, in whatever sense the same Holy
Mother Church now interprets that difficult saying, it is also
true, as has been observed, that there is no salvation outside the
soul. The hidden processes of growing in grace, of liberation
and enlightenment, take place nowhere but within the mind

[25] Quoted from Aldous Huxley, *The Perennial Philosophy,* p. 75.
[26] Chapter 4, p. 57.

and heart of each. "The mind in its own place and in itself can make a heaven of hell, a hell of heaven." The verbal propositions of the Church's dogma are assented to by all; but they are held and subjectively understood by each according to the distinctive character and equipment of his or her mind. Where final unity lies is not in articles of belief, but in penetrating through these to the Reality they inadequately represent. *Credo in Deum* . . .; that is, I believe in such a way that my mind goes out to God; or, more accurately, that God manifests Himself to my mind (John 14:21). To live continuously in God's presence, or in secular terminology, to be facing Reality with complete awareness, in terms of ought as well as thought, is the only condition required for every season to be a good season. Then we should be at the central point, the "standing now" *(nunc stans)*, round which the seasons turn in their recurring cycles; we should find ourselves quietly acquiescent in "the many ways of mystery and many things God brings to be."

A distinguished authority, R. H. Blyth, would have us believe that " 'Thy will be done on Earth as it is in Heaven' is the heart of Zen." He records also, with approval, the saying of Mother Juliana of Norwich, in her *Revelations of Divine Love:* "To seek God without already having Him, is of all things the most impossible." Finally, he states that "the Christian doctrine of Grace is identical with the Zen principle of 'Direct pointing to the soul of man.' "[27] These are suggestive ideas and there appears no reason to challenge them. They are indications, among many, that the spirit of Zen may find a congenial dwelling place within Catholicism; for the Church sees a continuity, not a radical break, between nature and grace. The Zen advice, to follow one's own nature, need not be interpreted as an encouragement to license; it could be a reminder that the Author of grace is also the Author of nature, and that provided one is in conscious union with God, to follow one's nature is to do God's

[27] R. H. Blyth, *Zen in English Literature and Oriental Classics,* p. 99 n.

will. There is more to be said than is often allowed for trusting one's instincts; they can on occasion prove a safer guide to appropriate action than the careful calculations of reason. Living in a continuous present, one need not be anxious about tomorrow (Matthew 6:34) ; acting as one's true self—the self that is always correspondent to the Holy Spirit—one will know by instinct what to say and do (Luke 12:11-12). We may record, by way of summary, a Catholic satori (= enlightenment) experience of Mother Juliana of Norwich:

And therefore the Blessed Trinity is ever full pleased in all His works. And all this shewed He full blessedly, meaning thus, *"See I am God: See I am in all things: See I do all things: See I never left my hands off my works, nor never shall without end: See I lead all thing to the end that I ordaine it to, for without beginning, by the same might, wisdom and love, that I made it with, How should anything be amiss?"* Thus mightily, wisely, and lovingly was the soul examined in this vision. Then saw I verily that me behoveth needs to assent with great reverence and joy in God.[28]

In bringing this series of suggestions to an end, I leave it to the reader to draw his or her own conclusions, if there are any to be drawn. One point, however, may be made with some confidence. Whatever be the import of the present widespread interest in Zen, any temptation to Westerners to turn for lasting enlightenment to Japan should be promptly resisted. The evidence points to the discovery of, at best, a mirage. Whatever is of permanent value in Zen is, I submit, not Japanese but Buddhist; and the Buddhist philosophy of life is of such universal validity that one does not have to leave home to find its application. One has only to look into one's own heart. As for Buddhism in its native setting, there are few signs of any vital spiritual renewal from that quarter. Dr. Edward Conze reminds us that

The creative impulse of Buddhist thought came to a halt about 1,500 years after the Buddha's Nirvana. During the last 1,000 years

[28] *Revelations of Divine Love,* conclusion to the third revelation.

no new school of any importance has sprung up, and the Buddhists have merely preserved, as best they could, the great heritage of the past. It is possible to believe that the lotus of the doctrine has, after 1,500 years, fully unfolded itself. Perhaps there is no more to come.[29]

With regard to Buddhism in Japan, in a recent press release from Tokyo, a prominent Buddhist religious leader is quoted as stating: "Unless we adopt the spirit and techniques of Christianity, specifically of the Catholic Church, Japanese Buddhism may soon be a thing of the past. . . . We have several movements in Japanese Buddhism parallel with yours in the Catholic Church. I have started a Buddhist 'Catholic Action' movement for lay people, which aims at bringing Buddhism back into daily life." In fairness, and as having an interest of its own, the following remark by the same authority should also be noted:

> But don't forget that for us, religion is culture and art, not dogma or ethics. Buddhism is the rice and Christianity the vegetables. Modern Japan wants to eat of both and mix them to her taste.[30]

What this witness has called Christianity's "slow but sure expansion" in Japan has its ironic aspect; it offers little comfort to disaffected Western Christians who might conceivably be seeking to salve their consciences by the cult of Zen on its native soil. Even Dr. Suzuki has some sad admissions to make:

> Institutions like the Zendo [*i.e.*, the Zen monks' meditation hall] are becoming anachronistic and obsolete; its tradition is wearing out, and the spirit that has been controlling the discipline of the monks for so many hundred years is no more holding itself against the onslaught of modernism. Of course, there are still monks and masters in the monasteries all over Japan, and yet how many of them are able effectively to respond to the spiritual needs of modern youth and to adjust themselves to the ever-changing environment created by science and the machine? When the vessels are broken, the contents

[29] *Buddhism: Its Essence and Development*, p. 68.
[30] Quoted from *The Catholic Review*, Baltimore, April 6, 1962.

too will be spilt out. The truth of Zen must somehow be preserved
in the midst of the prosaic flatness and shallow sensationalism of
present-day life.[31]

The spiritual problems of the West, it appears, are not essentially different from those of the East. Yet the truth of Zen,
like the truth of anything, must somehow be preserved! For in
Zen, as in Buddhism itself, there is, as Aristotle said of poetry,
"something more universal and of graver import than history."
The Zen intuition, so it has been argued in these pages, does
not have the uniqueness that many of its advocates suppose,
but what they say of it is important. It indicates a need, a goal
for which the human spirit seeks. Placed in the context of faith
in God and our dependence on His grace, the Zen insight may
cleanse the Christian mind a little—cleanse it from an over-
burdening sense of guilt (which is an inverted egoism: the
notion that God has somehow been frustrated by "me"!), from
anxiety and remorse, and in general from futile reminiscence
about past failures and mistakes, and no less futile hopes and
fears directed to the future. The mind being so clarified, God's
presence, adjustment to Ultimate Reality, is "realized"—now
where I am.

One final flight of fancy with which to end. Could Zen's chief
role in the West be that of peacemaker—the reuniting once
and for all of those quarrelsome sisters, Martha and Mary? The
antithesis between prayer and good works, action and contemplation, though based according to Catholic tradition on Luke
10:38-42, derives largely from the allegorizing tendencies of
some of the Church Fathers. This manner of dealing with
Scripture, kept within bounds, was legitimate and helpful—
it enabled St. Augustine, for example, to swallow what seemed
to him otherwise unacceptable portions of the Old Testament;
but the procedure is not in every case beyond the reach of criticism. Its application to the Martha and Mary incident has per-

[31] Daisetz Teitaro Suzuki, *The Training of the Zen Buddhist Monk* (New
York: University Books, 1959), p. 114.

haps become sacrosanct. Nevertheless it is worth recalling that
the commonly accepted interpretation owes as much to the
contrast, dear to the heart of Plato, between the life of intellectual speculation and the life of practical affairs, as it does to
the original Gospel.

A combination, as it was later to prove, of Platonic idealism,
Judaeo-Christian eschatology, and world-renouncing asceticism
constituted a formidable interpretative equipment to bring to
bear upon an exchange of words between two young women
and their Guest in a tiny house in an obscure Palestinian vil-
lage. The results of these concerted efforts, as might have been
anticipated, could not satisfy everybody. The life of union with
God came to be expounded in terms of a perilous ascent to
almost inaccessible heights, or as a future reward for a lifetime's
effort, or as a prize to be gained after a prolonged course of
asceticism. Obviously a case can be argued for each of these
positions; but what was apt to be forgotten was that the matter
had already been stated rather more simply. "He who loves
me shall be loved by my Father, and I will love him, and manifest myself to him" (John 14:21).

St. Thomas's opinion is here of special interest.[32] He follows
the tradition of the Fathers with respect to Mary, as the contemplative, having chosen "the *best* part,"[33] but then his
evangelical sense intervenes. Certain activities, "such as teaching and preaching," may proceed "from the fulness of contemplation"; in which case they are "more excellent than simple
contemplation." "For even as it is better to enlighten than
merely to shine, so it is better to give to others the fruits of
one's contemplation than merely to contemplate." The word
"contemplation" does not occur in the New Testament; and
it may be that the mind of the Church was, perhaps unconsciously, revealed in the selection of the Martha and Mary

[32] *Summa Theologica*, II-II, 188, 6.
[33] Luke 10:42, following the Vulgate. The Greek merely says "the *good*
part."

incident as the Gospel extract for a Mass on the Feast of the Assumption of the Blessed Virgin Mary. Mary, the Mother of Jesus, played at times the role of her contemplative namesake; but Our Lady was Martha also. How often must she have been busy, perhaps a little anxiously, about "much serving" for the sake of her Son in the homestead at Nazareth!

If Zen is to be the occasion of benefit to the Church, it can only be because Zen's essential insight—here understood as the insight of the Compassionate Buddha—is already latent in Catholicism. For Catholics to be made more consciously aware than they habitually are, is for them to be reminded, made more "mindful," of what they already know. To be made mindful, to be reminded, of what we know but have for all practical purposes forgotten is usually a greater need than fresh information. In this case the reminder is that *the Word has become flesh*. God is in us and all about us. No flight from the world is called for to discover Him; no particular austerities; certainly no high degree of learning—only to cleanse our minds and open our eyes. The virtues? Granted faith and love, the qualities that are always in demand are best: honesty, courage, integrity, perseverance, directness, simplicity. "Your every-day mind—that is the Way."

"To-day if you shall hear His voice, harden not your hearts" (Psalm 94:8; Hebrews 3:7; 4:7). It is as simple, and as difficult, as that. All we can do, all that is required of us, is not to harden our hearts. We harden them, not by malice only, perhaps seldom directly by that, but by being mentally asleep or abstracted, daydreaming, not living on the spot where we are. If in our minds or wishes we are not at the here and now, if we are dwelling on the past or the anticipated future, or absorbed in ego-regarding thoughts, we can neither hear God's voice nor see what is before us. To hear and to see we must "let go," that is, allow the flux of thoughts and feelings to evaporate into nothingness from our nonattention. When the mind is awakened to the point of cherishing no thoughts, then the challenge of vision will evoke, on the instant, the appropriate response. To be able to do this, through God's gift, continuously and by way of habit, is to be living as one's true self, egolessly. Then every day cannot but be a good day, every season a good season.

THREE
SUPPLEMENTARY
DISCUSSIONS

I • On Yoga

As with Zen, so with Yoga, one must distinguish the substance from the technique. Whatever is substantive in any philosophy or way of life should have its counterpart, even though as yet largely unrealized, in Catholicism. But the methods vary by which a philosophy of life may be brought, so to speak, to disclose its inner content. It would be presumptuous for a Westerner to say how closely, for example, the mental devices of *mondo* and *koan* are linked with Zen, or bodily posture (*asana*) with Yoga; but he may be allowed to think that these practices have unduly diverted attention from their basic purpose: which is to cleanse the mind of distractions, leave it unclouded by desires.

A brief mention has already been made of Yoga. Books on the subject abound; all that will be noted here is the author's impression of what Yoga is, and its relation, if any, to Zen. Yoga means, literally, "union." Yoga's aim is to bring the individual's life of thought and action into harmony with the ultimate Source of his being. From one of the chief authoritative texts, the *Yoga Sutras* of Patanjali,[1] it is clear that progress in Yoga depends on integrity of personal character and satis-

[1] Mircea Eliade, however, notes: "By far the greater part of modern yogic literature published in India and elsewhere finds its theoretical justification in the *Bhagavad Gita*," *Yoga* (New York: Pantheon Books, 1958), p. 161.

factory relations with others. The complexities of Yoga have
been summarized by Dr. Ernest Wood.[2] Yoga is intellectual:
its methods of meditation are applications of the powers of the
mind and Yoga offers reasons for its advice and procedures.
Yoga is ethical; its system of eight steps or limbs starts with
five virtues: (1) non-injury, (2) truthfulness, (3) non-theft,
(4) spiritual conduct, (5) non-greed. Yoga gives scope to the
emotions, prescribing friendliness, sympathy, and a benign attitude to friend and foe alike.

Yoga has many different schools and teachers, emphasizing
distinctive aspects of the doctrine. There are Yogas of action
(*karma*), worship (*bhakti*), and knowledge (*jnana* or *gnyana*),
and Yoga with the aid of ordered breathing and postures
(*hatha-yoga*), the raising of the spinal forces (*laya-yoga*), the
use of effective recitations (*mantra-yoga*), and Yoga by means
of meditation and contemplation (*raja-yoga*). It should be
noted that yogic practices, whether mental or physical, are
conscious and voluntary, not passive. Nevertheless, the higher
achievements of Yoga, we are told, are going to be attained
without knowing how. The beginner may know something of
the "how," but later, if and when he attains a state of "cosmic
consciousness," he will be aware only of having realized unknown potentialities within himself.

The aspect of Yoga which has attracted much popular attention in the West is *hatha-yoga*: the Yoga which utilizes ordered
breathing and bodily postures. In an interesting study, *Christian Yoga*[3] by Father J.-M. Déchanet, O.S.B., the author's treatment, complete with illustrations, was extensively reproduced
in the weekly press. Anyone who has practiced Father Déchanet's "gymnastic of silence" and experienced some of the results he claims for it will be happy to testify in its favor. But
a word of caution may be in order. The adaptation of a Hindu
technique to a Christian setting has its dangers, besides the
physical ones of possibly strained muscles. An undue cult of

[2] *Yoga Dictionary* (New York: Philosophical Library, 1956), pp. 175-77.
[3] A translation of *La Voie du Silence* (New York: Harper & Brothers, 1960).

the body could hide itself behind lofty spiritual motives. Any general advocacy of yogic practices is to be deprecated. Each individual should be encouraged to follow his own leading, and conservative instincts, suspicious of "novelty," are obviously to be respected.

In principle, however, the case for a healthy body as an aid to spiritual development can hardly nowadays be disputed. "For the love of God control your body and soul alike with great care, and keep as fit as you can." This advice is to be found, not in a Hindu treatise on Yoga, but in that mediaeval classic of Catholic spirituality, *The Cloud of Unknowing*.[4] Moderation in diet, together with appropriate amounts of exercise and fresh air, are the normal concomitants of sustained awareness. To employ the necessary means to keep oneself physically in trim is probably the most satisfactory of all forms of bodily self-denial. It renders adventitious austerities for the most part unnecessary.

Before leaving the physical aspects of Yoga, mention must be made of the *seated* posture of yogic meditation, since this is no less a characteristic of Zen Buddhism. It is hard to believe that a meditative posture, basically unchanged after five thousand years of trial, does not have an intrinsic fittingness to what is being aimed at. Archaeological evidence for the practice of Yoga is afforded by some small figures of men in the posture of yogic meditation excavated in the Indus Valley. They are said to date from at least 3,000 B.C. It is as seated in meditation that the Buddha is most frequently represented. Gautama did not repudiate the ascetic and contemplative traditions of India *in toto;* he completed them. "It was on the terrain of Yoga that the Buddha arose; whatever innovations he was able to introduce into it, the mold of Yoga was that in which his thought was formed."[5] Thus the following passage from the *Bhagavad Gita*, if not, as many scholars maintain, pre-Buddhistic, can be

[4] Chapter 41, p. 101.
[5] Mircea Eliade, *Yoga*, p. 162.

dated about 500 B.C., and clearly provides the setting for the Enlightened One's contemplation:

Day after day, let the Yogi practise the harmony of soul: in a secret place, in deep solitude, master of his mind, hoping for nothing, desiring nothing.

Let him find a place that is pure and a seat that is restful, neither too high nor too low, with sacred grass and a skin and a cloth thereon.

On that seat let him rest and practise Yoga for the purification of the soul: with the life of his body and mind in peace; his soul in silence before the One.

With upright body, head, and neck, which rest still and move not; with inner gaze that is not restless, but rests still between the eyebrows;

With soul in peace, and all fear gone, and strong in the vow of holiness, let him rest with mind in harmony, his soul on me, his God supreme.[6]

It was suggested on an earlier page that the conventional Christian attitude at prayer, kneeling, is the appropriate response to God as transcendent; and that the Buddhist convention is a response to God as immanent within the human spirit. Since the latter aspect of the Divine presence is also of Catholic faith, there appears, to say the least, no objection to the individual's adopting, given the suitable occasion, the posture best calculated to assist him in realizing God's nearness.

Anyone who has learned, after patient practice, to sit easily and for some time in a traditional yogic posture (*asana*) will usually find himself rewarded. Whatever the explanation—and one explanation is that the posture requires the minimum exercise of the heart, pumping blood to the extremities of the body (since these are now "folded in" to the center) —the results in terms of bodily and mental calm, together with intensified general awareness, are strongly perceptible. Too much can be made of precise postures at times of recollection, and many of the masters wisely leave their disciples to choose their own.

[6] *The Bhagavad Gita*, 6: 10-14, translated by Juan Mascaró, p. 70.

The best-known yogic posture is the *padmāsana*, or "lotus seat," involving "the left foot being on the right thigh, and the right foot on the left thigh, both with the soles turned upwards." But this is almost impossible to achieve by Westerners, unless they have learned it in their childhood.

For the benefit of any interested reader, here is a description of *siddhāsana*—the "adept's seat" or "perfect posture"—approved above all by some authorities. Father Déchanet[7] supplies the following helpful rubric: "In a corner of your room place a fairly large cushion, say thirty inches by twenty, preferably thick but not soft—more a kind of hassock, stuffed with horsehair." A folded blanket of similar dimensions will be found almost as convenient. On this one sits, both legs extended in front. Using one's hands to assist, place the left foot, instep turned down, under the center of the body, so that the heel supports the perineum; then place the right foot so that it rests between the left thigh and calf. In this position, swing forward slightly until one's knees rest on the surface on which one is sitting. The hands, thumb and first finger pressed lightly together, may rest on the knees or thighs; or the hands may be brought together directly in front, thumbs touching, right hand above left, wrists resting on the thighs. It will take some weeks of daily practice before a middle-aged person can assume this position painlessly and without effort. But given an initial suppleness—head, neck and back being kept in a straight line—this seat can be held for half an hour or so without trouble.

No book discussing Zen would have been complete without a description of one of the traditional sitting postures; for "sitting cross-legged on the ground" is one of Zen's characteristic activities. But it would be a mistake to look for any close links between Zen and Yoga. In his essay "Zen and the West," Julius Evolva draws attention to "the polemical attitude which Zen at times takes up with regard to techniques of the Yoga and to

[7] *Ibid.,* p. 123.

the *dhyâna* of the type practiced in certain Buddhist circles."[8]
According to a Japanese authority, "the Zen method is to sit
in meditation posture and swell with our breath and vitality
what is called 'the field of the elixir' (the abdomen below the
navel). In this way the whole frame is invigorated."[9] Such a
conception, though not entirely clear to a Western student, appears to be reflected in Rudolf Otto's "picture of Bodhidharma
himself, the prodigiously heavy man who 'sits before a wall ten
years in silence,' in concentrated, nay, in conglobate force of
inner tension like a highly charged Leyden jar."[10] Bodhidharma, lacking "slenderness and calmness," "the large eyes almost pushed out of his head by the inner compression,"
evidently did not possess the bodily perfections desiderated by
the authorities on Yoga. Where, alas, were the "correct form,
beauty, strength and very firm wellknitness" called for by Patanjali? Nowhere at all, it would seem.

And yet, in its dispute with Yoga, Zen on balance may have
the right of it. If Zen appears morally undisciplined, it is at
least open to God's grace in a way that Yoga, where it claims
to be a self-sufficient system, is not. The following speaks of
the effects of sitting in meditation (*Zazen*) especially in regard
to repentance and destruction of sins.

> Those who perform meditation for even one session
> Destroy innumerable accumulated sins;
> How should there be wrong paths for them?
> The Paradise of Amida Buddha is not far.[11]

It should also be noted that Zen "sitting" has a figurative as well
as a literal meaning. The Zen insight can come alive standing
or walking or lying down, or in any physical position compatible with being wide awake. The Sixth Patriarch, defining the

[8] *Anthology of Zen*, p. 210.
[9] *Ibid.*, p. 299.
[10] *Ibid.*, p. 71.
[11] A verse from Hakuin's "The Song of Meditation," quoted from *Buddhist
Scriptures*, p. 134.

word *Zazen*, says "Outwardly to be in the world of good and evil yet with no thought arising in the heart, this is Sitting (*Za*) : inwardly to see one's own nature and not move from it, this is Meditation (*Zen*)." It is interesting to find in Chapter 44 of *The Cloud of Unknowing* both the injunction to "sit quite still" and a reminder of a "stark awareness of yourself" which, in point of fact, needs to be replaced by a still more significant awareness. The *Cloud* speaks in the same context of what has to be supplied if Zen is to reach fruition—"God's very special and freely given grace, and your own complete and willing readiness to receive it."

By way of concluding these remarks, let it be emphasized that nothing could be more out of place than a patronizing attitude to Yoga, a spiritual tradition older by far than the written records of Christianity. Dr. Mircea Eliade reminds us[12] that not only are yogic practices accepted by the *Bhagavad Gita*, the apogee of Indian spirituality; they are elevated to the first place. Yoga is purged of rigorous asceticism and magic; its meditation and concentration become "instruments of an *unio mystica* with a God who reveals himself as a person." Nevertheless, from a Catholic standpoint, Yoga has too much the appearance of a personal achievement; it does not provide evident safeguards against pride and self-sufficiency. At least it may be said that Yoga was in need of being humanized by the insights of the Compassionate Buddha. The Awakened One was opposed alike to Brahmanic ritualism, exaggerated asceticism, and metaphysical speculations. The Buddha was concerned, not essentially with a mystical union with God, but with the basic human condition—suffering and emancipation from suffering. The Buddhist refrain "all is painful, all is transient" touches our common humanity at a level unattainable by Yoga. Zen, with its emphasis on the "every-day mind," though lacking, when allowed to float free from its Buddhist roots, in seriousness and depth, likewise confronts us with

[12] *Ibid.*, p. 161.

things as they are. Perhaps Zen will realize itself in the Western world by quickening our minds to the significance of another form of Yoga, often heard of but little understood. "Take my yoke upon you . . . for my yoke is easy and my burden light" (Matthew 11:29, 30).[13]

[13] Sanskrit, *Yoga;* English, *yoke;* German, *Joch;* Latin, *jugum;* Hungarian, *iga.* See Selvarajan Yesudian and Elisabeth Haich, *Yoga Uniting East and West* (New York: Harper & Brothers, 1956), p. 39, where the words of Jesus are quoted (Matthew 11:29, 30).

II • On Monasticism

What follows is neither an outline history of monasticism nor an analysis of its nature. Rather, we shall confine ourselves to a series of observations, based on over thirty years' experience of the central monastic tradition of the West. Monasticism is perhaps more closely linked with Buddhism than with Christianity. Thus many of the classical Buddhist texts are addressed specifically to "monks"; as, for example, "The Greater Discourse on the Foundation of Mindfulness."[1] Zen also has its monastic discipline, which has been described at length by D. T. Suzuki.[2] By Christians monasticism is commonly regarded as a more specialized vocation, calling for a lifelong commitment, whereas a practicing Buddhist will often embrace the monastic state as a form of lengthy retreat, on the understanding that it is only for a time.

Monasticism, it seems true to say, aims at achieving the religious life in its concentrated state. As an attempted distillation of the pure essence of man's communion with God, it should be worth study even by those who are not attracted to it. This is not by any means to suggest that monasticism necessarily represents religion at its best. The recorded practice of the monastic life, though supplying some grounds for edification, provides ample proof that monks, like everybody else, are per-

[1] See Nyanaponika Thera, *The Heart of Buddhist Meditation*, pp. 115 ff.
[2] *The Training of the Zen Buddhist Monk.*

petually in need of being reminded of what their true nature
is. Catholicism, as interpreted by Aquinas, is emphatic on the
point that the quality of an individual's goodness does not
depend on the state of life to which he is called but on the
measure of charity in his soul, that is to say, on his conformity
to God's will.[3] Likewise in the tradition behind Zen Buddhism, what ultimately counts is the individual's response to
the requirements of Truth.

> One in All,
> All in One—
> If only this is realized,
> No more worry about your not being perfect.[4]

The monk, according to the derivation of the word, is one
who lives alone. A capacity for being happy by oneself exists
more or less in every individual who is sane. Provided the pe-
riods of solitariness be not too prolonged, the mature person
often finds himself "never less alone than when alone." The
Christian ascetics of the third century, dwelling in the Egyptian desert, were originally hermits, that is, solitaries. Though
the numerous disciples they attracted demanded the organization of monastic communities, nevertheless the concept of a
monk as one having resources within himself, enabling him
to live in detachment from society, persisted. The suggestion
may here be offered that this concept is still basic to the monastic life, even though the monk now lives almost invariably,
and to his great benefit, with a community of brethren.

When St. Benedict of Nursia, in the sixth century, laid the
foundations of Western monasticism as it has endured to this
day, his organization had a cenobitical plan, but he still allowed a place of prestige to the life which he himself first embraced, that of anchorite. Several things are worth noting about
Benedictine monasticism, in the context of an essay touching

[3] *Summa Theologica*, II-II, 184, 3 and 4.
[4] Seng-Ts'an, "On Believing in Mind," 30, quoted from *Buddhist Scriptures*,
p. 175.

the matter-of-factness and unself-consciousness of Zen. It is relevant, when attempting to evaluate the monastic life, to clear the mind of any tendency to sentimental cloudiness; here as elsewhere we have to be on our guard against the illusions produced by *maya*.[5] Life in a monastery, like every form of community living, is bound up with a number of accepted and necessary conventions; but these, while being loyally observed, must be "seen through." There exists a considerable literature —the combined result of nostalgia for the asceticism of the desert Fathers, romanticism as applied to what Newman called the "Benedictine centuries," a strongly developed aesthetic taste directed to Church ritual, and a disgust at the modern world—which, whatever its other merits, does not always help us to fix our attention on the facts. St. Benedict, there are grounds for thinking, with his practical good sense and Roman *gravitas,* would have been surprised to discover how his carefully thought-out *Rule* could, in subsequent ages, fire the creative imagination of so many poetic spirits.

One of the first things to be noted is that St. Benedict, unlike many of his commentators, is not primarily interested in "monasticism." In the famous Prologue to the Holy Rule the word "monk" does not occur; and the word "monastery" is to be found only once, and that in the very last sentence. What absorbs St. Benedict's mind is the thought of God, and, as a corollary of this, how man is to be conformed to the will of God. Benedict's first biographer, Pope St. Gregory the Great, tells us that he who was later to become the Father of Western monasticism left Rome for Subiaco, not to enter a monastery, but because he desired "God only." So we find St. Benedict concerned in the first place, not with what has been called a "self-conscious monasticity," but with the fundamental human situation, namely, man's alienation from God by disobedience. Man's only hope of salvation, or even happiness, is that he return to God by the service of obedience. It is St. Benedict's

[5] See p. 99 ff.

interest in a practical plan to bring man back to God that makes the Holy Rule, in its substantial teaching, contemporary with all the ages.

There is, of course, plenty of evidence to show that St. Benedict gave careful attention to contemporary monasticism. He views it with qualified enthusiasm. He discusses four types of monks. Half that number he dismisses, not being sure which is worse than the other. Of the two classes of monks of whom he approves, the best he can find to say of the one is that it "has learned to fight against the devil," and of the other that it is "strong" and that it "lives in monasteries." None of this could be described as overlaudatory. The truth surely is that St. Benedict discountenances any preoccupation with monasticism for its own sake. For him it is merely a means to the end of a genuinely Christian life—good in so far as it assists in that purpose, bad in so far as it fails to do so.

St. Benedict combined the Roman instinct for administration, a sense of law and order, with the saint's intuitive understanding of what Christianity is. Thus he is distinguished from some of the outstanding representatives of monasticism before and after his time: he relegated to a subordinate place asceticism and physical austerities. Benedict believed in the asceticism of hard and useful work. A Benedictine monastery is not a place where one goes chiefly to expiate one's sins, or because life "in the world" has not been found worth living. Rather, a monastery is a "school of the Lord's service," a place where one learns to be more fully a Christian, a place, let it be added, where if one is faithful, one can enjoy the "bliss" which arises from selfless surrender to God, where "with unutterable sweetness of love, we shall run in the way of God's Commandments" (Prologue to the Holy Rule of St. Benedict) .

Appropriately, we may recall a tribute to Benedict of Nursia from a perceptive admirer of the tradition behind Zen Buddhism. Mr. Aldous Huxley writes:

It is worth remarking that the Benedictine order owed its existence to the apparent folly of a young man who, instead of doing the proper, sensible thing, which was to go through the Roman schools and become an administrator under the Gothic emperors, went away and, for three years, lived alone in a hole in the mountains. When he had become "a man of much orison", he emerged, founded monasteries and composed a rule to fit the needs of a self-perpetuating order of hard-working contemplatives. In the succeeding centuries, the order civilized northwestern Europe, introduced or re-established the best agricultural practice of the time, provided the only educational facilities then available, and preserved and disseminated the treasures of ancient literature. For generations Benedictinism was the principal antidote to barbarism. Europe owes an incalculable debt to the young man who, because he was more interested in knowing God than in getting on, or even "doing good" in the world, left Rome for that burrow in the hillside above Subiaco.[6]

It should be noted that St. Benedict did not discourage excessive austerity in order to make the monastic life "easier"; he aimed at providing scope for the observance of a more exacting rule than bodily retrenchment—the law of love. Christian penitential practices can themselves, of course, be performed in a spirit of love; but when they are deliberately chosen or imposed as a corporate routine, self-will is not necessarily excluded. The genuine Christian cross is the one that inevitably comes, like its prototype, in the course of a life lived, so far as may be, in response to God's enlightening grace. Thus Benedict urges his disciples, in the first place, to open their eyes to the "Divine light" (*deificum lumen*) and to listen to the voice of the Spirit.

Gautama Buddha, before his "enlightenment," had tried the path of severe asceticism, only to find that this was not the way to liberation. Over two thousand years later, St. François de Sales, in the Catholic tradition, was to express the same attitude to bodily mortification. "Our dear Saint," writes Jean Pierre Camus, "disapproved of immoderate fasting. He used to say that the spirit could not endure the body when overfed, but that, if underfed, the body could not endure the spirit." Non-

[6] Aldous Huxley, *Grey Eminence* (New York: Meridian Books, 1959), pp. 318-19.

attachment, including nonattachment to self-denial, is the condition of receiving the Truth that makes one free. Failure to appreciate this point has led to delusion, even disaster, in the spiritual life. The seventeenth-century Benedictine extravaganza of Port Royal, for example, illustrates how far a conventual existence, conceived chiefly in terms of world-renunciation and self-immolation, can go astray. Religion is apt to be replaced by superstition, humility by dedicated egoism. It was possible, as St. Paul had warned (1 Corinthians 13:3), to give one's body to be burned and still not have the root of the matter in one.

"Christianity in the cloister" might be a fitting subtitle to St. Benedict's Rule. The Benedictine concept of monasticism is that the individual should attain a state in which he responds, moment by moment, to the promptings of the Holy Spirit. By this faithfulness he will realize—to adapt the Buddhist terminology—his "Christ-nature"; that is to say, his separative ego, under the inflow of grace, will have yielded place to the condition of: "I live, yet no longer I, but Christ lives in me" (Galatians 2:20).

According to the central Western tradition, as represented by Benedictinism, the purpose of a monastery and the aim of every monk is, in the words of the Holy Rule, "that God may be glorified in all things." The achievement of this objective is striven for by the monks' devoting themselves to the "work of God," as St. Benedict calls the Liturgy, and to all the virtues needful to make the public worship of the Mass and the Divine Office, not only an outward ceremonial, but an expression of inward dedication of heart. The monastic life calls for the practice of recollectedness, humility, obedience, silence, simplicity, and self-denial. But more than anything else, a monastic vocation is a call to a life of love—a call to understand, at the deepest level, what it really means to love God and one's fellow men. Thus, in Chapter 4 of the Holy Rule, St. Benedict lays down what is the primary duty of the monk: "In the first place, to love the Lord God with all one's heart, all one's soul, and all one's strength; then, one's neighbor as oneself."

Benedictine life is communal in form, the brethren living together and sharing alike the goods (and the needs) of the monastic family. The most important daily work in the monastery is the singing or recitation of the Divine Office. Apart from the hours spent in church at public and private prayer, St. Benedict wished his monks to be fully occupied. Any kind of labor that can be done in a spirit of corporate prayer and Christ-like love is proper to a Benedictine monastery. So, for example, there can be no more suitable form of active labor for monks than the maintenance of a boys' school. Being so engaged, the communal and liturgical life of the monastery overflows into what is perhaps the most valuable of all contributions to the well-being of society, the Christian education of the young.

A school provides the type of fruitful work which enables the monk to avoid the danger, sometimes associated with monasticism, of spiritual self-centeredness, a kind of sanctified egoism. Being employed in a task that is fully human, he is neither an escapist from his social obligations nor a cultivator of "a fugitive and cloistered virtue." When his contemplative prayer issues in a constructive educational endeavor, he finds, moreover, that his own personality is strengthened and enriched. From teaching and being responsible for the young, he learns the ultimate selflessness—to be realized uniquely in the exercise of a spiritual fatherhood. Benedictine tradition has many instances of monastic educators, ripening through long years in the classroom and lecture hall, to that quality of mellow holiness depicted in St. Benedict's portrait (Chapters 2 and 64 of the Holy Rule) of the kind of man the father of the monastery should be.

Besides teaching, such occupations as farm work, arts, crafts, giving spiritual conferences and direction, writing, research, and many other forms of activity are to be found among members of a monastic community. It may not be out of place to recall that a Benedictine vocation is still, even in the world of today, a living reality. One who has such a vocation does not think himself particularly virtuous, or worthy to become a

monk; he is persuaded, often for no accountable reason, that
God, from an overflow of love and mercy, has called him, like
St. Benedict, to seek "God only," by a life of continual recollectedness, and by work done for one's fellow men as a form
of prayer in action. In order to attain this union with God and
likeness to Christ, the candidate for a monastery is convinced
that he, too, must live his life in conformity with the Gospel
precepts. He, also, has to learn the secret that, even here on
earth, ultimate happiness can only be gained through lowliness and self-abnegation, through obedience and patience and
the subordination of the flesh to the spirit. It is thus that he
strives, following the footsteps of Christ, to give glory to God
by conforming himself completely to the will of his heavenly
Father, becoming, at last, God-centered instead of self-centered.

To assist men to give this kind of glory to God, by becoming
Christ-like, is the reason why St. Benedict wrote his Rule, and
why Benedictine monasteries exist. Benedict withdrew from the
world to follow Christ wholeheartedly. He experienced first
the hermit's life and then turned to community life, as being
the surer and safer way. Today, as in the past, Christ calls men
to give up all things and follow Him (Matthew 19:21). Today,
no less than in the past, St. Benedict, the great Legislator and
Father of monks, throws out the challenge of his Rule. "To
thee, therefore, my words are now addressed, whoever thou
art that, renouncing thine own will, dost take up the strong
and bright weapons of obedience, in order to fight for the Lord
Christ, our true King" (Prologue to the Holy Rule).

In some such terms as these, articulated according to the
knowledge and insight of the individual, a Benedictine conceives his professional calling. Compared with all this, the life
of a Zen monk, to a Western mind at least, appears a jejune
affair. Dr. D. T. Suzuki offers a partial explanation. "Having
been nourished among nature-mystics and born metaphysi-
cians, Zen may seem to be lacking in religious feeling or in
the emotional aspects of the religious life. At least as far as
literary expressions go, Zen abounds in allusions to objects of

nature and statements indicative of philosophical aloofness."[7] In other words, Zen tends to be cerebral—since Suzuki will not allow us to call it intellectual!—and aesthetic; as often presented, it lacks a universal human resonance and so is apt to leave the heart unmoved.

Yet, once more, the Zen intuition, not being peculiar to Zen, with its matter-of-factness and realism, set in a Christian context, has its counterpart, it is here suggested, in the Benedictine way of life. Thus St. Benedict's Rule makes no allusion to the supposed antithesis between action and contemplation, the traditional contrast of Martha to Mary. The words "contemplation" or "contemplative" do not occur in the Holy Rule. Instead, St. Benedict simply requires, with specific reference to the work performed in the monastery, that matters be so arranged "that in all things God may be glorified" (Rule, Chapter 57; cf. 1 Peter 4:11). What the Rule does legislate for is a continuous state of recollectedness, corresponding to the Buddhist "mindfulness." The basis for humility, itself the condition of one's being aware of God's presence, is that one "completely avoid forgetfulness" (*oblivionem omnino fugiat*), that one "ever remember" what is God's will (Rule, Chapter 7). Given this fusion of awareness of God and consequent selfless motivation, it follows that every act, performed in what is now virtually a state of "enlightenment," will result from a kind of direct intuition of the thing to be done. Again, contemplation and action instantaneously are one, the part of Martha and that of Mary are no longer to be distinguished.

A monastery, today as it has always been, is a place of physical withdrawal; one called to be a monk instinctively seeks a separation, painful though it be, from his relatives, friends, and familiar associates; he hankers after a refuge "from the contagion of the world's slow stain." These are the material conditions, so to speak, of his achieving the nonattachment without which there can be no final "liberation." They provide, how-

[7] *The Training of the Zen Buddhist Monk*, p. 115.

ever, only the setting. In a monastery, as elsewhere, all depends on how the individual responds to his circumstances and opportunities. "The mind in its own place and in itself, can make a heaven of hell, a hell of heaven."

The Benedictine rule, conformably with the mind of its author, has been interpreted with a great variety of emphases. St. Benedict was preoccupied with God and God's self-manifestation in Christ. This is the master light in which the Holy Rule is to be read; such a light, needless to say, clearly allows of endless possibilities of development and adaptation in detail. Monastic archaism, a return to the "primitive" conditions of St. Benedict's own monastery, would no more give assurance of authentic Benedictinism than, say, a present-day reproduction of the life of the original apostolic communities at Jerusalem or Antioch would guarantee authentic Christianity. No phrase in the Holy Rule is of greater contemporary relevance, for those interested in monasticism, than that which reveals St. Benedict's conception of what he set out to do. It was to establish "a School of the Lord's service" (Prologue). He was not, therefore, concerned essentially with providing an escape from the world and its ways; or a quiet niche for the learned and devout; or a place of penance and mortification; or a habitation for saints. Rather, his concept of a monastery is that of a brotherhood made up of people who intend, in the first place, to learn how to serve God, and then to serve Him.

Accordingly, an almost fatal handicap in a candidate for the monastic life is for him to be full of ideas about monasticism. He is like the opinionated professor wishing to learn about Zen, puzzled at the Zen master pouring tea into his already overflowing cup; only to be told: "Like this cup, you are full of your own opinions and speculations. How can I show you Zen unless you first empty your cup?" Monasticism is, in this respect, like Zen. One may learn *about* it from books and conversation; but one cannot be shown it—or, rather, one cannot see it, even when it is before one's eyes—if one's mind is full of preconceptions and ideals about what true monasticism is. Here, again, the simple yet profound dictum applies:

> Try not to seek after the true,
> Only cease to cherish opinions.

The service of God is not something we make up our minds about, and then perform. God, in the first place, makes up our minds for us; if we let Him. That is our contribution—to let Him. A monastic vocation is a call to discipleship, that is to say, to become a learner in the art of Christian living. The lessons are learned, not notably from books or even other individuals, but through becoming a "child of time present," and so being shaped from moment to moment by God's manifest will. Which means, above all, avoiding living in the past or future, or nostalgically on some other spot than where one is; the call is to respond with total awareness to whatever happens to one, or to whatever one is called on to do—"Thy will be done."

A monastery, at least one that is in the central tradition of the West, has its well-tried customs, to which the newcomer is expected to conform; its long years, perhaps centuries, of practical experience, of which he will take account. But though pledged in loyalty to a usually very human superior, the monk's basic allegiance, within the framework of the Holy Rule, is to the light that breaks upon his own mind from God only. The monk may think that he has come to gain something for himself: peace, security, quiet, a life of prayer, or study, or teaching; but if his vocation is genuine, he finds that he has come not to take but to give—or, more accurately, to be shaped as an instrument of God's action. St. Benedict calls on his monks to expend their talents in God's service; so that "we may serve Him," to quote the Prologue to the Rule, "with the gifts which He has given us."

Service—could anything be more prosaic?—is the essence of Benedictine monasticism. But it is the service which brings us to the living heart of Christianity. "For the Son of Man Himself came not to be served, but to serve, and to give His life a ransom for many" (Mark 10:45). When St. Benedict comes to discuss what he calls "the instruments of good works," "the tools of the spiritual craft" (Rule, Chapter 4), to be diligently employed in "the enclosure of the monastery and stability in the community," he has nothing to preach but the Gospel. The monk must "deny himself in order to follow Christ"; the monk should "prefer nothing to the love of Christ." To learn how one may become the kind of person who manifests this self-denial, who exhibits this preference, is the opportunity offered in a Benedictine monastery. It is a call, not to a career, but to self-naughting, to the ultimate selflessness—"I live, yet not I, but Christ lives in me" (Galatians 2:20).

III • Saint Thomas Aquinas

The reader will have noticed that the Catholic positions touched on in the course of this essay have been elucidated, for the most part, with reference to St. Thomas's *Summa Theologica*. There is, of course, Holy Mother Church's own excellent authority for this procedure;[1] though, for the benefit of those who regard official endorsement in matters of the mind as the kiss of death, we may cite Father F. C. Copleston's pertinent reminder. "If we are considering Aquinas' philosophy from a purely historical point of view, the fact that he said this or that is obviously of prime importance. But if we are considering Thomism as a living and developing philosophy, it is the philosophical positions themselves which count, and the fact that Thomas Aquinas held them in the thirteenth century is not strictly relevant."[2]

"It is the philosophical positions themselves which count." They count particularly in the present case because, as can easily be shown, St. Thomas's mind moves at the same level of thought as the metaphysical tradition culminating in Zen Buddhism. He would, I think, have felt himself, along with his Catholic orthodoxy, at home with the *Upanishads* or the *Bhagavad Gita*. Indian thinkers themselves appear to find in

[1] *Codex Iuris Canonici*, cc. 589 #1, 1366 #2.
[2] F. C. Copleston, S.J., *Aquinas* (Harmondsworth, England: Penguin Books, 1955), p. 254.

Aquinas a kindred spirit. The work of such a scholar as Ananda Coomaraswamy reveals the author enriching his exposition with frequent references to St. Thomas.

Thomas Aquinas (1225-1274) was a creative thinker whose influence on Catholicism is much greater today than it was in the Middle Ages. It was in an inspired moment that ecclesiastical authority selected him as the Church's official spokesman, so to speak, on questions of rational debate; though this choice may have hidden from view the talent which most impressed, not always favorably, his contemporaries—the daring originality of his thought. Far from being acknowledged as the sage of his day, Thomas was widely regarded as a controversial and disturbing figure. Even so able a thinker as Duns Scotus took the view that the author of the now classical *Summa Theologica* had compromised himself as a Christian theologian by conceding so much to Aristotle. In 1277, the Bishop of Paris, Etienne Tempier, condemned 219 propositions, some of which touched Thomas Aquinas, who had been dead three years. St. Thomas, his theological reputation officially vindicated, came later to be looked on as a pillar of orthodoxy; but his courage and independence of thought are still insufficiently appreciated.

What enabled Thomas to keep his head amid the surrounding intellectual storm was the enlightened quality of his religious faith and his personal holiness. As Father Copleston has noted, "Aquinas' attitude throughout was one of serene confidence. There is no need to be alarmed by Aristotle or by any other non-Christian thinker. Let us examine what he has said with an open mind. Where he supports a position with valid reasons, let us adopt it. When he asserts conclusions which are in fact incompatible with Christian doctrine, the proper procedure is to examine whether these conclusions follow validly from true premises: it will be found that they do not."[3]

The clarity, precision, and architectonic scope of the *Summa Theologica* stood the Church's official hierarchy in good stead. Posthumously Aquinas supplied the thoughts to those who had

[3] *Ibid.*, pp. 63-64.

no particular calling to think for themselves. Thanks to his analysis of the concepts of faith and of grace, Catholicism could formulate a coherent position vis-à-vis the sixteenth-century Reformers. Following the crisis of Modernism, fifty years ago, the Thomist "revival," with its particular application to epistemology, reassured the more thoughtful Catholics and enabled them to retain their intellectual respectability. Anyone who had the good fortune, in the nineteen thirties, to traverse St. Thomas's chief works under the ablest Dominican supervision, surrounded by the mental ferment and humane learning of one of the world's greatest universities, will not easily forget the experience. "Bliss was it in that dawn to be alive," one might almost say. "But to be young was very heaven!"

Times, as they are apt to do, change. Outside such areas of learning as may be influenced by clerical seminaries and theological schools, St. Thomas is no longer much regarded. Occasionally one meets, even among devout Catholic intellectuals, a strong anti-Thomist bias. Students of the student mind can doubtless explain why many religious scholars apparently derive more satisfaction from edifying, if sometimes loosely written, essays on Ecclesiology, the Liturgy, and Scriptural typology, than from the type of writing which discusses the Christian revelation with the intellectual ability of a Plato or an Aristotle. Perhaps the explanation lies in the fact, pointed out by René Guénon, that "as a general rule, Westerners have very little natural aptitude for metaphysic." Their chief religious interest is moralistic and practical, aesthetic appreciation doing duty, in many cases, for philosophical understanding. "This inclination towards the 'practical' in the most ordinary sense of the word is one of the factors that were fated to become increasingly marked during the course of Western civilization, until in modern times the tendency became frankly predominant. Only the Middle Ages, being much more given to pure speculation, can be said to have escaped it."[4]

The same author points to this lack of a deeper insight as

[4] *Introduction to the Study of the Hindu Doctrines*, p. 41.

accounting for the incapacity of many Christians to arrive at anything more than a superficial understanding of their own religion.

A Hindu somewhere has written that the inability of Westerners to interpret the East is bound up with their failure to penetrate the deeper meaning of their own sages and even of the Gospels. Reciprocally, it may be said that by a genuine assimilation of the essential content of the Eastern traditions, they might be helped to recapture the spirit that dwells at the heart of Christianity itself, instead of restricting themselves, as generally happens, to a humanistic transcription of the doctrine many of them still profess, that relies for its authority almost exclusively on "historical facts" that can be placed and dated, thus relegating to the background the universal character of its fundamental truth.[5]

In his essay "East and West," Ananda Coomaraswamy has spoken of the need for Western man to regain an understanding of the "common universe of discourse," which enabled a St. Thomas, as if by second nature, to talk, without knowing it, the language of the *Bhagavad Gita*.[6] "We need mediators to whom the common universe of discourse is still a reality, men of a sort that is rarely bred in public schools or trained in modern universities; and this means that the primary problem is that of the reeducation of the western literati. More than one has told me that it has taken him ten years to outgrow even a Harvard education; I have no idea how many it might take to outgrow a missionary college education, or to recover from a course of lectures on Comparative Religion offered by a Calvinist."[7]

This situation may help to explain why, even to many intelligent Catholics, fortified by the best intentions, St. Thomas remains a closed book. Such students find themselves in the frustrating position of FitzGerald's Omar:

[5] *Ibid.*, pp. 11-12.
[6] "The Religious Basis of the Forms of Indian Society," *Indian Culture and English Influence*, p. 26.
[7] "East and West," *Indian Culture and English Influence*, p. 49.

> Myself when young did eagerly frequent
> Doctor and Saint, and heard great argument
>   About it and about: but evermore
> Came out by the same door as in I went.

That they come out by the same door as they went in may
partly be due to the well-meant efforts of the professionals,
the "man-eating Thomists." St. Thomas, being a philosopher,
must be left to persuade; he cannot be imposed upon the mind.
Admiration for his holiness and enthusiasm for his mental gifts,
even when reinforced by some acquaintance with what he
wrote, cannot be equated with an understanding of the task
he achieved. With explicit reference to, among others, Aquinas,
Dr. Walter Kaufmann's observations provoke thought:

> The difference between great philosophers who disagree is perhaps
> less considerable than that which separates them from their followers.
> Members of philosophic schools or coteries live on what others have
> seen, and the disciple usually applies his master's insights with a
> confidence which, most of the time, the master lacked.
>   The adherent of a philosopher is often a man who at first did not
> understand him at all and then staked several years on a tireless at-
> tempt to prove to himself that he did not lack the ability to gain an
> understanding. By the end of that time he sees clearly that his mas-
> ter's critics simply fail to understand him.[8]

A point made by Father Copleston should be kept in view by
all Catholic professors of philosophy and theology, anxious to
form their students "according to the mind of St. Thomas"—
ad mentem Sancti Thomae. "It is not my opinion"—nor could
it be the opinion of anyone who chooses to think about the
matter—"that the philosophy of Aquinas consists of a body
of true propositions which can simply be handed on and
learned like the multiplication tables."[9] What the student
needs to acquire is a mental quality which places him on the

[8] *Critique of Religion and Philosophy*, pp. 60-61. But see Postscript.
[9] *Aquinas*, p. 17.

level of abstraction and generality at which St. Thomas's mind habitually moved. Failing this ability, and it is rare, no amount of familiarity with the text will supply the necessary insight. One may become a loyal "Thomist," but hardly one who can pay Aquinas the worthiest tribute: that of becoming, in however modest a way, an independent thinker in the sense that he was, having learned from him to philosophize for oneself.

Before leaving the topic, a suggestion may be made with regard to stimulating interest in St. Thomas among the moderns. Those who are concerned with this ought to have a close acquaintance with contemporary philosophical fashions in British and American universities. Unless these modes of thought are understood, those who are influenced by them—in other words, many of the ablest American and British graduate and even undergraduate students—are likely to remain impervious to the appeal of St. Thomas. It should be noted that, however laudable the attempts at cross-fertilization between Thomism and Continental existentialism, the tradition of thought from Kierkegaard to Sartre, they are beside the point in meeting the intellectual problems aroused by, say, Wittgenstein, or the Anglo-American analytical philosophers in general. All this could not be better put than it is, again, by Father Copleston.

One can hear a great deal in Thomist circles about Heidegger, for example; one hears a great deal less about contemporary British and American philosophers of the empiricist tradition or about what can perhaps be called the linguistic movement in Anglo-American philosophy. This can, of course, be easily explained, if one bears in mind the difference between continental and Anglo-American philosophy in general, together with the fact that Thomism is far more widespread and vigorous in countries like France, Belgium, and Germany than it is in Britain. But I think that Thomist philosophy might benefit if its adherents paid rather more attention than they do to the prevailing currents of thought in Britain and America. For one thing, the influence of continental philosophy does not invariably contribute to the maintenance of that concern with preciseness and clarity that marked Aquinas himself and has characterized many of the older Thomists. For another thing, reflection on the foundations of their metaphysics in the light of modern empiricist criticism and of linguistic analysis might lead Thomists to achieve a greater clarification of, say, the nature of "metaphysical principles" and of their status in relation to pure tautologies on the one hand and to empirical hypotheses on the other.[10]

Of more direct concern to us here, however, is St. Thomas's approach to what he terms the *religio Christiana.* He sets out quite consciously, at the beginning of the *Summa Theologica,* to eliminate a "multiplicity of useless questions," to give instruction "according to the order of the subject matter," so avoiding presentations arbitrarily dictated by the requirements of the occasion or the plan of some book. He is attempting, in other words, to articulate Christian doctrine so as to show the proper interrelation of its various parts. The result of this effort, considered as a harmony of theological comprehensiveness and precision, is still insufficiently considered. The *Summa Theologica* is apt to be used as a source book of doctrinal texts, which can be adapted to the purposes of contemporary exposition or controversy. What is too often disregarded is the over-all plan, which reveals the gradations of importance and emphasis within the message of Catholicism. Matters are not reduced to one flat level; there is subordination and dependence of part upon part. St. Thomas's stresses and omissions—indicating, in many instances, quite different preoccupations from those revealed in popular Catholic thinking today—are alone worthy of study.

For example, St. Thomas has little to say about the juridical structure of the Church; he wrote no tractate *de Ecclesia.* His interest being theological rather than ecclesiastical, he discusses the Church in terms of Christ's headship of it as His own mystical Body.[11] The fact that the Church is administered through human agencies he properly takes for granted, but he does not apparently deem this aspect of the matter worth

[10] *Ibid.,* pp. 250-51.
[11] *Summa Theologica,* III, 8, 1.

lengthy discussion. Again, St. Thomas does not make frequent
use, as is nowadays the fashion, of the term "supernatural"[12]
as a synonym for grace. Needless to say, he never loses sight of
the truth that man has been raised above his own nature so
that he may share in God's (2 Peter 1:4) ; but St. Thomas prefers to discuss the implications of this transaction in the traditional Augustinian terminology of "grace" and "nature"—so,
it may be suggested, emphasizing the freely given quality of
grace and avoiding the unreal, or even magical, overtones that
can be projected onto the concept of "supernatural." St. Thomas's sacramental theology supplies a further example of his
capacity to keep all things in proper interrelation. God being
the sole Author of grace, the sacraments are simply His *instruments.*[13] This is true even of the Eucharist, whose "reality"
(*res*) is "the unity of the mystical Body"[14] of Christ. The
Summa Theologica comes to an abortive end in the middle of
the tractate on the sacrament of Penance. Tedium had overcome the author; what he had written, compared with what
he had seen by direct insight, appeared as so much straw.

Such, it would seem, was the climax of Thomas's "enlightenment," his satori. As a small boy at his Benedictine school
at Monte Cassino, the youthful Aquinas had kept asking his
teachers, "What is God?" His life was spent, one way and another, in exploring that question. The intellect, so he had
explained, concerns itself with things as they exist in the mind,
but the will goes out to things as they are in themselves.[15] For
this reason, though the intelligence in itself is more important
than the will, to love God in this life is of greater consequence
than to know Him. In his own case, Aquinas's preoccupation
with Ultimate Reality, always an affair of the heart as well as

---

[12] The word *"supernaturale"* is not listed in the index to the *Summa Theologica;* though St. Thomas does use the term in his treatise on Grace: *e.g.,*
"qualitates supernaturales," I-II, 110, 2.

[13] *Summa Theologica,* III, 64, 1.

[14] *Ibid.,* III, 73, 3.

[15] *Ibid.,* I, 82, 3.

of the head, had brought him to the point where all the holy realists[16] converge—"*Neti, neti*": "Not so, not so." Or, as St. Thomas had expressed it more formally: "In matters of Divinity, negative statements are to be preferred to positive, on account of our insufficiency, as Dionysius says."[17]

> Those who say do not know;
> Those who know do not say.

The *Summa Theologica* shows its author to be concerned with the basic realities of religion: the existence and nature of God, man and his condition, the constituent elements of the good life, the "way of truth" which man is to follow, as demonstrated by the Incarnation and lifework of our Lord and Saviour Jesus Christ. Within this general plan, all else—for example, the virtues and vices, the Ten Commandments, grace, and the sacraments—find their appropriate place. Nothing is taken out of its context or given disproportionate attention. The point may be illustrated by St. Thomas's relatively brief and, as compared to more recent authors, restrained treatment of the sacrifice of the Mass. He assumed as being obvious, what apparently escaped the attention of some later theologians, that the Eucharist as a sacrifice is to be considered solely within the framework of sacramental theology.[18]

This sureness of touch enabled him to preserve the links between his favorite sacrament, the Eucharist, and the total theology of the Incarnation, thus avoiding the confusion between sacramental and ontological categories which has given rise to so many elaborate "theories" of the Mass as a sacrifice.

[16] Sometimes, rather misleadingly, called "mystics"!

[17] *Summa Theologica*, II-II, 122, 2, 1. Referring again to Dionysius, wrongly supposed to be a disciple of St. Paul, St. Thomas has the following statement in his *De Veritate* (question 2, article 1, reply 9): "What God actually is [*quid est ipsius Dei*] always remains hidden from us; and this is the highest knowledge we can have of God in this life, that we know Him to be above every thought we are able to think of Him." Cf. *Contra Gentiles*, Book 1, Chapter 5.

[18] See *Summa Theologica*, III, 83, 1.

To the question: What happens to Christ when the priest pronounces the words of consecration? St. Thomas had already, in effect, given the only reply compatible with both reason and faith: Nothing at all.[19] As if to anticipate subsequent controversies, he answered in advance the charge that Catholic sacramentalism is a form of magic; he has nothing to offer those who would seek to season religious devotion with the excitement of the marvelous. "Your every-day mind," he might have said, "that is the Way." And why? Because it is there that the Holy Trinity dwells,[20] to enlighten that everyday mind, provided we do not stand in our own light.

Enough has perhaps been said to raise the question whether those who can think and articulate the thoughts St. Thomas thought have not much to offer in our time. Ananda Coomaraswamy, having linked certain passages in the *Contra Gentiles* with sections of the *Bhagavad Gita*,[21] takes the view that the opposition between East and West would not have been felt to exist before the Renaissance; "it is one of times much more than of places."[22] If we leave aside the "individual philosophies of today," and consider only "the great tradition of magnanimous philosophers, whose philosophy was also a religion that had to be lived if it was to be understood," it will be found that the distinctions of cultures between East and West "are comparable only to those of dialects. . . ." "There is a universally intelligible language, not only verbal but also visual, of the fundamental ideas on which the different civilizations have been founded."

Could it be the fact that St. Thomas holds a unique place, at any rate in the West, in "the great tradition of magnanimous philosophers, whose philosophy was also a religion," that has

[19] St. Thomas's doctrine on the manner of our Lord's presence in the Eucharist is expounded at some length in my *The Love of God* (Image Book edition), pp. 244-48.
[20] *Summa Theologica*, III, 8, 8, 1.
[21] *The Religious Basis of the Forms of Indian Society*, p. 26.
[22] *East and West*, p. 43.

led modern authorities on Zen Buddhism to find in him a kindred spirit? Surely it is interesting that a *haiku* by the greatest of Zen poets, Matsuo Bashō—most gifted in the art of not "putting words between the truth and ourselves"—should evoke the thought of Aquinas.

On board a boat

Octopus traps: how soon
they are to have an end—these dreams
beneath the summer moon.[23]

On this Mr. Henderson comments: "Here the religious implications are obvious, even if we do not go into the Buddhist symbolism of the boat and the moon. It is, however, worthy of note that whenever Bashō uses the word 'dream' he seems also to be thinking of human life; and perhaps it is even more noteworthy that to him the 'illusion' of the world does not seem to mean that it is in any sense unreal, but rather, as with St. Thomas Aquinas, that it is far more real than it seems."

Similarly, Professor R. H. Blyth, in his *Zen in English Literature and Oriental Classics,* pointing out that what excites desire is not the abstract idea but the concrete thing, remarks: "So in the *Summa Theologica,* Aquinas says, 'He who is drawn to something desirable does not desire to have it as a thought but as a thing.' "[24] Touching, by implication, on Buddhist compassion, *karuna,* the observation is made: " 'Shedding tears' is what St Thomas Aquinas calls grief, as distinct from mercy. In mercy we stand outside; in grief, for ourselves or for others, there is a complete identification with the other person and no feeling of *my* sympathy for *him*."[25]

We hear much talk nowadays of the need of "reform," for the Church to adjust itself to the realities of modern life. It may

[23] Harold G. Henderson, *An Introduction to Haiku* (New York: Doubleday & Company, Anchor Book edition, 1958) , p. 22.
[24] *Op. cit.,* p. 89.
[25] *Ibid.,* p. 233.

be so; I gladly leave such projects to those qualified to discuss them. From the standpoint of this essay, a more urgent need, and one less difficult to meet, is that we *realize* what we already know. To do this nothing need be changed, except perhaps our hearts. *"I show you suffering; and the way that leads to the stopping of suffering."* This dictum is, or could be, as much Christian as Buddhist. It tells us, in a sentence, what life is about. To understand and accept it is to have achieved the "ripeness" that is all. Granted this condition one may leave one's life hereafter, in God's good hands, to take care of itself. The problem is not to synthesize the various departments of knowledge, nor to analyze the "human condition," but to discover one's "self." Emptying the mind of nonsense, our true being must needs disclose itself, so that, by God's grace, with uninhibited awareness, we live *now*. Words, it would seem, are indispensable instruments on this voyage of discovery; but we must learn not to be taken in by them; rather, to see through them to the realities beyond. Then in quietness, with Thomas Aquinas and Matsuo Bashō, no matter how chilly the circumambient air, we may keep our hearts warm.

> When I speak,
> my lips feel cold—
> the autumn wind!

POSTSCRIPT

The famous Professor Challenger—whose adventures among the mighty saurians of the Lost World have been told so well by his biographer Sir Arthur Conan Doyle—has now at last retired from active life. He still retains his daring exploratory spirit, his irascibility and aggressiveness. We see him sitting attentive in his chimney-corner while a mixed gathering of intelligent and enlightened persons stand around exchanging views about the deplorable conditions of human affairs at the present time. Suddenly the professor intervenes. "In my opinion", he remarks disagreeably, "the contemptible triviality and utter sterility of this discussion are at least partly explained by your failure to take any account of Ethics as a factor in the situation". . . . "I only wanted to give myself the satisfaction of demonstrating that there are very few accepted ideas that cannot be challenged on some ground or other, and that even your most sacred shibboleths are not impervious to criticism."

—From a radio talk by L. M. Loring in *The Listener*,
October 18, 1962

A Critique of a Critique
THE CASE OF WALTER KAUFMANN

Dr. Walter Kaufmann's two recent books,[1] intended by their author to complement each other, *Critique of Religion and Philosophy* and *The Faith of a Heretic,* have deservedly attracted widespread attention among the more thoughtful. The aptness of some of his observations has already been noted in the text of the present essay. These quotations, however, should not be taken as indicating any general agreement with Professor Kaufmann's basic assumptions. He touches, sometimes at length, on Buddhism, with its development in Zen, and on Christianity, particularly as it is elucidated by St. Thomas Aquinas—in other words, on the chief themes of this book. And Mr. Kaufmann, so we are advised by no less an authority than a chairman of the Department of Philosophy at Harvard, is to be taken seriously. "No one writing or thinking on any of the book's [*i.e.,* the *Critique*'s] prodigious topics, now or for a long while hereafter, is likely to deserve our attention except as he

[1] Referred to respectively as C and H, followed by the section number. The books are: *Critique of Religion and Philosophy* (New York: Doubleday & Company, Anchor Book edition, 1961 [from which I quote], by arrangement with Harper & Brothers, copyright © 1958 by Walter Kaufmann), and *The Faith of a Heretic* (New York: Doubleday and Company, 1961, copyright © 1960, 1961 by Walter Kaufmann, copyright © 1959 by McGraw-Hill Book Company, Inc.)

comes to terms with Kaufmann." It is a formidable challenge. Nevertheless, I propose to accept it, and to do so without benefit of any presuppositions deriving specifically from Catholicism. The difficulties do not appear to be insuperable.

Dr. Kaufmann's first concern, if I understand him aright, is with honesty. "What is honesty?" he asks, and offers a reply as characteristic as it is salutary.

Some men readily persuade themselves that they have said what in fact they did not say, or that they never made a statement that in fact they made, or that you said something you never said. Such lack of scruple is extremely widespread and easy to cultivate. Many children and politicians are masters of the art of telling falsehoods with sincerity. (H, 7.)

Professor Kaufmann pursues the "quest for honesty" with something of the "rapierlike intellect" (C, 30) he so greatly admires in his favorite philosopher, Nietzsche. Many Catholics will make their own the questions raised with respect to the genuineness of the so-called "religious revival," will share the misgivings about certain presentations of the teaching of Jesus, will agree on the dubiousness of what Dr. Kaufmann describes as "holy relativism," and with his distaste for the politicians' professions of respect for "organized religion, no matter what shape it takes," or the advocacy of a "deeply felt religious faith —and I don't care what it is." (H, 85.)

It is common form nowadays for ecclesiastics to denounce Communist atheism. What is not so common, though it is a task perhaps even more important, is to make clear the nature of Christian theism. Professions of belief in God are not enough; we must know, and be able to state, what kind of God it is in Whom we believe. Not all religion is good; some of it —most of it, according to Professor Kaufmann—is bad. The widely held assumption that religion is the most effective support of sound morals is questionable. "A much higher percentage of Roman Catholics than of Unitarians or Reform Jews, agnostics or atheists, commit murder." (H, 69.) Though here it is added, "This does not mean that Catholicism predisposes men towards murder, but that more crimes are committed by the poor, the uneducated, and the underprivileged; and a greater percentage of the members of the Catholic faith are in this category. For the same reason, Baptists have more than their fair share of the worst crimes."

All this, though controversial, is well worth while drawing attention to. We should be grateful to Dr. Kaufmann for raising these issues so forcefully; even though they have long since been a matter for discussion among Catholic theologians. Unfortunately, the author of the *Critique* has an exceedingly low view of theologians, especially "dogmatic" ones. Among the dishonest multitudes that vex Dr. Kaufmann's spirit, easily the worst offenders are the theologians. What tries him most of all are the attempts by theologians, "always on the lookout for the newest wine to replenish their dry old skins" (H, 17), to relate theology to the ways of modern thought. Not that theologians are deliberate impostors, not that they lack ability—St. Thomas Aquinas, for example, may be acknowledged as one of the world's master minds, the greatest theologian of them all; but he, like the rest, was a manipulator of propositions in the interest of orthodoxy. He could not, as can Professor Kaufmann (C, 45), "cherish the open vistas" of his own thought. The characteristic occupation of theologians is "gerrymandering."

This is a political term, but unfortunately, politicians have no monopoly on dividing districts in an unnatural and unfair way to give one party an advantage over its opponent. Many theologians are masters of this art. Out of the New Testament they pick appropriate verses and connect them to fashion an intellectual and moral self-portrait which they solemnly call "the message of the New Testament" or "the Christian view"; and out of other Scriptures they carve all kinds of inferior straw men.

Theologians do not just do this incidentally: this is theology. Doing theology is like doing a jigsaw puzzle in which the verses of Scripture are the pieces: the finished picture is prescribed by each denomination, with a certain latitude allowed. What makes the game so pointless is that you do not have to use all the pieces, and that pieces which do not fit may be reshaped after pronouncing the words "this means." That is called exegesis. (C, 56.)

We shall presently consider the assumptions underlying these assertions, and examine briefly the integrity with which Professor Kaufmann discharges his role as stone-thrower. Meanwhile, the above-quoted remarks may be accepted as a useful warning to Catholics to avoid hasty and superficial apologetics, a reminder that nothing can be of ultimate service to religion except what is seen, according to the best light we have, to be true.

Dr. Kaufmann professes considerable respect for the Buddha and Buddhism. He sets forth the Four Noble Truths, "which are held to be literally true and were clearly intended this way by the Buddha himself." (C, 62.) Having noted the discipline recommended in the Noble Eight-fold Path, Dr. Kaufmann remarks that Nietzsche called Buddhism "the only positivistic religion in history." This, I gather from the context, is intended as a compliment. Nevertheless, Buddhism has definite limitations: it "does not by any means place a supreme value on truth." "The supreme concern of the Buddha was not truth but salvation: a state of being."

The development of Zen is seen by Dr. Kaufmann, citing a text from Suzuki, as a repudiation of the "four truths." (C, 63.) "The beginning of wisdom, according to Zen, is the recognition of the limitations, and indeed the futility, of all propositional truth, and above all of any dogma, any sacrosanct formulation, any rigid statement." The Zen masters "do not want to provide future theologians with sayings that lend themselves to quotation out of context or employment in a creed. They want to forestall the creation of systematic theologies." Oddly enough, when writing of Buddhism, Professor Kaufmann's train of thought does not turn to the all-significant doctrine of *tat tvam asi* ("That art thou"), which he nowhere mentions, but to Sartre and Nietzsche. " 'Life,' says Sartre in *The Flies,* 'begins on the other side of despair.' " "Nietzsche's ultimate concern is with truth. The Buddhist's is not." Is it possible that Professor Kaufmann thinks that Nietzsche has more to offer to our suffering humanity than Gautama Buddha?

The deplorable unconcern for "truth," to be found in Buddhism, is no less discoverable in Christianity, "organized" or otherwise. "The four evangelists agree in ascribing to Jesus evasive and equivocal answers to plain questions; some of the parables are so ambigious that different evangelists interpret them differently; and it was evidently unthinkable for a disciple to ask searching questions and persist." (H, 58.) With reference to the origins of Christianity, Dr. Kaufmann accepts the view that "Paul transformed Jesus' preaching and assimilated the crucified and resurrected Saviour to the mystery religions that were prevalent throughout the Roman world." Summarizing his position, Dr. Kaufmann tells us, "My Paul is neither the infallible saint of many believers nor the traitor to Jesus that many liberals have found in him. And my Jesus is closely related and indebted to Albert Schweitzer's." (H, 61.) Schweitzer's contribution had earlier been outlined as follows:

His study of the texts and his definitive work on outstanding previous interpretations led him to the conclusion that Jesus' moral teachings must be understood as a mere "interim ethic"—designed and appropriate only for the interim, which Jesus firmly believed to be quite brief, before the Kingdom of God would come with power. Schweitzer's result implies not only that Jesus' ethic is inapplicable today but that it has *never* been applicable and that Jesus' most central conviction was wrong. (H, 60.)

Taking up this position, Professor Kaufmann, one would have thought, could easily have absolved himself from the task of giving serious attention to Catholic theology. Why waste time discussing a science whose first premises have previously been dismissed as false? But Dr. Kaufmann is not the man to take the easy way; he has stern things to say to critics who "make things easy for themselves," by gerrymandering and assuming as true what needs to be demonstrated. So he examines carefully some of the things theologians, Protestant as well as Catholic, have said; and if his verdict is always unfavorable, this, apparently, is not due to his having antecedently rejected the premises on which they build their arguments, but because he has found them to be dishonest; they gerrymander. It is in this spirit that he approaches St. Thomas Aquinas, "probably the greatest theologian of all time." (H, 30.)

The section (45) in Dr. Kaufmann's *Critique* devoted to St. Thomas is obviously the product of some research, superficial and tendentious as it demonstrably is. Two of the best-known authorities, Gilson and Copleston, "who try to win friends for the saint," have been consulted and portions of the *Summa Theologica* examined at first hand. The "grandeur" of this work is acknowledged, particularly "the intricate planning which finds a suitable place for this sentence from Aristotle and that verse from Scripture." St. Thomas's arguments for God's existence are scrutinized and found wanting. "Here an analysis of the concept of causation, possibly along the lines suggested by Hume and Kant, could cause grave difficulties." But then, "Clearly, Aquinas would have burned both Hume and Kant, as well as most other modern philosophers."

Dr. Kaufmann's conception of honesty evidently does not allow him to keep separate the two distinct processes of exposition and interpretation. This, together with other idiosyncrasies presently to be discussed, may account for such observations as the following: "Even Aristotle himself was not a sufficient opponent for Aquinas. As he saw it, the dragon was reason itself; and the contest he tried to settle once and for all was the competition of reason and faith. He attempted nothing less than to pull the fangs of reason and to make it subservient to the church." "Aquinas gave all to his church, fortified its conscience, built imposing walls to protect it against storms, and was canonized." In a noteworthy paragraph, Professor Kaufmann indicates both the "style" of his own thought and his estimate of St. Thomas's achievement.

Linking Greek columns with walls to construct a church is, no doubt, an impressive feat, and Biblical mosaics can be stunning; but there are those who would still prefer the ruins of the unfinished Greek temple at Segesta, forsaken on a hill, with the wind blowing between the unfluted columns and the sun shining on grass, flowers, and life. Some of us might prefer to linger in the unfinished, open structure of Plato's thought, which certainly does not equal the grandiose single-mindedness of Thomas, rather than live in Aquinas' church. One might even cherish the open vistas of one's own thought. Thomas knows that in that case his arguments do not avail. (C, 45.)

Finally, Professor Kaufmann recalls the religious experience which brought the writing of the *Summa* to its premature end, quoting St. Thomas's words, "All I have written seems to me like so much straw compared with what I have seen." On this Dr. Kaufmann thinks it appropriate to comment: "One shudders to imagine his estimate of his prolific admirers." More to the point, I should have thought, would have been Dr. Kaufmann's conjecture on what it was that St. Thomas saw. There is a hint that it may have been "the God of the Bible." Which still leaves unanswered the interesting question, as do the two books under consideration, despite their eloquent tributes to the Old Testament in general and the Hebrew prophets in particular: Who or what, according to Walter Kaufmann, is the God of the Bible?

At the outset of these remarks it was laid down, and it is again stressed, that the validity or otherwise of the criticism that follows is independent of the distinctive tenets of the Catholic Church. The argument is philosophical, not theological; the reference is to verifiable facts, not to doctrines held by faith. If, for example, I were to state that a Catholic theologian is more interested in St. Athanasius's than in Schweitzer's view of the significance of Jesus, that would be to assert what is the case, and not to claim in this context that Athanasius rather than Schweitzer was correct: though without introducing theology, it might also be added that St. Athanasius lived over fifteen hundred years nearer to the event than Schweitzer, and was in much closer contact with the continuous Christian tradition. A further suggestion could be added, as an unimportant argument *ad hominem,* namely, that Athanasius should appeal to Dr. Kaufmann, if only because he was prepared to stand alone, *"contra mundum"*—an interesting case of orthodoxy being upheld *against* the conformists and men of the crowd.

Dr. Kaufman has much to say on the subject of "commitment," and there can be little doubt that he would regard himself as less "committed," having a more open mind, than the author of this book. An impartial judge, however, might take a different view. He would surely wish to ask why Dr. Kaufmann should be against so many things, and why his manner is so derisive. Do his ceaseless, though selective, probings, directed for the most part against the Christian religion, really represent an "honest" enquiry? Or are they, perhaps, little more than a device for airing his own all-too-evident prejudices? The matter is worth sifting.

A Catholic theologian, more consciously, I think, than Professor Kaufmann, at least knows what he is doing. He knows, for example, that his strictly theological reasoning has no more validity than the premises on which it is based. Such a theologian is committed to the Church's official teaching; but he is aware that this teaching is expressed in words, and that words inadequately represent ideas or mental concepts, and that these —as touching God, the very Object of theology—cannot even begin to comprehend what they relate to. The free play of the mind, so vast in its range, between the word, spoken or written, "true" though it may be, the mental concept or idea, and the extramental reality is something of which Dr. Kaufmann's two books contain no hint. His incomprehension of this point, we may note in passing, accounts for his naïve comments on the theologians' handling of the doctrine of Hell.

If it be urged that the present essay, having undergone the normal processes of ecclesiastical censorship, is not the result of independent thought, the reply is simple. It is in response to such light as the author has that, not wishing to misrepresent Catholicism, he has submitted his work to those officially responsible for upholding the Catholic "rule of faith." But the Catholic *regula fidei* apart—which means, for practical purposes, almost the entire contents of this book—there need be no meeting of minds. Those who grant a *nihil obstat* or *imprimatur* are no more committed to an author's expressed opinions than he is committed to theirs.

From this we may now pass to Professor Kaufmann's "commitments," to say nothing of his unacknowledged assumptions; though neither commitments nor assumptions are so described, or perhaps recognized, by him. Here are some of them, chosen almost at random: "Philosophy and art, religion and science, represent a revolt against common sense." (C, 32.) "A noun is not the name of a thing but an attack on a thing: a noun tears a thing out of its environment, strips it of its defenses, and hales it into court for an indictment." (C, 27.) "Bliss, despair, and ecstasy present fundamentally the same picture." (C, 72.) "The divine is not an object, it is a challenge." (C, 98.) "Reason can never be at home in this world. On the wings of searching questions, it transcends beliefs and facts and all that is." (C, 99.) "I am rejecting two clichés: that of the Judaeo-Christian tradition as well as the claim that Western civilization is a synthesis of Greek and Christian elements." (H, 58.) "There is a peace of mind born of transgression which is sweeter than that of a good conscience." (H, 59.) "Philosophy is always academic or upsetting. There is no middle ground." (H, 100.) "The original sin of religion is to objectify the divine and to accept as final some dogma, sacrament, or ritual." (C, 98.) "The primary concern of the great religions is not with truth, and least of all do they agree in teaching the same truths: they agree in considering truth secondary." (C, 61.) These are but a few of the categorical statements—some may consider them less philosophical than the Christian creeds—which have to be kept in mind when Dr. Kaufmann speaks of cherishing "the open vistas of one's own thought." (C, 45.)

Before placing a finger on the substantive weakness in Professor Kaufmann's approach to philosophy, a word must be said about his method. He can write succinctly and incisively, but not with accuracy or precision. His frequent lapses into loose writing are perhaps indications, despite an air (probably unintended) of omniscience, of a fundamental looseness of thought. "The same is true of some religious figures and of men like Lincoln and Freud." (H, 46.) Who are the men like Lincoln and Freud? "The theological virtuoso far transcends doublespeak and triple-speak to speak to each man's need." (H, 32.) Meaning? "Is an absolute morality possible? Most people assume it is." (H, 76.) Has Dr. Kaufmann consulted most people on the point? He speaks, twice on one page, of "self-styled absolute moralities." (H, 82.) Questions: Which are these? How can a morality "style" itself?

These complaints might appear merely captious were it not that Professor Kaufmann is an advocate of careful terminology and, in support of his case "against theology," cites an interesting statement from Wittgenstein's *Tractatus:* "Most of the propositions and questions that have been written about philosophical matters are not false but nonsensical." (H, 24.) Mr. Michael Novak (*The Current,* Harvard, May 1962), pointing out that Dr. Kaufmann attempts far too much, observes fairly enough that "It is gross to write a generalization purporting to cover Aquinas, Buber, Luther, and maybe Lao-Tze or Jesus, sometimes each by name, within the same paragraph. It would require consummate care to distinguish the countless intellectual possibilities within western Christianity alone; men have lived and died for differences of a word here or there, and intense intellectual concern for such detail is not at an end. Mr. Kaufmann seems to have read the requisite books, but he doesn't have much feeling for the care."

Perhaps it is this lack of care which accounts for another inconsistency of method. In the *Critique,* Dr. Kaufman repeatedly expresses dissatisfaction with Professor Arnold Toynbee as a historian. "Those who spurn accuracy, like Heidegger and Toynbee, find it easy to upset all previous knowledge." (C, 24.) "We may turn to Toynbee to be titillated, but if we want the truth we turn to men without a system." (C, 25.) Yet when Dr. Kaufmann is arguing his thesis that "The pagan sacraments found their way into the new religion" (H, 58), we find him referring to Toynbee for support. Citing Toynbee's query "In what sense did Christians, in those very early days before the statement of Christian beliefs began to be Hellenized, mean that Jesus was the Son of God, that He arose from the dead, that He ascended into heaven?" Dr. Kaufmann comments, "It is widely felt that this is the right question." One wonders whether it would be the right question to ask how this procedure differs from the gerrymandering, the making things easy for oneself, with which he is so ready to tax the theologians.

Nor is this the only instance of Professor Kaufmann's peculiar form of honesty. He makes much of St. Thomas's "support of the Inquisition." (C, 45.) He finds that the commonly held—though, to us, deplorable—viewpoint, that heretics must be "shut off from the world by death," is "an integral part of Thomas' system." The evidence points to Dr. Kaufmann's historical researches into the Middle Ages having been chiefly influenced by that outstanding authority G. G. Coulton, who is referred to as "the great historian" (H, 28) and extensively quoted. What was it, then, that prevented Dr. Kaufmann from setting the Inquisition in due perspective by citing the following passage from the same authority?

We must cast the main blame not on individuals, but on the spirit of the age, newly emerged from barbarism and lacking that respect for toleration which, after all, has come more from the practical experience of the last four centuries than from any speculation or argument. To us, the historical effect of past religious wars has brought conclusive proof that neither orthodox nor unorthodox can in fact exterminate each other, and therefore that agreement to differ is happiest for both parties. The Middle Ages had not that experience, nor sufficient knowledge of history to make up for their disadvantage. They erred, we may say, in invincible ignorance, and the most self-righteous among us may well confess that he himself might have erred with them.[2]

The most significant instance, however, of Professor Kauf-

[2] G. G. Coulton, *Inquisition and Liberty* (Boston, Beacon Press, 1959), pp. 117-18.

mann's one-sided methods appears in his central thesis, his attack on theology. He begins (H, 24) by spending much time with "Webster's New International Dictionary" and "the most complete dictionary of the English language, the twelve-volume Oxford English Dictionary," as the basis for an elaborate discussion on how theology is to be defined. "Much depends," he carefully points out, "on how we define theology." Could anything demonstrate more impressively how sincere is the quest for honesty? True, he finds most of the definitions to be no more than "comfortable ambiguities," since they "forestall a critical appraisal of theology, though this is badly needed." But at length he comes across one particular definition which he finds satisfactory. It is a definition which, as it so happens, prepares the way for the key statement to the whole discussion: *"At the crucial point, natural theology falls back on dogmatic theology"* (H, 25; italics in original). Here is the definition, from the Oxford Dictionary, which Dr. Kaufmann finds to his taste: *"Dogmatic theology,* theology as authoritatively held & taught by the church; a scientific statement of Christian dogma."

What, then, will be the surprise of the reader to learn, after all this, that Professor Kaufmann is not really interested in definitions! The point has been made abundantly clear in connection with a subject much nearer his heart than theology. "In the discussion of philosophy it is usually—and quite rightly—taken for granted that there is no need to begin with a definition." (C, 33.) Having touched on what he calls "pseudo-definitions," he observes, "The attempts at serious definitions are so vast in number that it helps to divide them into three kinds; and this subdivision shows at once how they have failed." This being so, why the elaborate pains to begin the discussion of theology with a definition? Could it be that Dr. Kaufmann, unconsciously of course, is gerrymandering, making things easy for himself? Given a convenient definition to start one off, the task of discrediting theology almost performs itself.

If one is merely researching into the word "theology," the dictionary is the obvious source; if, however, one is concerned about the *thing*, should not one turn to the experts? But perhaps Dr. Kaufmann thinks little of, or has forgotten, the Aristotelian distinction between a nominal, and a real, definition; and this may account for the peculiarly verbal quality of most of his discussions, except where his emotions are engaged. Honesty, one would have thought, should allow that St. Thomas Aquinas was better qualified to say what theology is than the compilers of a modern dictionary. He does, in fact, make clear his conception of theology (he calls it "sacred doctrine") in the opening question to the *Summa Theologica;* which, incidentally, Professor Kaufmann—his boast that he has examined Aquinas's "central claims" (C, 56) notwithstanding—shows no evidence of having read. St. Thomas regards sacred doctrine as being a science which "treats chiefly of those things which by their sublimity transcend human reason," whose first principles are revealed by God and held by man through faith. But how could Dr. Kaufmann possibly have reached the desired conclusion had he been obliged to handle such terms as "science," "principles," "transcending human reason," "God"? What he needs for his purpose are "authoritatively," "church," "statement," "dogma," which, though not considered worth mentioning in the discussion by "the greatest theologian of all time" (H, 30), lie conveniently to hand in the Oxford English Dictionary.

Despite appearances that might support the charge, it would be unfair to tax Professor Kaufmann with being unscrupulous. His deficiencies as an expositor and critic are due to a lack of intellectual grip; philosophically speaking, he hardly knows where he is. There are times, too, when he seems to have a qualm of conscience over what he is doing; his uncertainties are self-confessed. He is not really concerned to give "a balanced picture" (H, 61). "Still," he says, "I shall not plead guilty to gerrymandering the Bible." With engaging candor, he allows that, "My account of the New Testament is less positive than my analysis of the Old Testament. Even those who might concede that this makes for a wholesome antidote may feel that it is odd in a book that attacks the double standard and pleads for honesty." If these admissions indicate confusion, they do suggest a subjective regard for honesty; they are not without their pathos.

One can sympathize with Dr. Kaufmann's difficulties. They stem, I think, from a fundamental ambivalence in his own thought, which accounts for his mental aggressiveness. Intellectually, he is in sympathy with the philosophical analysts; or, to be more accurate, his interest is in the *use* of words; his hero is Wittgenstein. Though, significantly, Wittgenstein is reproached with "a tendency to be too respectful before the wisdom of simple people" (C, 20); he also "perhaps actually felt some slight nostalgia for the strong faith of Augustine." Emotionally, Professor Kaufmann's heart lies with the existentialists, from Nietzsche to Sartre. And Dr. Kaufmann's emotions operate much more powerfully than his intellect. "One can write with —and can remember that the men one writes about had—'dimensions, senses, affections, passions,' " he says, in his preface to *From Shakespeare to Existentialism,* "without embracing the profoundly unsound methods and dangerous contempt for reason that have been so prominent in existentialism." But there can be little doubt that the following sentence from his *Existentialism from Dostoevsky to Sartre* places its author himself pretty accurately:

> The refusal to belong to any school of thought, the repudiation of the adequacy of any body of beliefs whatever, and especially of systems, and a marked dissatisfaction with traditional philosophy as superficial, academic, and remote from life—that is the heart of existentialism.

Philosophers live by their mental agility, and it might conceivably be possible to run with the existentialist hares and hunt with the analytical hounds, as Professor Kaufmann heroically strives to do; but he lacks the necessary equipment. He has no ontology; he is without a theory of knowledge; he can apply no consistent logic. The goal which, presumably, he sets himself—"Philosophy has to be analytic and must explore the themes it takes up to the bitter end" (H, 100)—is beyond his powers of attainment. It is strange that he should claim to be a philosopher at all, as, in his own sense, he apparently does. "Let us see how a philosopher might deal with it, after repudiating dogmatic theology and endorsing the importance of the 'critical, historical, and psychological study of religion.'" (H, 38.) It is strange, because he has already made it clear that he does not regard philosophy as the love of wisdom, or even as an effort at coherent thinking, but as a literary exercise. "Philosophy is that branch of literature represented by Plato and Aristotle, Descartes and Spinoza, Hobbes and Locke, Berkeley and Hume, Leibniz and Kant, Hegel and Nietzsche, to name a few prominent exponents." (C, 33.)

In the field of philosophy Dr. Kaufmann is an incorrigible name-dropper; but his own preconceptions do not allow him to "place" his men. He thinks that Comte and Sartre, and, more generally, positivism and existentialism, have made "problematic" traditional philosophy, "as we know it from the works of Plato and Aristotle, Descartes and Hobbes, Berkeley, Kant, and Hegel, among others." (C, 11.) How easily, and how uniformly, the great names slip from Professor Kaufmann's pen! This lack of discrimination betrays significantly his limitations as a critic. Who would have thought, glancing at his closely packed pages and the copious entries in the index, that he has nothing to say of the distinctive contributions made to philosophy by Aristotle and Descartes? Dr. Kaufmann may be a man of letters with a flair for dialectic; he is certainly an able apologist for the currently fashionable Continental existentialism; but hardly a philosopher, or even a historian of philosophy, at least in the "traditional" sense.

There are eighteen references to Aristotle in the index to the *Critique;* but we learn nothing of Aristotle's criticism of the Platonic ideas (or "forms"), of his logic, of his theory of knowledge, of his ontology, or even, notwithstanding the portrait of the "magnanimous man," of Aristotle's original and vastly influential contribution to ethics. This last omission, incidentally, enables Dr. Kaufmann to make things easy for

himself in dismissing "absolute morality," as represented by
Plato, no account being taken of the empiricism of the Aristotelian conception of virtue. Perhaps it is ignorance of
Aristotle, rather than bias against theology, which leads to the
verdict that St. Thomas is "interpreting" or "adapting" his
Aristotelian sources. Dr. Kaufmann would hardly be in a position to appreciate Bertrand Russell's judgment that Aquinas
"knows Aristotle well, and understands him thoroughly."[3] Lord
Russell also points out that "Ever since the seventeenth century, almost every serious intellectual advance has had to begin
with an attack on some Aristotelian doctrine; in logic, this is
still true at the present day."[4] Since Aristotle's is a philosophy
rooted in objective *being*, rather than subjective thought, it is
not difficult to conjecture why Professor Kaufmann, despite his
partiality for attack, should be unequal to this challenge.

There are nine references to Descartes in the index to the
Critique. On consulting the text, one finds only two significant
remarks. "With Descartes, doubt came into its own once more,
and the analysis of human knowledge made cosmic and theological speculations problematic." (C, 1.) The point is not developed, and, in any case, Dr. Kaufmann amply demonstrates
that it is lost on him, by having already linked Descartes' name
with Bacon, Socrates, and the pre-Socratic sophists. He does
state later, with a view to giving Nietzsche the credit for the
"decisive break with the past" (C, 18), that "Descartes' doubt
never becomes fully existential," whatever that may mean. This
is the more puzzling, as Professor Kaufmann has himself
pointed out that Nietzsche was so consciously indebted to Descartes as to have named one of his own works after Descartes'
Meditations.[5]

Perhaps it is that Dr. Kaufmann is merely reluctant to acknowledge the philosophical rock from which he was hewn. He

[3] Bertrand Russell, *A History of Western Philosophy* (New York: Simon
and Schuster, 1945), p. 462.
[4] *Ibid.*, pp. 159-60.
[5] Walter Kaufmann, *Nietzsche* (New York: Meridian Books, 1956), p. 369.

must know that it was Descartes—rightly considered, according to Russell, "the founder of modern philosophy"—who broke with the intellectual tradition reaching back to Plato and Aristotle, by attempting to construct a complete philosophic edifice *de novo*. Descartes' *cogito ergo sum*, Dr. Kaufmann could have made clear, lies behind German idealism, influencing both Kant and Hegel. Descartes gave "thought" the primacy over "being," "subjectivism" over "objectivism." But could Dr. Kaufmann have made this clear, all "great philosophers" appearing more or less alike to him? A revealing phrase in his *Nietzsche* (p. 176) indicates that perhaps he could not. "Aristotle and Hegel tried to subdue the entire cosmos, without cavalry and cannon, by sheer force of mind"—as if Hegel's approach was the same as Aristotle's; as if Aristotle tried to "subdue" anything, other than his own mind to the realities of the external world.

Emotionally, Professor Kaufmann is deeply concerned with the world and its dishonest ways. Intellectually, he is imprisoned in the subjective dialectic of his own thought. How, then, does he bridge the gap between his thought and the world around him, which he "experiences" so keenly? How does he make sense of the life he wishes to lead so "intensely" (H, 98)? In so far as he makes sense of it at all, he does so by falling into the old Platonic fallacy known as hypostatizing the idea. He cannot sympathize with Christians, except the "great" ones (H, 100), because he is fighting against his own construct of Christianity. Thus, for example, Luther is devoted, not to his, or Dr. Kaufmann's, idea of Christianity, but to Christianity *tout court*. He was "thoroughly devoted to Christianity, which was the one constant of his life." (H, 59.) Having no coherent epistemology, Dr. Kaufmann disregards the fact that "Christianity," though it may be reified for purposes of convenience, is a mental concept, and that what exists are individual Christians, each more or less faithful to the Christian ideal, itself varying from Christian to Christian. He does not notice, despite his devotion to Wittgenstein, that "Christianity reversed

Plato's estimation of knowledge" (C, 69) is a nonsensical statement.

Behind Professor Kaufmann's erudition and gift for incisive comment, often both pertinent and just, lies an embarrassing crudity of thought. Not being able to concentrate on the same reality at various levels of abstraction, he fails to understand that others can. Hence his incomprehension of the manner in which theologians handle texts from Scripture. It does not occur to him that the theologians are, in effect, asking the question: How are the terms used and how did they acquire their use? Catholicism interprets its traditional doctrines, not merely on the basis of isolated Scriptural texts literally understood, but in the light of the total Christian revelation, still imperfectly apprehended. Because Professor Kaufmann envisages theology as the appropriate work of "philologists or historians" (H, 37), he must not conclude that this is the only view. Allowance should be made for the possibility that theologians have an interest, even perhaps some competence, in the field of philosophical criticism.

Never having grasped, or denying reality to, the concept of *being*, Dr. Kaufmann renders the Aristotelian "wonder," with which philosophy begins, by "perplexity"; which means, if I may quote Webster's Dictionary, "distracting uncertainty." Now this may well be a pretty accurate description of Dr. Kaufmann's state of mind; but it is not the same thing as "wonder." A child can look at something, apprehend it partly, but remain curious, and be often delighted at its part-knowledge, part-ignorance. That, I submit, is the *admiratio* with which philosophy begins. There already is the concept of *being*, with its depths within depths, yet assuring the mind that it is in touch with things as they are. Within the concept of being all our knowledge comes to birth; within that concept our potentialities to know are actualized, in varying degrees of completeness. The process is much helped by our being able to take our minds off our own thoughts, and our books.

Dr. Kaufmann's incapacity at this point may be illustrated

by his lengthy discussion of "Truth." Having criticized both Buddhism and Christianity for their unconcern with "truth," he cannot himself, notwithstanding the expenditure of thousands of words, tell us what he is talking about; basically, he has nothing to offer. "Even if we equate truth with correctness, the truth of many propositions is exceedingly difficult to determine." (C, 25.) "To communicate truth, a larger unit than a proposition is required; but that unit need not be a system, let alone, as Hegel thought, an all-inclusive system." Truth may mean "correspondence," or "coherence"; but it is not thought worth while to state of what with what. Nietzsche is brought in to assist: "The errors of great men . . . are more fruitful than the truths of little men." Which does perhaps raise incidentally the question: To which of these categories do Professor Kaufmann's writings belong?

It follows inevitably that he can make nothing of an age-long philosophy, based not on thought but on being, of which Aldous Huxley, for example, observes: "More than twenty-five centuries have passed since that which has been called the Perennial Philosophy was first committed to writing; and in the course of these centuries it has found expression, now partial, now complete, now in this form, now in that, again and again. In Vedanta and Hebrew prophecy, in the Tao Teh King and the Platonic dialogues, in the Gospel according to St John and Mahayana theology, among the Persian Sufis and the Christian mystics of the Middle Ages and the Renaissance—the Perennial Philosophy has spoken almost all the languages of Asia and Europe and has made use of the terminology and traditions of every one of the higher religions."[6] Or again, summarizing its contents:

Philosophia perennis—the phrase was coined by Leibniz; but the thing—the metaphysic that recognizes a divine Reality substantial to the world of things and lives and minds; the psychology that finds

[6] Introduction to *The Song of God: Bhagavad-Gita*, translated by Swami Prabhavananda and Christopher Isherwood (New York: New American Library, Mentor edition, 1954), pp. 11-12.

in the soul something similar to, or even identical with, divine Reality; the ethic that places man's final end in the knowledge of the immanent and transcendent Ground of all being—the thing is immemorial and universal. Rudiments of the Perennial Philosophy may be found in the traditionary lore of primitive peoples in every region of the world, and in its fully developed forms in every one of the higher religions.[7]

Dr. Kaufmann will have none of this. He thinks that we should ask, "what experiences, ideas, attitudes, or deeds appeared central to the Buddha, Jesus, Micah, and the men of the Upanishads, and what was the distinctive message of each." (C, 93.) "By exposing ourselves to the slings and arrows of diversity we should be changed." He warns us that "We are not in safe possession of the truth or of knowledge of good and evil or of the right standards, and able to apply them with sovereign wisdom to Mozart or Moses, Shakespeare or the Buddha, Michelangelo or Paul." We are invited to "Picture a youth who is troubled about his sexual desires seeking advice from Jesus, Socrates, the mystics, the Buddha, Lao-tze, and Freud: would they all tell him essentially the same thing? And how many of them would equate virtue with self-realization? These men were radicals, not eclectics." Here, as so often, Professor Kaufmann has found himself in what he looks at. By temperament a radical, he seeks to attach that label to those whose stature eludes his grasp, who cannot really be categorized at all.

Perhaps this is the key to our understanding. The dedicatory legends and opening quotations in his books, the passages of autobiography and his highly personalized ethical views, tell their own story. It would be impertinent to comment on these. They testify to courage, a sense of suffering, and an aspiration toward a somber, isolated nobility. Earlier, he had quoted from Lincoln, "If we could first know where we are, and whither we are tending, we could better judge what to do, and how to do it." (H, 11.) Dr. Kaufmann offers his suggestions about what to

[7] *The Perennial Philosophy*, p. vii.

do and how to do it, but because his mind is barren on the subject of where we are and whither we are tending, his "morality
of openness" (H, 83) appears singularly devoid of content.

One wonders how carefully he has examined the concept of
"happiness," and why he should find Plato's collocation of virtue and happiness "curious." Of course, it cannot be right "to
sacrifice man's moral, intellectual, artistic, cultural, potential to
his happiness." (H, 78.) But this does not contradict Aristotle's
view, that man seeks happiness—if only as a by-product, the
bloom on the flower—in everything he does, whether or not he
be aware of the fact. Dr. Kaufmann seems to think that his pursuit of honesty, since it lands him in trouble, precludes his happiness. But does it? Would he be happier, or, at any rate, less
unhappy, were he not to act out the image of himself as a modern Jeremiah, a twentieth-century Socrates?

Honesty, like charity, begins at home; as a response to the ancient, and extremely modern, imperative "Know thyself." Did
Dr. Kaufmann at any time entertain the thought that his two
books might constitute a collective piece of gerrymandering, in
the interests of his dogmatic skepticism and emotional satisfaction? How honest is he being with himself when he implies that
it is "easier" to propose "one's own 'philosophy'" (H, 85) than
to do what he does? I submit that for him to propound even the
elements of his own philosophy with the originality, let us say,
of a Descartes or a Kant, is a task which is not only not easier,
but completely beyond Professor Kaufmann's powers. Were he
able to break free from the bibliographies, the volumes on the
library shelves, and, above all, from the preoccupation with his
own "experience," and so open his eyes to the real world instead of his conception of it, he might make the attempt. But
then he would have learned, with Aristotle, that truth is gained
by submission to reality, not by an attack upon it. He might
even find himself in agreement with St. Thomas, that the heart
of courage is not in aggression but in endurance, patience.

These possibilities, however, are exceedingly remote; for Dr.
Kaufmann has strongly held, if chiefly negative, views. How

hard, then, it would be for him to take seriously the Zen advice:

> Try not to seek after the true,
> Only cease to cherish opinions.

Looking at all those books and card indexes, consulting the dicta of the Founders of religions, leafing through the Prophets, the Upanishads and the Bhagavad-Gita, recalling the innumerable names of philosophers, poets, existentialist novelists and playwrights, and even, for a brief moment, the dishonest theologians, what could he make of the Buddhist "nonsense"?

> The whole world is tormented by words
> And there is no one who does without words.
> But in so far as one is free from words
> Does one really understand words.

ACKNOWLEDGMENTS

The author and the publisher wish to thank the following for permission to use quotations from the books listed: Burns & Oates Ltd. and The Newman Press for *The Complete Works of St. John of the Cross,* translated by E. Allison Peers; E. P. Dutton & Co. Inc. and The Hutchinson Publishing Group for *The Essentials of Zen Buddhism,* edited by Dr. Bernard Phillips; Bruno Cassirer (Publishers) Ltd. for *Buddhism: Its Essence and Development* by Edward Conze; Luzac & Company Ltd. for *Introduction to the Study of the Hindu Doctrines* by René Guénon; Orientalia, Inc. for *The Religious Basis of the Forms of Indian Society* by Ananda K. Coomaraswamy; Philosophical Library Inc. for *Hinduism and Buddhism* by Ananda K. Coomaraswamy; Hutchinson & Co. (Publishers) Ltd. and Citadel Press for *The Heart of Buddhist Meditation* by Nyanaponika Thera; University Books, Inc. for *The Training of the Zen Buddhist Monk* by D. T. Suzuki; Grove Press, Inc. for *Anthology of Zen,* edited by William A. Briggs; Harper & Row, Publishers for *The Perennial Philosophy* by Aldous Huxley, *Grey Eminence* by Aldous Huxley, and *Critique of Religion and Philosophy* by Walter Kaufmann; Harcourt, Brace & World, Inc. and Faber and Faber Limited for lines from T. S. Eliot's "The Love Song of J. Alfred Prufrock" from *Collected Poems 1909-1935,* copyright 1936 by Harcourt, Brace & World, Inc.; Penguin Books Ltd for *Aquinas* by F. C. Copleston, S.J., *The Bhagavad Gita,* translated by Juan Mascaró, *Buddhist Scriptures,* selected and translated by Edward Conze, and *The Cloud of Unknowing,* translated by Clifton Wolters; Charles E. Tuttle Co., Inc. for *Zen Flesh, Zen Bones,* compiled by Paul Reps.

INDEX OF NAMES

Below are listed only persons and places. Subjects, as related to their context, will be found in the Analytical Contents.